IN SEARCH OF IRAQ

RICHARD
DOWNES

IN SEARCH OF
IRAQ
Baghdad to Babylon

NEW
ISLAND

IN SEARCH OF IRAQ
First published 2006
by New Island
2 Brookside
Dundrum Road
Dublin 14

www.newisland.ie

ISBN 1 905494 33 5

British Library Cataloguing in Publication Data. A CIP catalogue record for this book
is available from the British Library.

Book Design by New Island
Cover photograph: Scott Olsen © Getty Images
Printed by CPD, Ebbw Vale, Wales

10 9 8 7 6 5 4 3 2 1

Important Events in Iraq's History

1921: Britain, the mandate power for Iraq, installs Faisal I as head of state, incorporating the three Ottoman provinces into one nation, to be called the Kingdom of Iraq.

1941: Iraqi government sides with Italy and Germany in World War II. Royal family flees Baghdad and British troops invade from Basrah in mid-April. Regent restored to throne in June 1941.

1958: Army officers move against royal family and depose king on 14 July. Revolutionary government installed. Abed al-Karim Qasim becomes head of state.

1963: Qasim overthrown. The tiny Ba'ath party emerges as a key conspirator. Constant struggles engulf government.

1968: Ba'ath party seizes power and Ahmed Hasan al-Bakr emerges as president. Saddam Hussein becomes deputy chairman of the ruling Revolutionary Command Council and the key strongman of the regime.

1979: Saddam forces al-Bakr to resign and launches a purge of the party.

1980: Saddam sends forces into Iran, launching a bloody war which lasts for eight years.

1988: Saddam launches Operation Anfal to attack Kurds in the north. Halabja attacked with chemical weapons.

1990: Saddam criticises Kuwait for overproducing oil, forcing the price down. In August, Saddam invades Kuwait.

1991: Gulf War launched by twenty-eight countries to oust Iraq from Kuwait. Up to 100,000 Iraqis are killed in the war. Iraqi forces expelled from Kuwait. In March, Shia uprising is crushed by Saddam's cousin, Ali Hassan al-Majid, otherwise known as 'Chemical Ali'.

1998: Operation Desert Fox launched by United States and Britain. Baghdad attacked with hundreds of cruise missiles. Saddam remains in power. UNSCOM weapons inspectors leave Iraq.

2001: World Trade Center in New York attacked. Iraq says it was not involved.

2002: Referendum on Presidency in Iraq. Saddam receives 100 per cent vote. Release of prisoners from Abu Gharaib prison. In October, President Bush receives special powers from US Congress, seen as green light for war on Iraq.

2003: US, Britain and a small number of allies launch war against Saddam. War begins on 20 March and lasts until 10 April, when US announces end of Ba'ath party power in Iraq. In May, the Coalition Provisional Authority instigated as sovereign power of Iraq. In August, the UN building destroyed in suicide attack. Special Envoy Sergio Vieira de Mello killed.

2004: Transfer of sovereignty to Iraqi transitional authority. In March, following attacks in Madrid, new Spanish government pledges to withdraw forces from Iraq. In November, major offensive to retake city of Fallujah. Thousands killed.

2005: Elections in January are successful, but less than a third of Sunnis vote. New government pledges to crush insurgency but fails. Attacks reach new level of horror. In October, referendum on new constitution carried, but Sunnis vote against it.

2006: Shia shrine at Samarra attacked and destroyed. Nationwide sectarian violence follows. Death toll reported by Baghdad Morgue rises to more than 120 per day. Most are being killed by gunshots to the head.

PROLOGUE

I didn't want to go to Iraq. I had no interest in the Middle East; Africa was my abiding obsession. I read about and travelled around the continent during a three and a half year sojourn for the BBC, but my time there was coming to an end and with no other opening available, my bosses at the BBC decided to 'park' me in Jordan. Amman was a convenient place for a correspondent. A reporter could cover the Palestinian side of the Israeli conflict while also being available to go to Iraq when the opportunity arose. When I agreed to the job, I expected it to be a quiet posting, an interregnum, while I waited for another, more challenging job to free up. All I knew about Iraq could be summed up in a few sentences. I had read a little about Saddam. I remembered the Gulf War. I knew a little about the ancient city of Babylon and was determined to visit it at some stage. As events unfolded, Iraq dominated my time in the Middle East.

My first trip set a pattern that would repeat itself many times over the next eight years. My driver was Marwan, a cheerful thirty-year-old Jordanian from Amman. Marwan had a wife and three children and lived in a respectable working-class suburb. But like many settled Palestinians in that country, he regarded the Jordanian government and its king as a vile and unjust regime. He talked about this obsessively.

And so it went on for two hours: the thieving of the royal family; the stupidity of their government; the embarrassment of their begging for money from the Gulf countries; their recognition of the state of Israel; their kowtowing to America and Britain; the penal taxes they impose; their unIslamic lifestyle, etc., etc.

As we got closer to the border with Iraq, Marwan switched tack. The ranting about the Jordanian royal family gradually petered out and was replaced with praise for Saddam Hussein. He tapped his petrol gauge and again swerved dangerously on the road. 'Benzene, you know how much it cost in Iraq?' he asked. I had no idea. 'I fill up the GMC for ten dollars.' He looked at me, his eyes aflame with wonder. 'Ten dollars!' he shouted. 'And the King Hussein would charge a hundred and fifty. Liar, thief!' And we were back on the old hobby-horse again.

This was also my first exposure to the engineering marvel that is the GMC – a vast and ungainly vehicle the size of a small bus. Only a country with a devil-may-care attitude to petrol could produce such a hideous beast. Only a region with more oil than common sense could adopt the GMC as its totemic vehicle. It comes from a design universe whose clock stopped around 1976. Big, ugly and showy, it comfortably sped along the wide-open desert highways of Iraq at 160 km/h.

We passed through the Jordanian customs post in a blur of friendly handshakes and quiet efficiency, Marwan hugging and kissing the officials in a manner which surprised me after his lengthy diatribe on the evils of Jordanian officialdom. Then it was on through a no man's land before arriving at the Iraqi border. With much nodding and winking and hiding of US dollars in various safe hatches around the vehicle, Marwan drove up to the VIP section of the vast border crossing. This was a filthy place with an unkempt flowerbed that backed onto a chicken wire fence festooned with rubbish and discarded plastic bags blown up against it by the hot winds of the desert.

Marwan took my passport and $100 and marched me into the dark office. As my eyes slowly became accustomed to the lack of light, I realised that the waiting area to the left of the entrance was full of slumbering bodies covered by what appeared to be filthy blankets, laid out on a series of divans which doubled as benches for those waiting to be processed. Marwan told me to wait as he and one of the officials (who, because of the spectacular way in which he was greeted, had all the appearances of an old school friend) headed out to search the car. A tray of Pepsi and a plastic bag full of nuts, crisps and chocolates were handed over as a kind of acceptable bribe. Other cash bribes were paid in a more discreet fashion.

Marwan collected me and we headed over to another low range of buildings 100 metres further into Iraqi terri-tory – the dreaded medical centre. Here we were confronted with another slumbering official, this one lying in a cot against a mouldy wall. If one closed one's eyes, one could travel back in time – a slumbering official lying on a filthy divan in a filthy room with insects flying about the room and the mellifluous sounds of conversation in Arabic all around.

The official stood up and so the 'must be do the test' palaver began. The test involved was a HIV test and the only evidence that the medic involved could perform the test was the frighteningly large needle he picked up from the bench to our left. I looked on with horror at the prospect of being pricked by such an obviously filthy needle in such a decrepit place. In response to my protests, the bleary eyed medic simply replied, 'Must be do the test.' Shaking his head, he began flicking the needle with his index finger. Meanwhile, Marwan had changed into pleading mode and was talking intensely and sincerely to the medic.

The palaver continued. 'Must be do the test,' the medic stated blankly.

'Ah, no, there's no need,' I replied, showing him my Jordanian identity card which clearly indicated that I was HIV negative. But as far as the Iraqi medic was concerned, this wasn't sufficient. 'Must be do the test' was his insistent response to all the entreaties and appeals from Marwan and I.

At one point I lost the heart for the fight and began to roll up the shirt on my right arm and produced a clean syringe, ready to submit to the dreaded 'test'. I detected a change in the medic. No longer was he droning on ('must be do the test') and there was a distinct air of disappointment and reluctance in the air. It was then that the penny fully dropped. The medic wasn't really interested in performing a test. At this point Marwan took over, and linking arms with the medic, walked him outside the building, where they entered a deep and animated discussion, arms waving alternating with a cupping of hands in supplication and pleading. Marwan then returned and asked me for $200, the price of ending this ludicrous charade.

We headed back to the car and another $500 later, we were heading out on the Baghdad highway in our hideous GMC at breakneck speed. 'Must be do the test' became our watchword. If we were running low on fuel or coffee or water, it would be 'must be drink the coffee' or 'must be get the benzene' or 'must be do the piss'. Childish, it certainly was, but it helped pass the time and increase the sense between us that we were embarked on an adventure with numerous obstacles, many of them inexplicable. I was in Iraq.

⌒

I arrived at the Palestine Hotel on the banks of the river Tigris on an uncharacteristically cool October morning. The jagged nineteen-storey building towered over a once-charming plaza opening out to an esplanade which ran along the river.

The Palestine Hotel was a shock – a filthy, run-down flea pit of a hotel that hadn't had a cent spent on it in more than twenty years. I could hardly believe my eyes as the porter led the way down the dank, smelly corridor to my room. Just a single bulb illuminated the passageway, making it appear more like a basement than the eleventh floor of an international hotel. The walls were covered in a faded blue fabric wallpaper with sections ripped off and others caked in stains of unknown origin.

The door to my room opened and another hellish scene greeted me – the same blue wall covering and a filthy grey carpet which, because of the accumulation of stains over the preceding decades, resembled the floor of a Maze hunger striker from the early 1980s. Swirling patterns of dark brown leapt up and assaulted the senses while a strong smell of petrol – 'benzene', as the Iraqis call it – almost overpowered me. Years of sanctions, I was earnestly told by a minder from the Ministry of Information, meant that the import of strong cleaning sodas was prohibited. Petrol was used instead – yet another indignity heaped on the long-suffering Iraqis.

Before Marwan left, he promised to take me to Babylon. I imagined a glorious ruin, a picnic by the river and a day of leisure. He promised to pick me up at dawn and we would be back in Baghdad by lunchtime. He would then leave for the return journey to Jordan.

I awoke at five o'clock in the morning. There was a thumping sound at the door. I couldn't figure out what the noise was in the sleepy confusion of early morning. It was Sahdoun al-Janabi, my colleague from the BBC.

'Are you ready?' he said.

'Ready for what?' I responded.

'Ready for the big parade. We have to leave at six o'clock.'

'But I'm going to Babylon this morning,' I said.

'Babylon? Out of the question. You must come to the office and then we will go to see the president,' he said.

'Saddam?' I said, dazed.

'Yes. We will see him later today,' Sahdoun said excitedly.

I cancelled my trip to Babylon and instead headed off with a small official delegation to an obscure part of the city. We were dumped at an airfield. Two hours later, a convoy of black limousines came into view. They stopped about half a kilometre away from us. We were warned not to move. A man got out of the car and gave a salute. He was so far away from us that I couldn't identify him. The minders who were controlling us stood to attention. Moments later the man got back into his car and the convoy left. I was confused.

'What was that about?' I asked an official of the Ministry of Information.

'The president came to visit the foreign press,' he replied.

'You mean that's it?' I said, bewildered.

'It is a great honour for the president to come and allow us into his presence. This is very rare,' he said.

Back at the office in the Ministry of Information, I wrote my first news piece for broadcast on the BBC

World Service. It was a straightforward despatch about
the effect of sanctions and the recent arrival in Baghdad
of a group of Serbian engineers. They were in Iraq to
support the regime and to lend their expertise to what
was described as 'infrastructure projects'. I reported this
dutifully, adding that the Yugoslav delegation included
military experts. This titbit of information came from a
friend who had worked for the United Nations in the
Balkans and had had a conversation in Serbo-Croat with
some of the group about their mission. The delegation
told my UN friend that their main purpose was to
improve the accuracy of Iraq's short-range rocket
systems. This was perfectly legal, even under the sanctions regime that precluded Iraq from developing new
weapons systems.

After my news story was played on the main BBC
news programmes, a stern-faced man appeared at the
office door. I was on the phone and ushered him in and
asked him to sit down until I had finished my call. As I
chatted away on the phone, I noticed he was fidgeting with
his hands. On closer inspection I saw that he had no
fingernails. The tops of his fingers were horribly disfig-
ured and the places where the nails should have been were
dark red. I finished the call.

'So sorry,' he said, tilting his head sympathetically to
the side, 'the director of the Ministry would like to see you
immediately.'

I purposefully walked into the spacious wood-panelled
office overlooking the Tigris and shook hands firmly with
the director. Naji al-Hadithi was a short, stocky man and
was impeccably dressed in a sober blue suit and cream
shirt. He sat behind his desk and eyed me up while occasionally picking up papers, reading them and pushing
them around his desk. He had no moustache.

'I am deeply disappointed, Mr Downes. We invite you to our country and afford you all the facilities necessary to carry out your work, and what do you produce?' He looked up from a piece of paper he was reading for dramatic effect. 'Lies and propaganda.'

I was startled and began mumbling an explanation of sorts. He raised his right hand and read out a verbatim transcript of my report. He put the paper down and looked at me directly.

'We are fighting a war here. The enemy is the United States and Britain. You are Irish. You should know better. Now listen here. First. No more writings about our military. Second. No speculation of any sort. Any further breaches of this code and I will revoke your accreditation. Do I make myself clear?'

My colleague, Sahdoun, intervened on my behalf, explaining that I had only recently arrived and didn't know the rules very well.

'That is why I am taking a benign view of this episode,' he responded.

He then stood up and offered his hand. I smiled as broadly as I could, assuming the interview was now over.

'Do you play tennis?' he asked.

'Yes, but not very well,' I said.

'Good. Then we will have a match tomorrow at four o'clock. Is that a good time?'

'Yes,' I said, 'why not.'

I borrowed a racquet and some shorts and arrived at the tennis court in the grounds of the al-Rasheed Hotel at the appointed hour and began practising my serve. Minutes later a group of armed guards appeared and began fanning out around the court. Naji al-Hadithi arrived in full tennis whites, an aide carrying his racquet. Sahdoun was with him.

'You must let him win,' Sahdoun told me.

I looked incredulous, unsure whether to take him seriously or not.

'If he doesn't win, we will be in trouble. He is a very bad loser,' Sahdoun said.

Naji was a very poor tennis player. When he missed a ball, he cursed and whacked his racquet against his shoe. In the early games of the match, I played as if it was a normal game, but as his tirades grew in frequency and violence, I realised that this was not wise. Sahdoun stared at me and coughed and gestured every time I won a point.

At the end of the first set, which I had won, Sahdoun pleaded with me to stop winning.

'Naji is a very powerful man. You cannot beat him. It will go against us all if you win,' he said.

While up till then I had regarded Sahdoun's entreaties lightly, now I realised he was serious and that winning a tennis match could have an impact on my job and on the lives of the people in the office.

He won the next set easily. In the third set we were level at one game each and it was my serve. I served into the net for a double fault three times and he won the game.

'Three one,' he called out.

I stopped and looked at him.

'Are you sure that wasn't two one, Naji?' I asked.

'No. Three one,' he said and prepared to serve.

I looked at Sahdoun, who shook his head nervously and stared at me angrily. I was baffled. How could a grown man cheat so obviously? At the end of the game, I walked to the net to congratulate him. He smiled from ear to ear and shook my hand enthusiastically.

He gathered up his entourage and disappeared. Sahdoun and I sat drinking coffee in the foyer of the hotel. He congratulated me for doing the right thing.

'I have seen this before. If Naji loses in something, you will pay a price. I promise you. You do not want him as an enemy. He is close to Saddam and has a lot of experience. You did well,' he said.

I played against Naji three more times. Each time I lost and each time he shook my hand with great enthusiasm and beamed a triumphant smile. I tried hard to understand the mentality of someone who took such pleasure in cheating and failed each time. Sahdoun was surprised by my reaction.

'This is the way it is in Iraq,' he said by way of explanation.

Two years later Naji al-Hadithi was promoted to the high office of Minister for Foreign Affairs and held that post until the collapse of Saddam's regime in 2003.

1

THROUGH THE FIELDS

April 2003

My window on the fifteenth floor of the Palestine Hotel overlooked the widest bend in the river Tigris and the palaces of Saddam. Small plumes of smoke rose from the buildings that were spread out over 100 hectares. Most of the structures within the complex had been hit by American bombs over the previous three weeks. Some had been burning since the first attacks, the so-called 'night of shock and awe'. At the river's edge, a man was standing in his underpants stretching and exercising. He disappeared into the foxhole and returned minutes later, fully dressed. Others joined him. These were the Special Republican Guard, the most feared military unit within Saddam's army, the last line of defence for Baghdad. They appeared to be making coffee and busying themselves with morning duties.

The bombs fell without warning. Iraq's primitive early-warning sirens had ceased to function long before. The first one ripped open the ochre-coloured building that housed the Ministry of Planning and the offices of the deputy Prime Minister, Tariq Aziz. Others fell in less easy-to-identify buildings within the palace complex. It took me a moment or two to realise that the soldiers' foxholes had also been attacked. I took my binoculars and scanned the river's edge. Smoke billowed from a number of under-ground structures but there was no movement, no life to be seen.

On my bed were three bags, packed and ready to go. Over the previous two days I had been searching for something to help justify my decision to leave Baghdad, and now I felt I had found it. The defenders had given up the fight. The palace complex had been abandoned. The battle for Baghdad had promised to be a bloody affair, a new Beirut of grim urban warfare. The Iraqis claimed the Americans would have to take the capital street by street. This was clearly not happening. The Americans had occu-pied the airport with ease and were sending armoured columns to probe into the city, and meanwhile the aerial assault continued to attack the remnants of the Iraqi army. It would take another week to finish the war, but I had seen enough and was determined to go.

⌒

Spending weeks in a war zone creates a curiously detached attitude about death, particularly the deaths of others. It's easy to see why the military seems so blasé when using terms such as 'friendly fire' or 'collateral damage'. For them, death is the currency of fighting. So if you happen to kill person A rather than person B, that's not a failure or a tragedy. It's merely not a success.

Seeing mutilated bodies is bad for the human psyche. After you have seen ten, you need to see twenty before you have the same feeling of shock. If you see thousands you can easily turn into a monster. The mind works that way.

I had seen hundreds of dead bodies. Some were mangled and ripped to shreds. Others looked more complete. One man had been killed by a bomb that fell in a market. He was being prepared for his funeral in the overcrowded mortuary of a hospital. His face looked serene, as if he had died in his sleep of natural causes. The attendants cleaned him. As they lifted him into his cardboard coffin, his skull shifted eerily and the back of his head became detached from the rest. The workers scooped up what they could and sent the man to his grave with as much dignity as they could muster.

Hanging around in such places for long, the inevitable impression that takes over is that death happens to others. In a country where the targets are supposedly military, they aren't out to get me. Sure, there are people dying all around me, but I'm alive.

These were the unspoken assumptions I harboured at the back of my mind until I had my own encounter with death on the long journey out of Iraq to Jordan.

I had often thought that the closer you get to death, the more you would feel the love of life, the more you would want to cling on. All the better to fight this bastard; to scream and shout and rage and rail against the injustice of it all; how dare I be taken away so young, on the side of a rubbish-strewn, nondescript road with palm trees waving. How unfair.

But it wasn't like that. It was infinitely more mystical and strange. If I had ever given more than a passing thought to the possibility of dying, it was to see myself as the struggling hero.

In as much as I had ever considered it, I didn't think being close to death would be a spiritual experience. But it was. The shadows were soft, the edges like a gentle slope. At times, there appeared to be no shadows at all, just a granite greyness covering all but the most stark and angular structures and buildings.

As we drove through the detritus of the battle for Baghdad, a curiously relaxed and serene sense of resignation prevailed. Events happened very slowly, if not in slow motion. There was time to think, time to anticipate and then reflect. It wasn't an abstruse, out-of-body experience, but it had its moments. It lasted three hours and then it was over. It meant that I had survived a war and a number of near-misses, which meant in turn that I would have to go back to Iraq to make sense of it all.

Take away the cars and the telephone and electricity wires and the clotheslines and the other trappings of modernity, and the scene beyond the Al-Sha'ab district of Baghdad is probably the same today as it was thousands of years ago, when Mesopotamia was the cradle of humanity. This was the first place on the planet to cultivate crops on an industrial scale; the first place where humans produced a sufficient surplus to require towns and cities for their commerce and entertainment; the first place where laws were written down.

It was here that hunter-gatherers decided that the cultivation of wild wheat, barley, sorghum and other cereal crops was profitable enough for them to give up their endless wanderings and to arrange themselves into family, clan, tribe and finally urban communities. Vast herds of wild sheep, cattle and pigs were domesticated for the first time, allowing people to live in higher densities. The Fertile Crescent is how academics describe the swathe of land running from Iraq through Syria to present day Israel and beyond to the Nile delta in Egypt. It is a varied land-scape of burning sunshine, abundant water and, crucially, rivers that offer water, fish and life-giving silt to fertilise the land.

The empires of Mesopotamia were famously produc-tive places where the soil gave up an extraordinary bounty. Over the centuries the irrigation system had led to the establishment of an agricultural paradise, but the heyday of the region was probably as far back as the twelfth century. This was before the Mongol hordes swept through Mesopotamia wreaking havoc in the towns and wantonly destroying the dams and dykes that fed the agri-cultural bounty. After that catastrophe, the field systems never fully recovered, although the more easily accessible fields returned to productivity, making Iraq fully self-sufficient in food by the time the British took over the province from the Ottomans.

Modern Iraqis have been much less interested in agri-culture than their antecedents. Long gone are the days when Iraq relied on its own land to feed itself. Since the oil boom began in the late 1950s, Iraqis have imported much of their daily dietary requirements and the output of their farms has diminished in accordance with outside compe-tition. But there are still thousands of hectares of wheat swaying in the wind and thousands more hectares parcelled into small market gardens growing onions, tomatoes, potatoes, aubergines and countless other vegetables for local consumption. All around there are cattle, sheep and goats.

Snaking in between the fields and houses are irrigation trenches and canals. The complexity of the water system in this part of Iraq is bewildering. Some of the canals are fed from underground pumps, while other trenches flow with water that is tapped directly from the Tigris and channelled through thousands of rivulets, feeding fields as far as the eye can see. At intervals these runnels come to an abrupt stop, halted in their tracks by stoutly made dams from which yet more water gates allow the precious liquid to flow to higher ground. All of this happens under an unforgiving sun that raises temperatures above fifty degrees centigrade for most of the summer months.

The system of sluices, dams, channels and canals looks so complicated that it's clear that it could only have evolved over thousands of years. No Brunel designed this watery matrix, because no single designer could possibly know the ebb and flow of water levels in the river and its tributaries or the subtle undulations of land and the tiny variations of field structure and water table. Only the slow evolution of people and their land over countless generations could give rise to a land of such beauty and bounty today. In a parched and barren region, the green fields of Iraq are a true wonder of the world.

The Americans had captured the international airport and were now in the city, although they hadn't taken complete control of the capital – if they ever did. In the David and Goliath battle between the most sophisticated military machine on the planet and a poorly equipped and uncertainly motivated army of a fading despot, the favourite won the day. Iraqi weapons systems were hopelessly inadequate in the face of the all-seeing modern radar and satellite technologies employed by the coalition.

As we approached the main western desert highway, huge industrial earth movers with their digging arms fully extended were knocking down the directional signs from the overhead highway gantries and traffic was being diverted away from the main routes into the Mesopotamian wetlands to the north-east of the city.

The men doing the traffic work were a cadre I hadn't seen much of before. They wore black from head to toe but a number of them had balaclavas rolled up so their faces could be seen. They carried Kalashnikov rifles over their shoulders, hung at a jaunty angle. They were silent and didn't interact with the drivers or passers-by and exuded an air of authority and purpose that was rarely evident among Iraqi officials. The drivers reacted in a submissive fashion. No one opened a window to remonstrate with these men. No one tried to break through the cordon. The men motioned us off to the slip road on the right. Within a few hundred metres we were in an area of waving wheat fields and tomato plantations. I knew my driver, Basim, reasonably well. We had made the journey in and out of Baghdad a number times since my first visit in 1998.

'Feddeyin Saddam,' Basim said.

'Oh yeah? What are they up to?' I wondered.

'Trying to confuse the Americans with the signs,' he said, pointing up to the gantries. 'Getting ready for the final defence of the city.'

'But it's over now. The Americans are at the airport and in the city. They've won,' I offered, somewhat provocatively.

'Yes. But these men will fight to the death. They will be fighting the Americans for a long time yet,' Basim replied.

We sped on as the traffic thinned out and the area became less city and more farm. Herds of sheep and goats were being moved along the side of the road and every patch of land was cultivated. Until, that is, we changed direction slightly and came into a wide and open area of scrubland. Here there was less evidence of farming and few, if any, houses. Even though we were travelling at around 100 km/h, I began to realise that the field to my right was a well-disguised military encampment, bristling with hidden armour and tanks. Fresh clay was visible and one could make out tunnel systems for troops to move unseen between emplacements. Occasionally one could see a soldier moving above ground, but from afar it must have looked like an empty field.

Every hundred metres or so I noticed the large barrel of a gun or mortar or tank. They were dug into the ground and well camouflaged, some completely shielded from view by an elaborate arrangement of trees and foliage. All were pointed in the direction we were travelling, north-east. As we drove on and the reality of our location sank in, I looked at Basim, shook my head and said, 'Oh shit.' Basim returned my look and all the sentiments it contained.

Presently we arrived at a point where the dual carriage-way we were driving on met another at a T junction. In front of us and beyond the road was a small settlement with a market square to its front. It was busy and in partic-ular I noticed a number of young men pushing handcarts. As we waited at the junction for a clearance in the traffic, I saw that one of them was trying to cross the road, watch-ing vigilantly for cars and trucks. Sitting on top of the handcart was a mass of meat, apparently recently slaugh-tered, the muscle and organs wobbling in the burning sun like a giant, grotesque jelly, blood dripping from the sides. I could have sworn that I smelled the stench of this heap of flesh, but as he was at least 100 metres away from our vehicle, that wasn't possible.

Gradually I became aware that this domestic scene at the market was not all it seemed. Amidst the coming and going, I noticed yet another barrel of a large gun, this time a tank hidden in a house on the edge of the market. The vehicle had been reversed into the car parking space under the first floor, causing the rest of the house to collapse around it, creating the perfect disguise. As we moved on I noticed another tank hidden in a house in the same fashion and then more mortars and artillery scattered around the hamlet in a similar fiendish ploy to conceal weapons deep in civilian districts.

One greenhouse seemed to hold two pieces of artillery, the plastic covering pierced by the barrels of the guns, each pointing in the direction of the advancing American troops.

The more one looked, the more the armour revealed itself. I noticed the sharp crack of an aircraft moving low overhead and saw the people in the market look up and almost simultaneously begin to scatter with their belongings. As I looked to my right I saw explosions ripple across the open space of this ramshackle market. The detonations were regular, in a linear pattern as if choreographed by a Hollywood director, throwing up huge plumes of dust and soil, some of which now started to fall on our car. Many of those left in the market had now fallen to the ground, some obviously wounded or killed by the explosions. I looked on in a state of shock.

I turned around to check our accompanying vehicle and saw that they, too, were frozen by the encounter. A hundred metres behind their car I saw the raw meat cart and beside it what appeared to be a heap of human remains, blood-spattered and unmoving. The hand cart was still dripping blood, the meat still wobbling.

Just then another shower of bombs fell fifty metres behind the handcart. Again they fell like rain and in a regular pattern, exploding around the house with the tank embedded within. The sound of the explosions followed the visual event with a tiny delay, making the experience all the more eerie and difficult to reconcile with any sense of reality.

An air of serenity – or was it resignation? – took hold. The strange, almost slow-motion quality of outside events reinforced this. Weeks of watching explosions in the distance had made me somewhat blasé about the awesome physical power of weapons. I had watched whole buildings collapse in seconds after they were hit by Tomahawk cruise missiles or other laser-guided bombs, but seeing the effect of these weapons at such near remove chilled me. The fact that the salvos followed each other so closely also made it difficult to respond. If there are two distinct points of reference on the spectrum of reactions to close-quarter war, namely blind panic and frozen terror, I was closer to the latter.

We were now stopped, Basim frozen in fear. Fifty metres in front of us and to our left, another shower of explosions was unleashed. This time I saw the individual bombs dropping. They fell in a graceful arc that reminded me of something I had seen in southern India. There the fishermen wade out into the waters carrying a net. They then throw the net powerfully and skilfully and it lands on the water in a series of regular splashes.

As the bombs fell, I could make out the colour of the bomblets. They were blue-black, a colour that is often called gunmetal grey. It was as if the bombs had been thrown from some primitive catapult at a great distance and were falling in our path. I was mesmerised by the spectacle. Television and the movies prepare one for explosions, each individual detonation producing a perfect V, throwing up dirt and smoke. But images have no smell and the air around them isn't disturbed by the explosion, nor can you feel the heat generated by bombs while watching a Hollywood movie. There is an abiding sense that one has seen this before, but that was a rehearsal. This was the real thing.

Red and orange and yellow and green flames flared up from the orchards to our left, followed by secondary explosions as the targets detonated, throwing up clumps of soil high in the air. Some of this material made a terrifying noise as it crashed on the roof of our car. At times we thought we'd been hit by a bomb, such was the noise, but mercifully this hadn't happened.

The car behind us carrying a small group of journalists from the Reuters news agency drove sharply into our rear, causing me to wake from my catatonic state. I looked back and one of the occupants, Nadeem, was gesturing wildly and shouting instructions for us to drive forward. I turned to Basim and said, 'Let's go now. Forward. Drive, drive, drive!'

Basim held his hands out in front of him as if in prayer or worship. He tried to speak but nothing intelligible came out. I realised quickly that Basim was in a deep state of shock and was unable to comprehend the demands now being made of him.

'Okay, Basim. Come on now. We've got to get out of here,' I said, slapping the dashboard to emphasise the urgency.

He turned to me and tried to speak, but his English failed him and he couldn't think of the Arabic words to describe his feelings. All that came out was a series of half syllables, gulpings and mouthings that made no sense in any language. He continued to try to speak but failed.

I could see trauma in his dark brown eyes. Once he took his right hand and wiped his face from his hairline to his beard and back up to his eyes as if trying to wake from a momentary slumber. He blinked repeatedly and took a long, deep breath.

Nadeem's car hit us again and I looked back to see an even more hysterical Nadeem screaming and gesticulating wildly for us to drive on.

Something deeply ingrained, visceral, urged me to hit Basim, and to hit him hard. Perhaps it was something dark and unpleasant within me, but I felt that violence was the only way to snap Basim out of his hazy trance.

So I hit him with my fist very hard indeed, striking him squarely at the top of the arm and shoulder. He winced and drew back and adopted a look of deep offence. I shouted at him to move, this time screaming and beginning to show some of the hysteria that had gripped Nadeem in the car behind. I hit him in the same place again and then struck him harder, shouting all the while. I opened my fist and slapped him on the face with some violence. He looked terrified and began to cower in the corner of his seat, trying to avoid my increasingly violent blows.

It's difficult to say how long this episode lasted, but I hit Basim at least twenty times. At this point a series of explosions occurred about 100 metres in front of us. Again they fell like rain. This time some of them exploded in the canal, sending up huge plumes of water that drenched a large area.

Almost simultaneously there was a huge explosion behind us that caused a massive air change between the vehicle and the outside air. It almost lifted the car off the ground, such was its ferocity. It was at this point that the sharp ringing note in my ear before became prolonged. It was as if someone had clapped their hands loudly right beside my right ear, causing a shock to my hearing. It was only then that I realised that I had been hearing this noise intermittently since the start of the bombing.

Nadeem banged us from behind again and suddenly Basim woke up from his torpor and pulled the gear lever down to the drive position. In an instant the car jerked forward violently and we were moving at last. However, gripped by the fear of imminent death and the disorientating ringing in my ears, I continued to thump and punch Basim, shouting at him to drive faster.

'Faster, faster!' I screamed. 'Get a move on! Come on! Put up some speed! Get going!'

At this point I took out my notebook and scrawled a last letter to my wife.

Dear Mairead,

I'm sorry that I was killed on the side of the road in Iraq. I have always loved you more than anyone else in the world and I hope that you will always remember that. I am writing this having just been attacked by the Americans on the way out and I think they are going to kill us all. I will not forgive them and you shouldn't either. Please tell Luke that I love him. He must be strong for his little brother and you must be strong for them both. You have made my life so happy and I am sorry that it end (sic) this way.

I love you
Richard.

The handwriting was shaky and my only concern was that it would be illegible, so I went over it again, carefully rewriting the words that were difficult to make out and underlining sentences. I looked up from my notebook and after a brief moment of inactivity resumed my violent attack on Basim. At this point he had snapped out of the haze and started to punch back at me, telling me to calm down.

'Mr Richard, you're gone crazy. You must stop and calm down. Take it easy. Please, stop punching me,' he said.

I punched him again but there was no power in the blow and I slowly came to my senses.

I took out my notebook again and started to write up the events of the last hour. The road we had resumed travelling on was the main highway out of the area. It followed the line of the canal and was flanked on the left-hand side by a large berm or embankment obscuring the water from the road, presumably designed as flood protection. On the right-hand side the characteristic settlements of the area were clearly visible – homes with messy courtyards and fields and glasshouses and square block houses of no architectural merit.

However, the Iraqi military had another use for the embankment at this time of war. At intervals of about 300 metres, small clusters of tanks and armoured personnel carriers were arranged. Mortar shooting positions had been set up on the upward angle of the berm pointed out to the north-east, towards the airport. The first knot of vehicles we passed was still functional, and in the grass below, Iraqi soldiers wearing camouflage in the form of tree branches lay in waiting, clearly prepared for the approaching Americans. We heard more explosions in the near distance, ear-splitting detonations which restarted the ringing in my ears.

As we moved on, the picture changed dramatically. Three or four hundred metres later we arrived at a scene of carnage, smoke and flames shooting out from a knot of five APCs and a tank, the turret of which had been blown off. It lay forlornly upturned on the road. This was the result of the explosions we had heard less than a minute earlier. Around the vehicles, the victims of the attack lay in varying states of injury and distress.

We approached slowly, the earlier panic returning as we took in the scene of carnage before us. The debris of the attack was all around, covering the road and blocking our progress. The smouldering remains of the inner parts of the tanks and APCs were scattered over a wide area. To my left I saw a blackened body, only recognisable as such by his uncovered arm and hand, which was a bright beige while the rest of the body was a blackened stump.

We came to a halt ten metres before the wreckage. The scene reminded me of a famous photograph I had seen a decade earlier from the Gulf War of 1991. As the Iraqi army retreated from Kuwait in some disarray, their convoys were attacked at will by coalition forces – mainly American airplanes and helicopters. The pictures of the 'road to Basrah', as it was called, showed hundreds of burned-out Iraqi armour and tanks with the charred bodies of Iraqi soldiers scattered about.

The most chilling of these photographs showed the blackened torso of an Iraqi soldier halfway out of his tank, the ghostly image of his teeth and eyes putting a human frame on an otherwise abstract image.

Our scene of carnage wasn't on the scale of the death seen on the 'road to Basrah', but it was equally upsetting and a reminder of how close to annihilation we were.

What could we do? The area in front of us was littered with burning remains. Behind us there were more targets and further danger. To our left was a high embankment that we couldn't surmount and on our right was boggy farmland.

As we rolled these facts over in our minds, another enormous explosion rang out, this time from our rear. I looked back and saw the leaping flames of another inferno. The group of soldiers we had just passed was scattering in all directions as more bombs fell on the ordinance and tanks behind us. We were trapped.

Again the initiative was taken by the Reuters crew that was travelling in the car behind. They bumped us again, urging us forward. Basim looked at me and I at him. Was it really a good idea to hurtle through a still-smouldering battle scene? The first thought to enter my mind was the possibility of driving over the remains of soldiers or even driving over troops who were still struggling for life. Inured as I was to the suffering and carnage around us, this still seemed to me a move too far.

Then there was also the possibility of detonating further explosions by driving over Iraqi shells scattered from the vehicles or unexploded bombs dropped by the Americans. At this point, indecision had overcome both of us and the friendly but insistent bump from behind was all that brought us to a quick decision. We had to move forward, simply because we had no other option.

We pushed ahead and Basim expertly steered a careful course through the carnage, jerking the wheel sharply when necessary to avoid a large piece of shrapnel or a body. This part of the drive lasted no more than a minute, but it felt like an age. American warplanes were constantly circling around the area and the strange droning noises and unsettling sonic booms they made pushed me to the edge of a nervous attack each time.

It was then that I decided that there was little point in pushing myself to a heart attack by my hysteria and heightened state of anxiety. As we emerged from the smoke and remains, I started to take deep breaths. I closed my eyes and deliberately tried to slow my racing heartbeat. I opened the window and let the warm air of the river valley flow over me. Basim looked puzzled.

'You okay, Mr Richard?' he asked.

'Fine, Basim. I'm just trying to calm down and not have a heart attack,' I replied with irony.

'Oh, don't have heart attack. Please, we have too many problems,' he said.

How right he was. Ahead and for the next ten kilometres we were faced with similar scenes of carnage in progress. Every few hundred metres, tanks and fighting cars were destroyed or were in the process of being destroyed. The troops had scattered, discarding their rifles, mortars and rocket-propelled grenades in a chaotic fashion around the fields and ditches.

⌒

I often wonder how it looked from the air – two large GMC vehicles weaving their way through the battlefield, speeding up, then slowing down, bumping into each other and travelling erratically. There were hundreds of American and British warplanes in the sky. Above them were AWACS aircraft that provided mobile radar cover over a vast area. Below them were the unmanned drones, small armed spy planes which acted as television cameras beaming high-resolution pictures back to base.

This was the 'kill zone', the military area in the combat arena where forces have discretion about when they can attack. When all was ready, the monitor would signal that we were now available to be hit by blinking its parameter borders and emitting a high-pitched intermittent bleep. However, if the gunner crew was uncertain about the target – if he thought we were innocent civilians caught up in the chaos, if he thought we were friendly special forces or others not worth killing – he would be obliged to call in to his commanding unit to clear the assault.

The call would be made to the Al-Udaid air base in the Gulf kingdom of Qatar, where the United States and United Kingdom had set up their forward command base. A controller would be asked to authorise a strike.

Perhaps that controller was a thirty-year-old engineer from Idaho, or maybe a forty-year-old computer operator from New York City or even a twenty-five-year-old trainee from Texas. Possibly, he was a young recruit from South

America using his service in the military to acquire United States citizenship.

We couldn't see them, but they could see us. We were the moving dot on a heat-sensitive image, the dark grey object on a monitor, barely distinct from other shadows. We must have looked suspicious as we swerved around the broken-up Iraqi military hardware. There we were, plain for all to see, accelerating sharply, then braking and swerving around a burned-out tank, then manoeuvring around a mini-crater created by a big bomb.

Later I found out that the Russian ambassador and his convoy had taken the same route through the Mesopotamian wilderness half an hour earlier. They had been directly attacked by US forces. Five in their convoy had been injured. We were lucky.

Amid all the chaos, I mulled over the possibility of dying in this muddy wasteland, amid the detritus of battle. Would I feel any pain? Would my last few moments on earth be spent counting my fingers and toes and hoping against hope for medical assistance? I thought this unlikely, although still within the bounds of possibility. The most likely scenario would be that a bomb would fall from the sky and hit the vehicle, which would instantly explode due to the heavy fuel load. I probably wouldn't even know it had happened. The detonation would deaden the senses and the ensuing inferno would finish me off in a fraction of a second – not long enough to feel pain or to think. That would be the optimum outcome.

Alternatively, one of the little cluster bombs could fall near the car, causing a large explosion, but not one big enough to finish us off, leaving me cut apart by shrapnel and seriously burned. I could be covered in third-degree burns but still tenuously clinging to life, writhing in agony as the nerves on my body screamed for relief after the searing heat of the detonation. How horrible that would be.

What would happen next? I would be taken to a clapped out, filthy Iraqi hospital overflowing with thousands of angry, injured Iraqis. I would be the only foreigner in their midst, competing with them for the meagre supply of bandages and medicines available. I would be screaming for pain relief only to be told by overworked doctors and nurses that there was none because of the decade of sanctions which the Western world had imposed on this suffering country.

Or perhaps there would be no hospital, no treatment at all. Maybe the Iraqis would leave me where I fell and laugh and guffaw about my condition and jeer at me and enjoy my extreme discomfort.

Such was the see-saw of emotions and self-pitying thoughts that washed over me in this situation. I saw little room for heroism or bravery. In fact, the very notion seemed absurd. At no time did the impulse to do something that that could be characterised as selfless or brave even occur to me.

There were bombs and guns lying about everywhere. Explosions were going off near to me and further away and I concluded that there was a serious danger that I would go the way of the meat seller in the market, or the soldier burning in the tank.

I broke my prospects down to a one-third, one-third, one-third chance – I could survive unscathed; I could survive but be injured; I could be killed.

As we moved on through the battleground, the feeling that I had worked out my chances of survival brought comfort and the anxiety ebbed away. I slipped into a reverie akin to the one that people report during a near-death experience. It brought me a curious calm. This pleasant state lasted two or three hours. Rather than dwelling on painful experiences or personal shortcomings, it was full of pleasant, even happy, memories.

What was the point in railing against death if I had no say in whether I could cheat it? If the American bomber pushed the button or the controller gave the signal or the corporal leading the cluster bomb troop added another salvo, I would be gone. I had no responsibility in this. It was out of my control completely. I could see no way of avoiding such an outcome if fate had ordained it, so I had better resign myself to my destiny. My previous hysteria, my extreme vigilance and fear had gone, replaced by a strange idyll, a pleasant repose that lasted for those few odd hours and beyond.

We hurtled out of the fertile alluvial plains of Mesopotamia and the landscape changed. We moved into the scrublands and before we knew it we were in the desert, bleak and delightfully empty.

With Baghdad at a safe distance behind us, Basim pulled the GMC over at the side of the highway, a signal I understood to mean that we were to take a break, to take on some fluids and to stretch our legs. When the vehicle stopped I jumped out and went to the back of the bus to get some water and snacks. I noticed there was almost no traffic on the road as I slid down the side of the embankment to relieve myself. As I was down there a strange noise rose up. It was human but not immediately recognisable, as if it were a child whining or a person in pain complaining.

I clambered back up the ditch and the sound I had been hearing became apparent. Basim had unfurled his small *salat* mat and was pointing towards the Ka'baa in Mecca (qibla for Muslims), deep into his prayer of thanks: '*La ilah illa llah. Mohammed rasul Allah.*' ('There is no god but God. Mohammed is the messenger of God.') He repeated the statement a number of times, raising his voice in an almost musical fashion before falling prostrate on the ground. I had heard this Muslim prayer (*shahada*, or witness of faith) hundreds of times before in Iraq and elsewhere, but nowhere had it struck me as more heartfelt and sincere as here on the side of a road in the empty western desert of Iraq.

Basim finished his prayers, rolled up his mat, put it away under the driver's seat and joined me for a glass of water and some nuts. We smiled a warm greeting at each other.

'I'm sorry about hitting you back there, Basim. I'm afraid I thought we were going to be killed and I lost control of myself. I'm really sorry,' I offered.

'I thought you had gone mad,' he said. 'You had a crazy look in your eyes. Pure crazy, like a crazy man. I was more scared of you than the bombing.'

We both laughed and embraced.

'Thank you for driving us out of that, my friend. I thought that was the end,' I said.

'*Hamdullilah* (God be praised), Mr Richard. Allah will not abandon us now,' he replied.

At the border, the guards who were still working were more sheepish than usual – less inclined to demand bribes. After a cursory search we arrived at the gate which marks the end of Iraq and the beginning of Jordan. In normal circumstances, this is where the final bribes are requested, but that day the two characters manning the barrier were in jovial mood. One was tall and the other short and extremely fat.

'Looks like we've got a regular Laurel and Hardy here, Basim,' I said.

He smiled in agreement. Just then a squadron of military jets flew high overhead. We all looked up.

'Heading to Baghdad?' I asked the guards.

'American planes. Coming from England,' the short one said.

They jointly raised the barrier, half-saluting.

'Bush. He a donkey,' the fat man said.

'Blair. He a dog,' the thin one said.

The double act erupted into uncontrolled laughter as we sped into the neutral area in the direction of the Jordanian border post.

After some cursory form-filling there, we regained the road and headed out on the Jordanian highway, to a country with soft beds and fluffy pillows. We were going to a place where the hotels had bars that were stocked with beer, to a country that has never seen cluster bombs and to a city where restaurants served something other than chicken kebabs, stale bread and hummous.

How joyous it was to be in this dull place. How delightful not to hear explosions and the rat-tat-tat of Kalashnikov gunfire and the screaming of wounded soldiers and civilians. The mundane sounds of a normal city seemed magical. With the window in my hotel room wide open, I laughed as I heard two doormen cheerfully talking about the tips they had received. I smiled as I listened to the sounds of cars speeding by, people driving home after a day of work, oblivious to the mayhem going on just a few hundred kilometres away in their nearest neighbouring country, Iraq.

I took a yellow pill and cut it in half with a knife. Iraq was someone else's problem now. I would go back when it had calmed down, when the coalition had brought order; when the Iraqis elected a new government – in a few months' time. But first to sleep.

2

MISTER FIXIT

October 2002

It was my first time to fly into Baghdad after years of hurtling up the desert highway in a retro-styled GMC, and what a strange experience it was. If the city was an austere 1970s brutalist macho timepiece, all boxes and rectangles, then the city's Saddam International Airport was its full long-haired feminine alter ego. Constructed at the end of the 1970s and early 1980s by a French company, the airport buildings were all wavy walkways, curving concrete screens and long strips of lighting. The dominant colours were green and orange – psychedelia in the desert. The moustaches worn by the hundreds of officials added to the 1970s ambiance. I marvelled at the surroundings as I was passed through customs, then currency control, then visa department, then immigration until finally I arrived at the press accreditation desk.

No doctor in a filthy coat urged me 'must be do the test'. No slumbering customs official demanded a bribe.

I had left behind the medieval atmosphere of the Jordanian border crossing and was now in the twentieth century – even if the rest of the world had moved on to the twenty-first.

I emerged into the baggage hall after the bureaucratic ordeal and made my way to the carousel. A man with a large sign marked Amman Flight walked around the machine and shouted 'Royal Jordanian' every thirty seconds or so at the top of his voice. This struck me as odd, bearing in mind there were no other flights that day. Another man stood at the console that controlled the carousel with a walkie-talkie pinned to his ear. Everyone was impeccably dressed in the secret service uniform of choice – black baggy slacks, shiny black shoes and a black leather jacket.

Someone touched me on the shoulder. I turned around. There was a shortish man in his late forties. He smiled – the first sign of human warmth I had seen since my arrival.

'Good afternoon, sir. My name is Abu Aseel. Anything you want, I can do,' he said, with great emphasis on the word 'anything'. 'I can take you to Basrah. I can take you to Mosul. I can take you to Kirkuk. Anywhere you want and anything you want. I can provide. My name is Abu Aseel.' He broke out in a broad smile, showing a gap where an incisor tooth was missing on his otherwise perfect smile.

'Which department are you from?' I asked.

'Department? I not from department. I am Abu Aseel,' he said, somewhat indignantly.

I looked at him again. He was short, slightly rotund. He wore the characteristic moustache beloved of all Iraqi men but he didn't have the government stooge uniform. Instead he wore a grey jacket and blue trousers. His shoes

were brown. Such a dress sense struck me as a manifesta-
tion of wild individualism in the Iraqi context.

'You are offering to drive me around Baghdad,' I said,
'but I am a journalist and only drivers from the Ministry
of Information can escort me.'

It was a lie and something of a test. If he knew that it
was untrue, then he must be a plant or an agent of some
sort. Insisting on the use of one of the ministry's drivers
wasn't a requirement, but the bureaucrats did foist a
'minder' on you for the duration of your stay. They also
put pressure on your driver to give information on your
movements, attitudes and opinions. It was all part of the
extreme police state that operated under Saddam.

'If that is so, then I will go to the ministry and get a
special order to be your driver. They know me there. I
have done many, many things for them. I have a friend
there. He will help me,' he replied, and again broke into a
hugely warm and apparently genuine smile. There was
something gentle and pleasant about this man, Abu Aseel.

I felt powerless to resist and in any case I needed a
driver to take me from the airport to the al-Rasheed Hotel
in the centre of Baghdad, and so I agreed.

'Fantastic,' he replied, 'fantastic, fantastic, fantastic.'

We picked up our bags and headed for the centre of the
city. Visiting Baghdad wasn't like arriving in other cities.
The metropolis had a hang-dog look to it. While entering
other cities, one notices newly constructed buildings and
billboards advertising the latest products. Baghdad
presented the same dreary, rundown face it had done on
my first visit in 1998. It was like a city preserved in aspic.
At every significant traffic junction there were huge billboards showing Saddam in various poses: Saddam the
warrior (in military uniform); Saddam the modern-day
incarnation of King Nebuchadnezzar of Babylon (in

flowing costume beside a Babylonian structure); Saddam the father of the nation (in a crouching position with an unfeasibly broad grin listening to adoring children); Saddam the leader (on horseback at the head of a cheering crowd), and so on.

I turned to Abu Aseel and nodded towards a billboard showing Saddam holding out his gun and grinning obscenely. 'I see he's still around,' I said.

'Yes, he seems very happy for himself,' he replied, and darted a quick knowing look at me.

'You are a Shia, I think, Abu Aseel,' I said.

'Yes. I am Shia and my family is originally from the south, near Nasariya,' he replied.

'I don't see any posters of Saddam with the Ma'adan,' I offered tenuously. The Ma'adan, or Marsh Arabs, had been brutally suppressed by Saddam after the 1991 Gulf War and I thought Abu Aseel would know about this, coming as he did from their heartland.

'No, Mr Richard, there are no Marsh Arabs in Tikrit,' Abu Aseel said, referring to Saddam's hometown from where he drew his elite fighting force and the senior ranks for all government services.

He again looked at me and I at him. I didn't want to completely show my hand as a hater of Saddam and the regime and Abu Aseel certainly couldn't make any statement that would land him in trouble with the authorities. And so our shadow play over Saddam continued and would last right until the day he was finally toppled. We would refer to Saddam as the 'big guy', 'your man', 'Eric' (I can't remember why) or if we were feeling particularly jovial, 'Harry the Horse' (again, I can't remember why). But most of the time we didn't refer to him at all. I would simply nod my head in the direction of the palace and we would know who and what we were talking about. We were learning to communicate without speaking – by gesture, through a slight change in tone, by raising an eyebrow. It was subtle and it was safe. Nothing dangerous needed to be said. It was all in the inflection or the curl of a lip.

I presented myself in due course to the Ministry of Information's foreign journalist section and was granted an interview with the head of the service, Shakar al-Najri, who remembered me from my BBC days. He scratched his head as he looked at the list of 'minders' available to supervise my activities. He called out the name of one of them. A man arrived in the office and we shook hands. Abu Ali would be my minder for the duration of my stay in Baghdad this time. He didn't look promising. He was short and fat and had the distinctively cold eyes of a true Ba'ath party believer.

Mr Shakar looked at me and asked me who would be driving me during this visit. I told him it would be my old friend Abu Aseel. He asked to see him. I fetched Abu Aseel and told him of my conceit.

'Pretend that we know each other,' I told him.

He seemed bemused. Mr Shakar spoke to him sternly and on one occasion pointed to me and spoke very directly. My Arabic is rudimentary, but it was obvious even to me that Mr Shakar was warning Abu Aseel about me and telling him to keep a close eye on my actions or he would be in trouble.

'Mr Shakar,' I interrupted, 'you need not have any worries about me. I'm just here to do an honest job and to report on the forthcoming presidential elections in a straightforward manner. You should have no concerns. My friend Abu Aseel and your colleague Abu Ali are well capable of looking after me.'

He looked at me for a moment, frozen in mild surprise by my interjection. I could read his face and it seemed to be saying 'this fellow can understand Arabic and knows what I just told the driver about him'. He recovered his composure.

'As you wish,' he said, dismissing all three of us with a wave of his hand.

I was only in Baghdad a few hours and I had already been forced to tell half a dozen lies.

The presidential election of November 2002 was drawing near and I needed to produce an item for RTÉ television that gave a sense of the tensions that lay just beneath the surface in Iraq. Everyone was prepared for the poll to be a sham. The United States was sabre-rattling and the sense of an imminent war was in the air. To bolster his position within Iraq and to enable him to present some spurious evidence of his popularity to an international audience, Saddam dreamed up the idea of a presidential election. There would be only one candidate for the top job. When I asked, Ba'ath party apparatchiks presented the election as a referendum on who the Iraqi people wanted to govern them. Did they want their own home-grown Arab hero or did they want their president chosen by a criminal in Washington? It was a rhetorical question and I nodded to show I understood what was expected from me by way of reaction.

The ballot paper would have a box beside the name of Saddam Hussein. The voter had the option of ticking the box or not. That was the extent of the choice available. One could spoil the paper by not marking it at all, but in such a closely policed society, only a fool would dream of spoiling a ballot paper. Our minder from the ministry, Abu Ali, told me that this had happened during the last such exercise in Iraqi democracy. A few hundred votes across the country were left blank or had obscenities scrawled on them.

'But we found these deviant people and dealt with them. It will not happen this time,' he said without irony.

Later that evening, Abu Aseel came to my room to plan our programme.

'Abu Aseel, I want to go to watch the people voting in Najaf,' I said.

'Impossible,' he replied.

'Why? I thought you said you could do anything.'

'Mr Richard. The people in Najaf no like Saddam Hussein. If we go there, it could be trouble. The ministry will not let us go. I promise you. But I will try,' he said.

Najaf is one of the holiest shrines in Shia Islam. Even though most of the Shias in the world live outside Iraq (and the vast majority of them in neighbouring Iran), Iraq has the honour of hosting almost all of the significant holy places within the Shia sect. Najaf is such a special place that millions of Shias are buried there in what is reckoned to be the largest graveyard in the world. A vast city of mausoleums and graveyards stretches far into the horizon and the caravan of funerals continues on an almost twenty-four-hour-a-day basis.

Abu Aseel told me the legend of the founding of Najaf. Nothing existed before Ali, the founding figure in Shia Islam, was buried there. After he was murdered/martyred in the town of Kufah, his body was put on a camel and turned loose in the scrubby desert. Those that supported him in Kufah said that wherever the camel came to rest, there his remains would be interred and a simple shrine constructed. These supporters felt a great guilt, as they were the ones who had betrayed Ali and failed to come to his aid when he was being attacked by his rivals in the Islamic succession. The camel wandered across the wide open desert and came to a halt at high ground, called the Bahar Najaf. There he was buried, but the location was kept secret, lest his enemies return and desecrate the grave. Centuries later, the great caliph of Baghdad, Harun ar-Rasheed, was hunting in the area when he chased a gazelle to a high point, but a strange thing happened. He was unable to shoot his arrow. The gazelle stood on the mound and showed no fear. His strength had left him. The gazelle escaped. An old man came along and the caliph questioned him about this strange place. The man said that it was the resting place of Ali. He told the caliph that the gazelle took sanctuary on the mound, knowing that he would be safe. The caliph ordered an excavation of the mound and found a simple slab and the bones of Ali. He ordered that the spot should be marked as holy and soon a mosque and then the town of Najaf rose up in the dusty desert.

Abu Aseel enjoyed telling me the story and kept repeating that although it was legend, it was believed by all of the Shia people of Iraq.

'It is the most special place for the Shia,' he said.

Virtually all of the major Shia religious and political figures of the modern era have spent significant amounts of time in Najaf, teaching in the madrassas or studying theology. The best-known in the west was Ayatollah Khomeini, the leader of the Iranian revolution who arrived in Najaf from Qom in Persia in 1964 and was hunted out by Saddam Hussein in 1978. Following a brief exile in Paris, he subsequently returned triumphant to Iran in 1979. Saddam attacked Iran months later.

Najaf's long antipathy to the Sunni Muslim order manifested itself in almost continuous rebellion and insurrection. The city's rebellious heart asserted itself most recently after Saddam Hussein's defeat at the hands of the international coalition in Kuwait in 1991. Shia loyalists attacked and murdered Ba'ath party members and chased the security forces out of the city before Saddam put down the rebellion, sending his cousin Ali Hassan al-Majid and the Republican Guard to suppress the uprising. Even though Saddam's forces committed atrocities on a massive scale across the south, it was here that the rebellion was crushed most ruthlessly.

Abu Aseel arrived back from the ministry looking a little glum. 'They refuse us to go to Najaf,' he said.

I said I wasn't surprised and told him not to worry. We would find somewhere else interesting to visit for the election.

'Yes, Mr Richard, they refuse us to go to Najaf, but they say we can go to Kerbala,' he said, smiling broadly. He threw his hands in the air and said '*Hamdilillah* (praise be to God)'. We embraced.

'Why refuse Najaf and agree to Kerbala?' I asked myself. It didn't make sense. Kerbala is the other central shrine in Shia Islam. Buried under the dome of the golden mosque is another of the Shias' greatest heroes, Husain, whom Shias like Abu Aseel revere as a sort of intermediary between man and God. Along with Najaf, a visit to his holy shrine is almost as important for many Shias as the *Hajj* (pilgrimage) to Mecca. It was also a hotbed of anti-Saddam activism. I thought it likely that the town was under the close control of Saddam's security apparatus.

By the time we left for Kerbala, we had been joined by a small posse of journalists, some of them friends from previous trips. They included correspondent Lindsey Hilsum and cameraman/producer Tim Lambon, veteran journalists from ITN's Channel Four news programme. They were by far the finest broadcast journalists operating in Iraq during that time and they were doubly unusual in being thoroughly decent and kind human beings to boot.

The Ministry of Information laid on a tour bus for us – a bad thing, as this meant our arrival would be flagged in advance and there would be a smokescreen of Ba'ath party hangers-on at every turn. Abu Aseel was tremendously excited by the prospect of travelling to Kerbala. For the average Shia, a pilgrimage to Kerbala is one of the spiritual highlights of life, and permission was difficult to get. The government didn't want groups of Shias congregating in such a centre of sedition and intrigue.

We were greeted by a corpulent Ba'ath party official who welcomed us to the city. 'Kerbala loves Saddam and Saddam loves Kerbala,' he assured us. It was all we could do to stifle our giggles at such an improbable statement.

He escorted us into a large courtyard where people were voting in the elections and then, apparently spontaneously, roaring out loud, 'My life, my blood for Saddam Hussein!' He smiled and thanked us for coming. It appeared that the idea was that we would interview the voters for five minutes or so and get back on our bus and head back to Baghdad. But we had other ideas.

I asked Abu Aseel to go off into the town to find out what was really going on while I stayed at the voting station and took stock of the scene there.

'I must go and pray at the shrine for Imam Husain also, Richard. I will buy you special rosary and prayer disc,' he said.

He left for the golden domed mosque while I made do with what was available at the voting station, which doubled as the Ba'ath party offices in the city. The whole charade was comical. The secret police and the Ba'ath party faithful were everywhere and the voters who did arrive in the shabby courtyard were either party stalwarts or members of the public who had been cajoled or even bullied into casting their vote.

One man extravagantly produced a curved knife and brandished it above his head while holding the ballot paper in his right hand. He then cut his right thumb and as the blood started to flow, made an imprint on the ballot. Again, he called out the Ba'ath party slogan: 'My life, my blood for Saddam Hussein!'

Tim Lambon was filming while Lindsey Hilsum and I interviewed all and sundry. It was a most unsatisfactory experience because of the close supervision of the government heavies, but we had got used to this sort of thing in Iraq. We packed up our equipment and headed back to Baghdad. On the journey, Abu Aseel looked sheepish and withdrawn and didn't make eye contact with me. As we got off the bus, he approached me: 'Very important information for you, Mr Richard. I will see you later.'

He gave me a rosary/worry beads made from fragrant sandalwood and a small round tablet inscribed with Qu'ranic verses featuring the golden dome of Kerbala. While saying their daily prayers, Shias will finger the rosary, and as they prostrate themselves, will touch their head on the tablet of sacred soil from Kerbala. It was the only time Abu Aseel demonstrated the slightest interest in religion. While he believed in his faith, his observance would be best described as sporadic. He was steeped in the mentality of Shia Islam without being overtly religious. If Abu Aseel was a Catholic, he would be described as an 'à la carte Catholic'.

Later that evening, as Tim was reviewing the tapes, he noticed that something was amiss. One of the voters – a particularly vocal one – had come back to vote a second time, to emphasise his devotion to the great leader. The old Irish adage 'vote early and vote often' was clearly well known in these parts. We filed our stories and headed off to our respective hotel rooms.

An hour later there was a knock on my door and I let Abu Aseel in. He seemed excited and wanted to talk. I turned on the television and pushed up the volume. We formed a conspiratorial huddle in the corner as Abu Aseel told me of a meeting he'd had in Kerbala. He wouldn't say who he had met but indicated that it was a number of distant relatives. He told me the astounding news that the Shia opposition group based in exile in Iran, the Supreme Council for the Islamic Revolution in Iraq (SCIRI), had infiltrated into Kerbala and Najaf. They were using agents of the Badr Brigade, their armed wing, for this infiltration. The actions had been approved by Grand Ayatollah Ali al-Sistani, the highest religious authority in Shia Islam and the supreme source of law and instruction for Shias in Iraq. They were convinced that we were in the last days of Saddam and that the Americans would eventually attack and they had sent in a large number of organisers to get ready for the post-Saddam era.

I was amazed. At that remove it didn't seem possible that Saddam would be overthrown easily. Abu Aseel told me he had met a number of men who talked to him of the plan to take over the holy cities when the Americans arrived and to run them according to strict Islamic principles. They would also deal with the lackeys and stooges of the Ba'ath party who had exerted close control over the shrines since the uprising in 1991.

I looked at Abu Aseel and tried to figure him out. His story seemed so removed from the immediate situation in Iraq that I questioned Abu Aseel's judgment and, I'm ashamed to say, his honesty. Was he telling me things that he thought I wanted to hear? Was he spinning me a sensational story so that I would continue to employ him? I really didn't know and so I never filed a report based on the conversation. I kept it at the back of my mind and thought of it as a test of Abu Aseel's reliability. What a fool I was. Experience would teach me to listen to Abu Aseel very carefully when dealing with such serious subjects. As time went on I learned to take what he had to say with the utmost seriousness, especially when it came to information about the Shia.

We greeted the results of the elections with a wry smile. One hundred per cent of the voters had cast their ballot and one hundred per cent of them had voted for Saddam. No one dissented. '*Hamdillilah*,' we exclaimed and shook hands in mock congratulations. At the Ministry of Information building, the mood was buoyant. Abu Ali smiled from ear to ear.

'A great result. Now George Bush and his warmongers can't attack us. We have proved our great democracy loves our president. It is wonderful news,' he exclaimed.

Three months later, I found myself back in Baghdad, and again Abu Aseel was my helper and guide. It was early March 2003, and the coming war was on everyone's mind. Abu Aseel had begun preparations for what he told me would be a long period of chaos after the fighting. He invited me to his home to meet his family and to witness the work going on.

As he showed me around the modest house, one of his helpers, Abu Ra'ad, was manipulating a huge drilling machine and there was much discussion about where exactly the well should be sunk. Abu Ra'ad was a ruddy-faced man in his late fifties with an open, welcoming smile. I got on reasonably well with him but his relationship with Abu Aseel was regularly testy. Abu Aseel suggested he move his machine to another part of the garden. Abu Ra'ad muttered to himself and flicked his eyes to the heavens.

'The water will be the first to go, then the electric. This is the generator and in this shed, I have spare,' Abu Aseel told me.

He had stored enough rice, pasta, petrol and provisions to keep his family of six in basic comfort for about four months. I asked whether he needed so much. Surely the war wouldn't last that long?

'The last time the fighting with the Americans didn't last long, but afterward we had a difficult time. There was no food. There was nothing. It will be the same this time,' he said.

He showed me his basement, a shallow space about one metre in height, used for storing hard goods. He dismissed it with a wave of the hand. 'This is not proper basement. Not like in the older houses,' he said, referring to the deep excavations most Iraqis made to create underground rooms. In the stifling heat of a Baghdad summer, families would head below ground and sleep in the cool of their underground. The difference in temperature was more than ten degrees centigrade, Abu Aseel claimed.

'Nobody has these basements now. In the summer now, we go onto the roof and sleep under the stars. It is not as cool as the basement, but it is better than the bedroom,' he said.

Abu Aseel ushered me into the family parlour, a long room with a low ceiling and comfortable armchairs on either side and a huge painted portrait of the pater familia on the wall. A small vase with plastic flowers sat on the small occasional table in the middle of the room. Two uncles and a cousin joined the party. The children arrived at the door to look at the stranger. They giggled and pointed and eyed me up in the way that young children do. I smiled and nodded and when I got the chance pulled a grotesque face, which sent them into paroxysms of laughter. Abu Aseel scolded them gently and shooed them out to the kitchen, but to no avail. They were back five minutes later and kept us company for the duration of the visit.

Aseel, the eldest girl of fifteen years, served tea. The Iraqi and Arab tradition is that the father takes on the pet name Abu (father) and the name of his firstborn and his wife Oum (mother) at the same time. Depending on the tradition in the family, they may be called by this name forever. In stricter, more Islamic families, it's rare for a father to carry the name of a girl, even if she is the first-born, but for Abu Aseel this wasn't an issue.

We settled into a long discussion about what the imme-diate future might hold. The war was coming. Of that there was no doubt. The Americans would win. Abu Aseel was sure of that. But, to my surprise, it wasn't the dangers of the war that concerned them, but its uncertain after-math. Oum Aseel joined us for the discussion. She wore the standard black *abaya* of a conservative Shia woman and didn't offer an opinion until invited to do so. But when she did, her opinion carried a considerable force. She was clearly very respected in her own home.

'The Americans do not speak Arabic. They come from a place many thousands of kilometres away from here. What do they know of our Iraqi life?' she asked. We all nodded in agreement. 'There are very many bad people in Iraq and if the Americans do not show a strong hand, there will be chaos for a long time. I promise you this,' she said.

I thanked her for her opinion, which was similar, although expressed differently, to that of the men in the room. I appreciated their frankness. No other Iraqi had offered their honest assessment in such a straightforward way to me before and there were huge risks for them in doing so. It was, after all, sedition to even consider the end of the Ba'ath party regime, and to openly discuss the demise of Saddam was dangerous indeed. But I quickly learned that even among the least political families in the Shia community, there was a seething resentment about their treatment under Saddam. They were almost uniformly awaiting his early demise.

Soon afterwards, Abu Ra'ad arrived and spoke to Abu Aseel. They looked worried about something. Abu Aseel explained that they were having difficulty locating a source of clean water in the garden. We all went outside to inspect the work.

The small garden looked like it had been infested with moles. There were large holes and mounds of soil everywhere. In places a dark liquid substance had formed a pool around the excavation. Abu Ra'ad puzzled over the problem and then addressed me.

'You see, Mr Richard, this is why this war is going to happen. Oil. There is oil everywhere and this is what the Americans are greedy for. They want to come and take the Iraqi oil and use it for themselves,' he said.

I was incredulous. I inspected the holes and the dark bituminous substance oozing from the ground and had to concur that it looked like oil. In truth I had no idea what crude oil looked or smelled like. I had heard that there were places in Iraq and Saudi Arabia where oil could be found bubbling to the surface, the so-called 'fields of fire' which had been alight since biblical times because the oil was so close to the surface. But it seemed incredible to me that it could be happening here in my friend's garden.

'Is it really oil,' I asked, 'this close to the surface?'

Abu Aseel explained that we were very close to the Baghdad East Oil facility, which was the only oil facility in the capital, and that there is oil all over that part of the city.

'I think this is not any good for refining, this oil. But we cannot drink it so we will have to find another place for water,' he said.

Moments later, another two men arrived with more pipes and a more powerful drill and the prospectors moved to another part of the garden to try to find water. I asked Abu Aseel if there were water diviners in Iraq who could pinpoint a source of clean water. He looked at me in disbelief.

'Water diviners, what is this thing? You have these people in Ireland?' he asked.

I told him that we did and explained that no farmer worth his salt would even think of digging a well on his land without consulting a diviner first.

'Yes, I think we have them here,' he replied, 'but I have never had to dig for water before, so I never thought of getting one.'

I thought it a curious sign of how Iraqis saw themselves. More than once Abu Aseel and other Iraqis expressed surprise at the weirdness of certain aspects of Western culture. One story particularly amused Abu Aseel. He laughed for hours after I told him about the concept of the pet stone. I explained that people bought these stones and spoke to them and put them to sleep in specially constructed nests. I told him it seemed to come from California in the 1970s, like a lot of these ideas. He was flabbergasted that people would actually pay money for stones and that they would treat them like an animal.

'Are these people mad? How could this happen? It is very strange,' he said, bewildered.

At a more serious level, the pet stones and water diviners offended Abu Aseel's belief in Western rationality. In spite of decades of Ba'ath party propaganda in support of the non-aligned countries of the developing world, Abu

Aseel, like most Iraqis, felt that the Western system was far superior to any other in the world. He regarded Chinese goods as inferior and wouldn't even entertain the idea of buying Indian-made equipment. There was a hierarchy in his mind and at the top of that was Europe and the United States. At the bottom was the Third World. In many ways this was an old-fashioned view of the world, post-colonial in character. But it also spoke of that other legend about the Iraqis, that they are the 'Prussians of the Middle East', a strong-minded, work-orientated, ambitious nation with high standards. That trait manifested itself in many ways and it was always strongest when the Iraqis compared themselves to others in the region.

Later that afternoon, after we had left, the team struck a source of sweet, clean water. Abu Aseel brought me a bottle of it to drink later, and although it was more brackish than the bottled water I had been consuming, it was perfectly good for drinking and bathing.

'They drilled nineteen holes and out of number twenty came sweet water. *Hamdilillah*,' he said.

'*Hamdilillah*,' I rejoined.

Our preparations for war were now at an advanced stage. Abu Aseel had built a small wooden office for me on top of the Ministry of Information. It was a shack in all but name but we sheltered from the sun in it and plotted our strategy for surviving the war there, far from the prying eyes of the ministry's officials. It was our hideaway and we drank endless cups of coffee and gossiped. Abu Aseel produced iced pastries one day and colleagues flocked to our shack. So many turned up that the group spilled out onto the untidy roof. It was almost a party.

Abu Aseel asked me if I wanted a gun. I replied that I couldn't use one and that I didn't think it was wise for a journalist to be armed in a war situation.

'But Mr Richard, everything will go bad here when the bombing happens. The law and the order will stop. You have to have something to protect yourself,' Abu Aseel said.

I thanked him for his concern but reiterated my opinion that journalists shouldn't be armed. Abu Aseel countered that everyone else was.

'Even the children have the gun. I am teaching Mohammed to use the gun. I can teach you also,' he said.

'But he's only fourteen years of age. How can you give him a gun?' I asked.

'Believe me, there will be a great need for the gun when the Americans come. There will be big problems,' he said.

Two days before the war began, Abu Aseel brought me back to his house to show me his military preparations for the war. He had modified his flat roof to include a kind of sentry hut so that a guard could keep watch on the family home at all times. From a secret hiding place in his house he showed me the family's arsenal of weapons. They had four AK-47 rifles and at least half a dozen handguns. Boxes of ammunition were stored carefully in another safe.

Back in the parlour, Mohammed demonstrated his prowess with the AK-47. He was thin with round, deep brown eyes like his father, but he looked much younger than his fourteen years. I could have easily mistaken him for a ten-year-old. Under the close supervision of Abu Aseel, he loaded then unloaded the gun and removed the barrel and cleaned it. Abu Aseel taught him the military drills associated with these weapons, skills he had learned during his time in military service. The boy was delighted to show off his prowess and beamed proudly as he wiped the rifle with an old rag.

'I will protect my family with my father. Nothing bad will come,' he said.

Abu Aseel touched him gently on the cheek, took the gun away and put it back in its hiding place behind a display cabinet. Mohammed skipped out of the room to play football outside with his friends. He was a child again after his brief sojourn in the dangerous adult world.

Driving back to our shack at the Ministry of Information, Abu Aseel confided that he didn't like the idea of having to expose Mohammed to weapons.

'You know the guns, they are no good. But what choice do we have? If someone come to my house and I am not there, what can we do? Mohammed is a good boy. He will help the family until I come home,' Abu Aseel said.

The pace of work had become hectic. There was constant demand for material back in Dublin and I had been afflicted with sharp headaches as a result of the workload and hours spent in the open with no sun protection. Abu Aseel urged me to visit a pharmacy to stock up on medicines in advance of the combat. I had put it off for a few days, but time was running out and the task was becoming urgent.

'When the bombing comes, the shops will all close and there will be a big problem with things like medicine. Let us go together and get what we need,' he said.

We stopped on Sa'adoun Street and looked around for a pharmacy. Many of the shops had already closed. Others looked empty of stock. We eventually found a ramshackle pharmacy. When she saw us, the assistant behind the counter called for the proprietor, Gulam Khatib, who greeted me warmly and talked of his fears of the forthcoming conflict.

'There are many sick people in this city and they will suffer when the war comes. Many live on small pensions. How will they survive? Will the Americans give them money to live? It is very difficult. Up to now we have had a few problems. I spoke with other pharmacists and we are all worried about thieves coming to steal the drugs. There are many who will do this after the prisoners were freed,' he said.

He was referring back to an extraordinary event that had happened after the sham election of the previous year. After his victory – 100 per cent voted for Saddam with a turnout of 100 per cent – the president ordered that the prisons be emptied of all but the most serious political criminals. More than 30,000 were freed. At Abu Gharaib prison alone I saw up to 5,000 running out of the jail amid chaotic scenes. Afterwards there was a small demonstration outside the Ministry of Information by mothers of prisoners who had failed to appear. Apparently these prisoners had been authorised for release, but when the families went to find them they were told that they had been taken to other detention centres or killed by Saddam's security forces.

A crime wave followed the amnesty. There were many stories in Baghdad of burglaries and hold-ups, events that were almost unheard of before the prisoner releases. Pharmacies in particular were targeted and Mr Khatib told me that every single premises in the city had been burgled at least once in the previous three months. Drug addiction was a taboo subject in the old Iraq, although it was obvious that the country had a major problem. The opium smoking habit is at epidemic levels in neighbouring Iran, and although Iraq's problem isn't of that order, it's still significant. He reckoned that this was behind the rash of crime.

The pharmacist told me that he had studied in London in the 1970s and had returned in 1980 to set up business in Baghdad.

'That was a different time. Everyone had some money. The country was peaceful. No one was threatening us. Iraq was one of the leading countries,' he smiled.

He spoke as if it was a distant time, halcyon days. He had sent his family to Jordan to escape the worst effects of the war. He would not be joining them.

'I cannot leave the pharmacy. It is all we have,' he said.

I purchased some Paracetemol and some aspirin and asked if he had any mild sleeping tablets.

'You are having trouble with the sleep?' he asked.

I explained that my sleeping pattern had become somewhat broken and I was sure that it would get worse when the bombing began.

'You are not alone, my friend. The biggest tablet we are selling at this time is this one,' he said, picking a jar of yellow pills from the shelf behind the counter.

He explained that they were low-dosage diazepam pills for people with mildly disturbed sleeping patterns.

'The parents mostly buy it for the children. It is safe for the little ones and makes them sleep through the bombing. We used it in the last war with our own children, who are now grown up,' he said.

'This is what I came to buy, also,' Abu Aseel added, to my surprise.

We collected our medicines and parted with the firm promise that I would visit again when the war was over. I kept the yellow tablets in my room for the duration of the war and never thought it wise to use them. My sleep pattern was thrown into chaos by the constant bombing. The fear of being killed in an attack would set my heart racing and I would feel adrenalin coursing through my veins. At that point I would be bolt awake, unable to contemplate sleep for at least another three or four hours. I never knew whether I would have to flee the hotel because of a stray bomb or an attack or a fire or an accident. Even though I was tempted to take half a tablet every now and then to enjoy the uninterrupted bliss of four or five hours' sleep, I convinced myself that it would be foolish and maintained that resolve throughout the whole war.

Abu Aseel finished his family's supply of yellow tablets at the end of the second week of bombing and I handed over half my supply. He explained that the routine in his house was the same every day. After a late supper the children would gather for night-time prayers. Abu Aseel would talk to them and reassure them before giving each of the four children half a yellow pill and sending them off to bed for the night.

'All of the families are doing this. It is not good for the children to be awake all night crying. The bombs make them very scared,' he said.

At the beginning of the war I saw less of Abu Aseel and urged him to attend to his extended family. I was swamped with pointless press conferences and endless work reporting the early stages of the war back to Dublin. There was a huge appetite for material on the human effects of the war, and with only twenty or so reporters in Baghdad to produce stories, I found the going tough. I missed Abu Aseel's help and insights, but he had more important work to do at home.

Abu Aseel turned up after the second night of bombing with a large vat of home-cooked food and a small stove.

'Oum Aseel is worried that you are not eating well enough. She will make the meal every three days and I will bring it to you. You can heat it on the ring,' he said.

The first instalment of Oum Aseel's cooking was a revelation. Chicken had been cooked in a thick tomato-based broth with vegetables added and a large bowl of scented rice and almonds. It was delicious and I shared it with my South African friend Bonny Schoonacher, correspondent of the Johannesburg-based *Sunday Times*. He had his own secret supply of goodies too.

Bonny had dual Dutch/South African nationality and had become friendly with the Dutch ambassador to Iraq before the war. Before he left Baghdad, the ambassador had given Bonny keys to the embassy residence in the wealthy suburb of Mansour and told him to use it as he saw fit. The residence had the biggest television I'd ever seen – it almost covered a whole wall. When it was turned on it went immediately to a pornography channel with buxom women screaming in ecstasy while we scrambled around, looking for the correct remote control unit, fearful that the security agents outside might misunderstand our reasons for visiting. Bonny had discovered thousands of Dutch meal packs (MREs, meals ready to eat, as the Americans called them) in the basement, along with an endless supply of beer.

The meal packs contained sachets of stew or curry that could be warmed up by a chemical heater which was provided, and lots of packs of peanut butter, tea, chocolate, salt, crackers and other luxuries. The deal we made was that I would provide morning coffee in my room (Habibe Coffee, we called it) while Bonny would provide lunch and Oum Aseel dinner. We felt very organised and pleased with ourselves.

As events unfolded, breakfast was the only sure meal of the day, as for much of the war we were out in the afternoons and evenings attending press conferences or inspecting bomb sites or hospitals. Even though our hours were long and irregular, not once did we fail to finish Oum Aseel's dinners.

Abu Aseel took me aside after the press conference on the afternoon of the fourth day of the war.

'There is a lot of fighting in Nasariya. I spoke to my brother–in-law who is a senior officer in the air force defence and he tells me that there are a lot of attacks going on there. The tribes have been given many guns and many bombs and money and the Feddeyin Saddam are fighting there. They have killed many Americans. But my uncle, he tells me that the ordinary soldiers are not fighting. Many, many of them have left and are gone home,' he said.

Abu Aseel told me that the war had become a guerrilla war almost immediately. His brother-in-law had informed him that almost all of the troops under his command had deserted and he himself had been brought under the control of the Feddeyin Saddam. He had less than 300 soldiers left. This Feddeyin was notoriously ill disciplined and chaotic and was outside the normal military hierarchy, being controlled by Saddam's two sons. The Feddeyin was designed to be the last line of defence for Saddam's regime. In the event of an army coup or an Iranian invasion, they would secure the al-Tikriti clan's power base. It was drawn almost exclusively from the Sunni heartlands around Saddam's hometown of Tikrit, including the significant cities of ar-Ramadi and Fallujah.

'My brother-in-law is worried. The Feddeyin want to take the Americans into a street fight in Nasiriya, but this is not good. The Americans will catch them all and kill them. My brother-in-law wants to leave Nasiriya. Can you contact the Americans and maybe they can meet him?' Abu Aseel said.

I thought about it for a short time and then realised it was out of the question. How would it look to the Baghdad authorities if it were found that I was organising the surrender of Iraqi troops? Apart from the obvious safety concern, there was also the simple matter of journalistic independence. I was in Baghdad to be a witness to the war, not a participant. There are many compromises for a journalist in war time, but this was a compromise too far.

Abu Aseel was disappointed, but he understood the problem. Yet again, the information he provided about the Iraqis proved invaluable. Like all the journalists covering the war, I was having great difficulty in putting the news from Nasiriya and the other hotspot of the war to date, Um Qasr, in context. This wasn't helped by the misinformation coming from both sides and the paucity of detail about the battles going at such a great remove from Baghdad. The only map I possessed was a tattered affair, twenty years old and based on too small a scale to be useful. As ever in Iraq, there was another complication. It was illegal to own a decent map. In the paranoid world of the dictator, a good map was considered to be a classified document. It could be used against the state itself, and so anyone found with one was immediately under suspicion as a saboteur or foreign agent.

Abu Aseel brought me down to the lobby of the Palestine Hotel and we walked past the throng of agents and minders to the untidy mini-market that flourished in the plaza outside. Abu Aseel shuffled up to a man who was standing alone carrying a large briefcase. He spoke to him briefly and motioned for me to follow them to the wasteland area between the hotel and the river. We sat on a bench near a long-abandoned fountain that was overgrown with shrubs.

The man was taller than Abu Aseel but looked considerably older, perhaps sixty. He had previously worked in the Iraqi equivalent of the Ordnance Survey office and was now hawking maps of Iraq to the foreigners in the hotel. I looked at the merchandise and agreed to purchase a large-scale map of the country for the outrageous sum of fifty dollars. I noticed that the map was old and asked him when it was produced.

'All of the work for this map was done in 1989, but there were some updates after that but we were not allowed to see them. That was only for the military and the *Mukhabarrat* (intelligence service).' Abu Aseel translated his answer.

Before we left him, he insisted on drawing two new roads on the map. These were key highways from the south and were normally closed to civilian traffic. I subsequently found out that they had been constructed after the 1991 Shia uprising as a means to deliver elite fighting units to the south should the need arise. The map man pointed to the highways and told Abu Aseel, 'That is how the Americans are coming.'

Back in the hotel I opened the map on my bed and Abu Aseel began filling in my knowledge of the war so far. He knew little about the north, but he had heard a steady trickle of information from his ancestral lands in the south. The picture was clear even after the first few days of fighting. He pointed to the British advance on Basrah and showed how they were advancing in an arc around the city. A clear pattern was obvious. He then followed the wave of American attacks on Nasiriya and beyond to Ur, Samawa and Najaf. Another pattern emerged there. The Americans were moving fast up the country, following the line of towns and settlements on the Euphrates.

'They are not coming into the cities. They are going around and around and chasing to the next place. It is very strange tactics. You agree?' he said.

I had to agree that it seemed very risky for the Americans to bypass so many strongholds of the regime in their march to Baghdad. It seemed to leave their rearguard vulnerable to a breakout attack. Abu Aseel disagreed on that point. There would be no organised breakout attack by the Iraqi forces. The pattern in Nasiriya would be replicated everywhere, he explained. The Americans would bypass a town, encircling it while the Feddeyin Saddam would snipe and attack them using guerrilla tactics.

'The time will come for the terror attacks. There will be bombings and suicides and snipers. My brother-in-law tells me they cannot fight against the Americans because of the radar and the satellite. The Americans can see everything and the Iraqis can see nothing. Every time they turn on a machine or a radar, within five minutes it is destroyed. They cannot fight like a strong army, so they are fighting like bin Laden,' he said with a laugh and a clap of his hands.

It was at times like this that I could see the dilemma of many Iraqis. Even though they despised the regime, they still retained pride in being Iraqi. They wanted to see the overthrow of Saddam, but at the same time they felt the humiliation of defeat very acutely.

Abu Aseel worried about the speed and character of the American advance. He saw that it could lead to instability for a long time.

'You see, we all thought Saddam was strong. He invaded Kuwait. He killed the Shia in 1991. He killed all the opposition since then and he threw all the bad people into prison. But now we see him against the Americans and he is nothing. There is nothing he can do. If there is nothing, the bad people can do anything they want. I tell you, Richard, this is very dangerous,' he said.

Early the next day, Abu Aseel arrived at the hotel out of breath. He looked tired and upset. He'd had another phone call from his brother-in-law.

'Abu Ali is in big trouble. His soldiers turned on him and he had to flee. He called me from a small town north of Nasiriya. The Americans are everywhere and he cannot move. What can I do? I am here and he is there and I cannot go to get him,' he said.

I had never seen Abu Aseel so upset. His face was flushed and he was short of breath. I thought he was close to having a heart attack. He explained that he hadn't been sleeping and every bomb that fell at night increased his anxiety. I took him to the rooms of a doctor from Medicine du Monde (an NGO that was in Iraq to support the hospitals during the crisis) and asked for help. The doctor briefly examined Abu Aseel and told him to go to the Yarmuk hospital, which was still functioning. The doctor confided in me that he thought he was suffering from very high blood pressure.

Abu Ra'ad drove us to the hospital through a deserted Baghdad. The street traders had all gone and most of the shops had been closed. Many of the shop fronts were boarded up and some had even bricked up their front windows.

At the hospital we headed straight for the emergency section. I noticed a higher than normal presence of military and police around the facility. I didn't take any notice of this, as Abu Aseel's condition worried me so much. Eventually we got to see a doctor, who took Abu Aseel into a cubicle and examined him. I wandered around the ground floor. I had heard a commotion earlier and went to find out what was going on. The noise came from a large ward which had spilled over into the corridor. There was blood on the floor and many of the patients were in uniform. Between the low moans of the barely conscious and the screams of the walking wounded, the scene was one of true bedlam. Nurses were attending to the victims as best they could. I saw a doctor and asked him what was going on. He looked at me sternly and advised me not to stay. I was puzzled. Normally Iraqi doctors are most sympathetic to foreigners and to journalists in particular.

'These are all soldiers from the Republican Guard who were bombed out near the military airport. Many were killed and we have many, many injured here. It is not wise for you to stay,' he said in impeccable English.

Just then a soldier in full uniform approached, carrying a rifle. He had the dark, hard looks of a true fighter and I stepped back. He spoke to the doctor brusquely, and by his demeanour and stance, I realised I was not welcome. I took a few steps back. The doctor turned to me and in an urgent voice told me, 'Go. Go now. Before there is trouble. Go. This is a hospital. Please go,' he said.

The soldier moved to get his rifle and shouted something. I fled back towards the emergency room as fast as I could, the sounds of soldiers apparently pursuing me spurring me on. Abu Aseel and Abu Ra'ad were sitting in chairs in the filthy waiting room. I told them we had to leave quickly and we headed out as fast as we could. Abu Aseel pushed us out the door and went back to negotiate with the angry soldier.

We waited anxiously in the vehicle with the engine running. Abu Aseel came out of the hospital fifteen minutes later.

'He was coming to kill you. He said you were American and you had killed his brother soldiers and you deserved to die. I told him you were Irish and not American. I turned him back,' he said.

I thanked him for again saving my life.

'It was easy,' he said with a smile. 'I gave him some of your money.'

For all his coolness under stress, Abu Aseel's high blood pressure had caused severe strain on his heart and under normal circumstances he would have been admitted to hospital for observation and rest. But there was nothing normal about Iraq at this time and so he had been given a handful of pills along with a prescription and told to come back after the war. The pills had the immediate effect of reducing his blood pressure, but I insisted that Abu Aseel went home and rested for a few days.

He initially refused, pointing out that I would be alone in Baghdad in the middle of a most dangerous part of the war.

'It is better for me that you are alive in three days' time, Abu Aseel, rather than dead tonight,' I said.

Abu Aseel looked at me for a moment and then smiled. 'This is the Irish sense of humour again, Richard,' he said. We embraced and he went home to rest.

The three days that Abu Aseel was absent saw an intensification of the war and a growing realisation that the end would come sooner rather than later. I also had to acknowledge how dependent I had become on him. At a practical level I found it difficult to navigate around Baghdad without his sure knowledge and instinct for danger. My meals were a lot more Spartan in the absence of Oum Aseel's superb home cooking. At a more profound level, I found myself at sea, unable to interpret events without the sound judgment of Abu Aseel to guide me.

Explosions in the distance were just that now. Whereas before Abu Aseel would be able to tell me precisely what had been hit and why, now I was relying on the government and the same rumour mill as the other journalists. Without Abu Aseel, the war had become a guessing game.

When he returned to work at the end of March, our reunion was warm and happy. He looked less drawn and told me he had slept better with the help of some of the small yellow tablets I had given him earlier. He may have spent the time relaxing, but he had also gathered a huge amount of information about the course of the conflict. He shared his insights with me as we sat in our familiar conspiratorial huddle in my hotel room overlooking the palace complex at the bend in the river.

When the day came for me to leave, I wrote Abu Aseel a long testimony and handed over what was left of my money. I prepared to leave Baghdad with a heavy heart. Abu Aseel tried to return some of the money and reassured me that all would be well.

'Remember, Richard. The Americans come along and they take over Japan. Look at it today. They come along and take over Germany. Look at it. The same with Korea. Everything will be fine. Go home to your family and I will see you in a few weeks,' he said. I promised I would come back soon to check on the progress he had been expecting.

⌒

September, 2003

The airplane banked alarmingly and the South African captain announced over the tannoy that we were descending into Baghdad.

'Don't be alarmed by the approach. It has to be done this way and we'll get you all safely down in no time,' he said.

I looked at the man beside me and raised my eyebrows in mild alarm. The descent into Baghdad was not so much an approach as a controlled fall. The plane began to go down in ever decreasing circles like a corkscrew. My stomach heaved but I wasn't yet sick. I looked out of the window and saw the horizon in a place it shouldn't have been. The engines roared and we continued our alarming descent. Buildings flashed across my field of vision through the window. The manoeuvre was executed this way to avoid missile and small arms attacks by insurgents. At the last turn of the corkscrew, the plane violently righted itself and we hammered the ground.

'Welcome to Baghdad International Airport. The time is 11:35,' a disembodied voice announced.

The security men waved us on. An immigration official stamped a tiny circular impression on my passport. It read, 'Baghdad International Airport. Entry. CPA. Sept 8 2003.' There was no mention of Iraq.

I made my way to the rendezvous point and waited for Abu Aseel. Moments later, a short man with wavy gray hair wearing his left arm in a sling approached me.

'Richard. Richard. *Habibe*. Abu Luke. How are you, my friend? How nice to see you again,' he said, embracing me warmly, kissing me on each cheek three times.

I looked at this man with his familiar voice and scrambled my brain to try to figure out why I didn't recognise him as Abu Aseel. It appeared as if he had aged ten years in less than five months. I snapped out of my trance and we walked arm in arm to the car while I related our adventures on the journey to him. I asked him what had happened to his arm.

'Bad story, Richard. I was coming home from the office. I had lovely Mercedes car. A real Mercedes. Not one of those stolen from Kuwait. As I neared my city, I hear some men shouting at me from the car behind. I speed the car up. Then they are shooting in the air and chasing me. Believe me, I didn't know what to do. So I speed up very fast and go towards my home. They are following me all the time. Now they are shooting at me in the car. I get one bullet here in the shoulder first of all. Then I turn the corner very sharp and head up to my street. I am blaring the horn and flashing the lights and shouting "help me, help me". My neighbour, he saw what was happening and he got his gun. I had no gun in the car. Then I am shot again. This time it hit me here in the arm and the bullet go up my arm and out here at my wrist and I stop the car. My neighbour came running up the street shouting and shooting the gun in the air. Then everybody came and started to shoot at the robbers. I went to hospital and here I am now. *Hamdilillah*,' he said.

He told me things were very bad in Baghdad. 'Ever since they bombed the UN building and the Jordanian embassy, everything has got bad. Very bad. There is Ali Baba everywhere. The Americans, they are doing nothing. Just taking the oil,' he said.

I reminded him of his parting comments at the end of the war about the Americans turning Iraq into a Germany or Japan.

'Yes. Turn us into Germany? They are welcome to do this. Turn us into Korea? Welcome. Turn us into Japan? Welcome. But turn us into Somalia? No!' he said. It sounded like a rhetorical flourish he had rehearsed on a number of occasions.

After checking into the Palestine Hotel, Abu Aseel took me back to his home. Oum Aseel greeted me as a long-lost son. She took my hand, touched her heart and kissed her hand. For a conservative Shia woman, this was an impressive demonstration of affection. Aseel served us tea and food in the parlour. I thought she had grown taller and said so. It was the right thing to say and all joined in to admire her. She was becoming a woman, Oum Aseel told me, smiling. Aseel was embarrassed by the attention and pulled her veil across her face slightly. She skipped out of the room moments later, smiling.

Abu Ali, Abu Aseel's brother-in-law, joined us. I greeted him as an old friend and explained that the news of his exploits in the south of Iraq during the war had kept me well informed and entertained. He smiled warmly and welcomed me back to Baghdad.

'The country has changed and we are all changing with it, my friend,' he said.

Oum Aseel catalogued the chaos that was going on around their suburb. 'Everyone in the street has had something happen to them. One family had their daughter kidnapped and had to sell their car to pay for the ransom. Another family lost the father. Everywhere there is chaos and people are being killed or kidnapped. It is incredible. We have never seen anything like this. Not even after the invasion of Kuwait was it this terrible. We never see the Americans except in tanks on the big roads and you must avoid them because they can shoot you. There are no police. They have destroyed the country and they are taking the oil. Why did they come?' she asked plaintively.

Abu Ali sat silently as Oum Aseel went through the catalogue of woe. While in the West it has always been assumed that women have a low status in Islamic countries and that their opinions count for little, I always found in Iraq that the situation was more nuanced and subtle than the outward picture would imply.

When Oum Aseel spoke, everyone listened with respect and took what she was saying with the utmost seriousness. The impression gained was that her opinions mattered. When she had finished, Abu Ali took up the baton.

'I was a big man in the old air force defence corps, but now I am nothing. They have abolished the army and the police and replaced it with nothing. Now I live on the charity of my brother-in-law, Abu Aseel. He keeps the whole family going and I don't know what we would do without him,' he said.

Abu Aseel looked proud and embarrassed at the same time. I asked how many people were relying on him for survival. Abu Ali counted up the numbers for me.

'There are twenty-five members of the family relying on Abu Aseel. There are no jobs for us. I am forty-eight years and I am not finished yet,' he said with a tone of defiance.

Early the next morning, Abu Aseel picked me up from the hotel and we went out to meet Abu Ali. Like many former soldiers and officers, Abu Ali was entitled to a small monthly payment of fifty dollars. This small stipend had been finally agreed by the CPA after it was reported that a large-scale uprising of former soldiers was imminent. There had been riots at former army bases in Baghdad and Baquba. The money for the new pensions (as they were called) came from Iraqi assets abroad that had been frozen after the invasion of Kuwait more than a decade before.

We met Abu Ali as he queued with thousands of others to collect the pension. He was subdued, slightly embarrassed that we wanted to see him in this position. The military base where the money was doled out was opposite the dilapidated Baghdad Zoo on a busy main road. The zoo had been one of the few places of leisure in Baghdad. Now it was a ruin. All the animals were gone. As we crawled along in the traffic, I absorbed the changed atmosphere of the city. The charm and common courtesy that characterised life in Baghdad before had disappeared, replaced by a sharp edge.

A man driving a taxi drew up beside our vehicle in the boiling heat of mid-morning. All our windows were closed to extract the maximum benefit from the air conditioning system in the car. I looked at the driver, smiled and nodded my head in greeting – a normal occurrence in the old Iraq. The man looked at me with real hatred in his eyes. He rolled down his window, coughed and spat on the road.

Abu Aseel was deeply embarrassed by the episode and remonstrated with the driver. He apologised on behalf of the spitting man and explained that with little electricity or water and few jobs, Baghdadis were becoming more and more angry.

'Maybe you can die in an argument at a benzene [petrol] station. Maybe someone will kill you for your car. Maybe you will be shot because you look at someone the wrong way. Any way you can die. Just like that,' he said and snapped his fingers.

As temperatures rose into the mid-forties centigrade, the line of ex-soldiers grew longer and longer. By midday there were more than a thousand waiting in line. American military police officers kept order in the queue, wandering up and down the line swinging their metre-long batons, calling out instructions in English. Abu Ali bought a glass of water from a waterseller and bemoaned the passing of the previous regime.

'I do not want Saddam back. Not Saddam himself, but the time of Saddam. The quiet life of the old government. Everything was not good then. Especially for us Shia. But if we stayed out of politics, we could buy food and we could walk on the streets. Now everything is bad. The Americans have made a big mistake,' he said.

I asked him if he had been approached to join the growing Resistance movement.

'No. They do not want me. I am Shia and the Resistance is Sunni. They are Ba'ath party men and Salafia and Wahhabi [two fundamentalist traditions within Sunni Islam]. But they try to recruit all my friends from the air defence because they know how to make bombs. Many, many of these men are joining the Resistance. But not the Shia,' he said.

I asked Abu Aseel if he had witnessed this. He explained that in his neighbourhood there had been growing tensions between Shias and Sunnis. The Sunnis were blamed for attacks against Shias in Kerbala and Najaf and for kidnappings and murders around the Sunni Triangle.

'They [Sunnis] think that the Americans will put the Shias in government. They say no to a government of Sistanis,' he said, referring to the Shia Grand Ayatollah Ali al-Sistani, undisputed leader of Iraq's majority community.

I questioned him about the tensions in his district. He explained that a mullah in the local mosque had attacked the Sunnis in a Friday sermon the previous month. He berated them for supporting Saddam in the past and for fuelling the current insurgency. Sunni families in the street adjoining Abu Aseel's were attacked the next day and their property burned to the ground.

'This was a nice family, but some of the people are jealous and want their house, so they pretend to follow the mullah's advice and attack the homes. It is very bad. The families that were kicked out will come back and there will be revenge. Then we will have small war in my city,' he said.

I looked at Abu Aseel. He seemed ill equipped to live in this dangerous new Iraq. He had a fierce side to him that I had witnessed on occasion, but his overwhelming traits were gentle ones. While I'm sure he would defend himself and his family ferociously, his instincts weren't tuned to the subtleties and the sinister dangers of this new disintegrating country.

⌒

I returned six months later and my visit coincided with an unexpectedly secretive handover of powers from the Coalition Provisional Authority – the American-appointed commission that took over the country after the war, headed by L. Paul Bremer – and a new Iraqi transitional government.

As ever, Abu Aseel had got wind of what was about to happen the day before the event. He managed to smuggle me into the CPA's headquarters in the middle of the

Green Zone on the morning of the signing ceremony. The Green Zone was the area in the centre of Baghdad that the Americans had secured for themselves. It was envisaged that it would host the Iraqi government and the American Embassy in the future. Sitting in a corridor waiting for news of the momentous event, an Iraqi military band walked by, tuning up in advance of the big occasion. We all expected a ceremony and some pomp. There would be a formal handover, music, festivities – even a celebration. In the end, it all happened behind closed doors in secret for fear that the event would provide a focus point for the insurgents to launch attacks. Hours later, we were given a video tape of events, including the departure of L. Paul Bremer out of the Green Zone by helicopter to the airport and thence to Washington. A day which should have heralded a decisive change in the status of the country and an end to the formal administration of Iraq by a foreign country turned out to be a non-event, a damp squib.

Perhaps this was fitting. There were still 150,000 foreign soldiers in Iraq and the new governing council was independent only in as much as it operated under the cloak of security provided by the Americans.

Abu Aseel brought me up to date with the state of affairs in his suburb. In the intervening six months, all of the Sunni residents had been burned out or chased out of the suburb. There was a struggle between the various factions within the Shia community, and the radical cleric Moqtada al-Sadr had planted people in the area. They were behind most of the attacks and had taken to manning checkpoints at all entrances to the area.

'Believe me, Richard, these are just boys. They know nothing and they abuse the people. But what can we do? If we challenge them, they will kill us,' he said.

The transitional plan for Iraq envisaged elections within six months, followed by a referendum on a constitution, ending in a full and final election to a parliament with a five-year term. Abu Aseel despaired at the prospect of so many elections.

'Each time we have elections there will be more killing and more bombing, and what will we get at the end? The same as we have now,' he said.

He shared the opinion of most of the Iraqis I spoke to. What is the point of having a democratic system when basic security is not guaranteed?

'Sure, I can have my own opinion. I can start my own party, but I cannot send my children to school because they may be kidnapped. If this is democracy, then take it away,' he said.

Not for the first time I realised that democracy had very limited appeal to many Iraqis. It was merely an abstract notion, unrelated to the problems they were experiencing. When Iraqis thought about things in a political way, they worked it out as follows. How does this affect my clan? After that, how does it impact on the tribe? Following tribe comes the question of how the action influences the group, in effect, the religion of the person – Sunni, Shia or Kurd. Iraqis still have a 'group consciousness'. They identify more with their clan, tribe, ethnic group or religion than with political parties with policies that could be voted on in an election. This was at the heart of the insurgency. Many Sunni insurgents believed that democracy was a ruse to deny them access to power. Even if they accepted that Shias were more numerous (and many did not), they saw their actions as a vindication of tribe and group, rather than an attack on a fair democratic system.

As word spread throughout the city about the handover, the violence started up again. Within an hour of the ceremony I counted five loud explosions in the vicinity of the Green Zone, some of which shook the ground underfoot.

We again visited Oum Aseel at home and I handed over some trinkets for the children. We arrived at dusk and I crouched down in the back of the car so that no one would see me. A foreigner visiting their house could bring unwelcome attention. Their modest home in the middle-income suburb had become a fortress. Abu Aseel had hooked up two cameras to keep a watchful eye on the street. He used the picture-in-a-picture facility on his high-tech television to observe the boundary. Whenever the family watched a television programme, a small box in the corner showed a mini picture of the outside. It did not make for relaxed viewing.

A distant cousin kept vigil on the roof equipped with an AK-47 and a box of hand grenades. Oum Aseel confided that she was deeply worried about her husband.

'He is not sleeping and he has a very bad temper. He has high blood pressure but he will not go to the doctor. He will not let the children go out,' she said.

Early the next morning, Abu Aseel came to my room in the Palestine Hotel and we talked about his situation. He agreed that he had become short-tempered and was neglecting his health.

'Believe me, Richard, I cannot leave the family for very long. I cannot go to the hospital. I worry about it all the day and all the night. I thought everything would be okay after the war, but it is getting worse and worse. I really don't know what to do,' he said.

I was unable to give any useful advice except to point out that he was needed by his family. If anything should happen to him because of his neglect of his health, they would be severely affected.

'You mean it is better for them that I am alive in three days than dead now,' he said with a smile.

'Yes,' I said. 'That Irish sense of humour is rubbing off on you'.

We parted company a week later with much sadness. The country was at a low ebb. The number of attacks in the Baghdad area had risen to more than seventy per day. One could sit at night in the garden of the Palestine Hotel and listen to almost unceasing gunfire. At least every half an hour there would be an explosion, perhaps a suicide bombing or a mortar attack. The coalition soldiers had more or less withdrawn to base and it was left to the hapless new Iraqi police and security forces to cope with the mayhem. They were not doing a very good job.

One service that did function was the mobile phone system. Before the war it was illegal to carry a mobile phone, even though no such system existed in the country. Now they were ubiquitous. I gave Abu Aseel money to keep his phone in service and left Iraq with a very heavy heart.

A month later I phoned Abu Aseel's number. It didn't ring. I assumed there was a problem with the cell phone network and tried again a few days later, but again there was no result. This pattern continued for a number of weeks, until, frantic with worry, I rang another Iraqi friend and asked him to find out what he could.

A week later he sent an e-mail detailing a tale of woe. He had asked around for Abu Aseel, but no one in the journalistic community had seen him since my last visit. He found his address and visited one afternoon. As he approached the house, a man in a *keffiya* (Arab headscarf beloved of the insurgents) appeared on the roof of the house and told him to leave, pointing a gun at him. My friend explained his mission, but another person appeared at the garage door with a gun and told him there was no such family there. My friend managed to get a glimpse inside the house while this commotion was going on and saw that there was no furniture. He surmised that the house had been abandoned and subsequently taken over by insurgents of some sort.

Months went by and with great reluctance I agreed to return to Iraq. There was no word from Abu Aseel, and because I no longer had the comfort of knowing and trusting a secure contact in Baghdad, I agreed to become embedded with British forces in the south of Iraq. After ten days in Basrah, I moved up to the British base in Baghdad to report on the Royal Irish Battalion that was on duty there. The day before I arrived, insurgents had launched one of the most audacious attacks on the capital. Their target was my old home, the Palestine Hotel, and its sister, the Sheraton.

Firstly, a large pick-up sped towards the concrete barriers that surround the hotels and exploded. The aim was to destroy or at least knock over these giant obstacles. Moments later, a car laden with explosives and full of steel ball bearings sped into the square and headed for the gap in the blast walls created by the first explosion. The aim here was to blow up the car, using the ball bearings to kill as many rescue workers as possible. The third bomb was designed to take down the two towers completely. A huge cement mixer full of commercial explosives arrived exactly five minutes after the last explosion and headed directly for the gap that had opened up in the barrier. Luckily, the British sniper team on the roof of the Sheraton Hotel was alert to the danger and shot the driver dead as he drove the vehicle into the centre of the square. The bomb exploded with an almighty force, but it had been stopped some distance from its intended target and much of the force of the explosion was dissipated. Had it got through the barrier, the death toll would have been very high. In all likelihood, it would have brought down the hotel buildings. This would have been a great symbolic victory for the insurgents. In all, fifteen were killed and 100 injured.

In the comfort and relative safety of the British compound in the Green Zone, I looked across the river at the aftermath of the bomb. The Green Zone is the most protected place on earth. Tens of thousands of soldiers and contractors guard its entrances. There is constant monitoring by helicopter and spy planes overhead. The guards have a simple 'shoot first' policy to protect the perimeter. It should ensure a haven of peace and tranquillity in an otherwise violent wasteland, but it does not. Even with this phalanx of security agencies and units, the Green Zone is regularly hit by mortars, rockets and small arms fire.

I reflected on this chaotic new country, with its massed ranks of crazed suicide bombers and jihad-inspired religious zealots. A melancholy thought occurred to me. Where would Abu Aseel – if he was still alive – fit into this insane mixture? Even though he is the ultimate survivor, I didn't think he would fare well in this unpredictable new country.

As if by magic, an hour later my mobile phone started to ring. I looked at the identity of the incoming number and it read 'Abu Aseel'. Incredulous, I answered the call.

'I have been trying to call you for months. What has been going on? Are you all right?' I asked.

Abu Aseel relayed a uniquely Iraqi tale of chaos and mayhem. He had again been attacked and shot, this time in the chest. The assailants were after his car, but again they were foiled by his neighbours, who came to his rescue. After a week in Yarmuk hospital, Abu Aseel went home and packed up his family and brought them down to his ancestral village near Nasiriya. He had left a cousin to guard the house. Late one night, the guard had been attacked and injured. The house was taken over by unknown men. Abu Aseel reckoned they were former criminals who had hooked up with elements of the insurgency. It was at that time that my friend had visited the house, at my request.

Abu Aseel then raised a group from his homeland to return to Baghdad to reclaim his only asset. Cousins and uncles drove up to the capital in convoy, armed to the teeth. They attacked the men in the house, who fled, leaving behind only a pair of shoes. They had systematically looted the house, taking all the fittings and furnishings and even the light bulbs. His beloved house was a total mess.

'We injured one of them. There was blood all over the garden,' he told me.

Over the last month, Abu Aseel had started rebuilding the house, but he reckoned that Baghdad was still unsafe. Oum Aseel had stayed in the country with the family.

'I would love to see you, but I know you can't come into the Green Zone, Abu Aseel. I don't think I can leave here and go out to you. It's too dangerous,' I said.

'So you are a prisoner of the British and the Americans and I am a prisoner of the Iraqis. This is the life. A curse on them all,' he said.

3

WE WERE HERE FIRST –
THE CHRISTIANS

March 2004

When he said his name, I did a double take – David
George. Could there really be someone in Iraq called
David George? It sounded like a name from the British
high street – David George Menswear, or David George
Camera Supplies.

'Yes, my name is David George,' he said, giggling at my
puzzlement.

And yet the young man standing in front of me had the
thick-set good looks of an Iraqi. He had the same dark,
almost sunken, eyes of countless other Iraqis I had met.
He was cheerful and youthful yet he possessed the
manners of a courtly official when necessary. But David
George? Surely it must be a translation or an approxima-
tion from the Arabic.

But wait. Hadn't I met someone else with the surname
of George before in Iraq? My mind turned this over as I

chatted away to the young man. Then the moment of real-isation dawned.

'Dr Donny George from the Iraq Museum,' I said out loud.

'Yes. He's my uncle,' David said. 'Well, not my uncle exactly, but I call him uncle. He is my father's cousin and a wonderful man. We are Christians,' he said.

I had met Donny George on a number of occasions before and after the war. He was one of those 'must-meet' people in Iraq. His demeanour was jovial and pleasant and his depth of knowledge of Iraq's complex history was unsurpassed. When I met him first in 1999, he was deputy director of the Iraq Museum, and even though he was head and shoulders above the others at that institution, he was modest about his status. Any request for an interview with him had to be channelled through his boss. The director of the museum was a short, wiry man with a Saddam-clone moustache and an arrogant demeanour. He was a Ba'ath party apparatchik and looked like a jumped-up colonel from a third-rate army. When I requested the meeting with Dr George, he shook his head.

'Impossible. You need to see Dr Ghanar. She will supply all the information you need,' he said.

I detected a prejudice against Dr George. I suspected it was partly because he was a Christian, but perhaps also because of his free and easy way with Westerners.

After an hour with the nervous Dr Ghanar, I was screaming for mercy. I'm sure she was a fine academic, but she wasn't very communicative to a foreign journalist looking for information about the museum and its exten-sive collections. After my tortuous time with Dr Ghanar, I returned to the director's office and asked again to see Donny George. The director finally capitulated and agreed to let me see him.

As I entered his office, Dr George sprang from his chair and greeted me in fluent English, shaking hands warmly and offering tea. And so a five-hour conversation started. One moment he would be talking about old Babylon, while the next he would whip out a paper on Abbasid architecture in Baghdad. I would ask about Nineveh and its famous guards, the winged bulls that towered over its gates. Dr George would sketch out a plan of the city, outlining the various dynasties and how they met their end. I would mention the ziggurat of Ur, and within seconds he would be in full flow, drawing sketches and explaining the importance of the ruins there and the dangers posed to the site by the American bombing of the Iraqi air base nearby. This whirlwind of enthusiasm and knowledge was almost unique in Iraq and I couldn't get enough of him.

That was 1999, and it was now 2004 and Dr George's nephew was standing in front of me and I was interviewing him for a job as my translator. The previous incumbent, Mohammed Tawfeeq, had been offered a job by CNN, the American news network, and was now their main translator and fixer. He brought David along and recommended him to me. I asked David a few rudimentary questions and listened as he did some simultaneous translation. He was bright, clever and well able for the job.

I introduced David to Abu Aseel, who was clearly taken aback at the idea of my employing a Christian in Iraq. David noticed his reaction. Under Saddam, Christians were perceived to have a privileged position in Iraq. A small number had been employed in the upper echelons of the public service. Saddam was said to believe that they were more honest than other Iraqis. This didn't stop him from brutally oppressing their community at times, but the impression most Iraqis had was that the great leader liked Christians.

In business, they were successful and their hospitals and schools were reputed to be the best run in Iraq. Other groups were jealous of the Christians' success – one of the reasons why, in the new Iraq, their position was very uncertain.

The new Shia-led authorities were actively hostile to any remnant of the old regime. Even though many Christians despised Saddam and actively worked for his overthrow, the perception that they had thrived under him led elements in the new government to seek to exclude them. They either chose to ignore the evidence of the suppression of the Assyrian culture and language that had occurred under Ba'ath party rule or they were unaware of it. If they paused for a moment to reflect on the fall in Christian numbers, they might have thought otherwise. Gertrude Bell, Mora Dickson, Freya Stark and many others put the percentage of Christians in Baghdad in the 1920s to 1940s at between 20 and 40 per cent. Now it's estimated to be less than 5 per cent and is more likely 2 or 3 per cent. Abu Aseel was merely reflecting the new atmosphere in Shia-majority, post-war Iraq. He offered to find me another translator. I refused, saying I had offered the position to David in good faith and would honour the commitment. After that, David was wary of Abu Aseel.

When I got Abu Aseel on his own, I remonstrated with him over his comments about David. How dare he interfere in such a way? What did he think he was doing trying to stop a young man like David getting good experience with a foreign broadcaster? It was one of the few times I had been genuinely angry with Abu Aseel. He took a step back and looked at me carefully, pursing his lips.

'I am sorry you feel this way, Richard. I am only trying to help you. This David will be a big problem for you. The Shia will not talk to you with a Christian there, an Iraqi.

The Sunni will not talk to you with a Christian. There is no one else. You will only be left with the Christians and they are all leaving,' he said.

'What about the new Iraq and everyone together united and all that?' I asked.

'Believe me, it is all shit, Richard. Shit,' he said before leaving me, confused and still a little angry.

I approached David and asked him if he felt comfortable translating with Shias and Sunnis. He was surprised and it took him a little while to understand what I was getting at.

'You mean they won't want to talk to me because I'm Christian and they are Muslim?' he said.

'Yes. They might think you're an American spy or a collaborator with the former regime,' I said.

'You think this?' he asked, looking a little angry, his brow furrowed now.

'I don't know what to think, David. You tell me,' I replied.

'This is not true. I am Iraqi. They are Iraqi. That is enough. I know the Iraqis and they all accept me. They never say, "you are Christian, go away". No. This has never happened. My friend Mohammed. He is Sunni. Basim. He is Shia. We have no problem with each other. Maybe with the insurgents, we have a problem, but with the insurgents everyone has a problem. We are all different, but really, Mr Richard, we are all one. If you don't think so, then you should not have me as your translator. This is the truth,' he said.

I was stung by his implied criticism of my comments and a little ashamed of my clumsiness. Once again in Iraq, I had jumped in boots first and trampled over an individual's sensibilities. I showed myself as lacking the requisite subtlety to understand such a complex culture.

I apologised and said I hoped this wouldn't be a barrier between us. David smiled and agreed that it wouldn't be a problem. We shook hands warmly. I showed him my African handshake, an elaborate four-move manoeuvre, which soon became our daily greeting. He seemed to genuinely accept that I was merely trying to be safe and careful. If he had been an older man, perhaps his reaction would have been different, more resentful.

The young in Iraq seemed to stay young in attitude longer than elsewhere. Maybe the decades-long isolation brought about by war and sanctions had cut them off from the 'smart alec' world of international youth culture. Like his friend Mohammed, David was genuinely wide-eyed about the world and was full of curiosity and interest in Western manners and culture.

They would ask me about meeting girls in Ireland and how it was done. I told them that when I was on the scene, you went up to a girl at a disco or a club, started dancing with her, bought her a drink, chatted her up and either went home with her or made a date for another night. They marvelled at the apparent ease of it all and laughed uproariously at the idea of this happening in Iraq.

'We don't even have clubs any more,' David said.

They said they liked Michael Jackson. I raised an eyebrow. They were unperturbed. They asked about the music scene and whether live music was available in Dublin. I bragged about the various venues in the city and regaled them with stories of early U2 concerts I had attended. They were hugely impressed that I had met Bono and asked a lot of questions about him. Why does he wear those glasses? Has he got glaucoma? I told them I didn't know and agreed that it was strange for an Irish guy to be wearing sunglasses at all hours of the day and night in rainy, gloomy Dublin.

They were less impressed when I described the drunken orgies that Irish youth go in for. David laughed and asked why. I smiled and said it was all too complicated to explain. I said I didn't really understand it myself.

'It's got something to do with the climate. All the countries where people go out and get hammered like that are northern European countries with awful weather,' I said.

They nodded as if they understood.

They asked about access to the internet and e-mail in Ireland. I gave them the rundown of how the system works. David asked if there was anyone in charge of the World Wide Web in Ireland. I laughed, much to his bewilderment. No. There was no one in charge. No censorship. He smiled and nodded.

'So it's free,' David asked.

'Well, you have to pay for it, of course. But in terms of what goes on there, yes, that's free, except that the normal laws apply. No child pornography. No libel or defamation. Otherwise you can say or read what you want, really,' I said.

David nodded slowly and earnestly. It was a kind of innocence – one of the many charms of Iraqis. It was almost as if he could intellectually understand the concept of freedom, if not its practice. But it was also a sign that the old Iraq of state control and oppressive censorship still held a powerful sway over the imaginations of even the young. Decades of dictatorship aren't that easily cast off.

David was twenty-six years old and looked even younger. His skin was darker than that of many Iraqis and he was hairy. One of our longest-running jokes was for me to ask him how many times he had shaved that day. He would look away in mock disgust and turn back and ask, 'Chicken kebab for dinner tonight, my friend?' Cue African handshake and laughter. Apparently David thought my skin looked like a chicken's.

Our first task was to organise a trip to the Iraq Museum and a long interview with his 'uncle'. I had high hopes that this time my visit there would not be derailed by bureaucratic meddling and interference. David assured me that his 'uncle' would be more than happy to see me and would give me a lengthy and entertaining interview. I asked him if he thought Donny George would survive the American occupation and their control of the civil service. He assured me that he would.

'He is a very clever man, but he is also very honest and respected. If the Americans want the Iraqis to work with them, they will have to understand people like my uncle,' he said.

My view of Dr George had been influenced by a BBC film I had seen prior to my departure for Iraq. It had been made soon after the capture of Baghdad by coalition forces and its focus was on what had happened to the thousands of items looted from the collection of the Iraq Museum in April 2003. The atmosphere in Baghdad at the time was euphoric but full of confusion. The unmistakable impression the film gave was that the staff at the museum were involved in some way in the disappearance of many treasures. The presenter, the eminent British historian Dan Cruickshank, repeatedly questioned the bona fides of Dr George. I could see why this was done. Dr George repeatedly fobbed the presenter off when asked about various aspects of the looting. The presenter was puzzled. Thousands of items had gone missing. Dr George had been a member of the Ba'ath party. He wasn't being straightforward when asked about the whereabouts of the objects. Add it all up and the answer was obvious. Except that it wasn't, as I found out when David brought me to the museum.

I greeted Dr George warmly and he apparently remembered me from my previous visit five years before.

He even remembered the difficulty I'd had with the former director.

'It was very difficult at that time. I had to become a member of the party to survive. As a Christian, they watched me very closely. I had to be very careful. When I suspected senior members of the party were involved in looting archaeological sites in the south [after the Gulf War in 1991], I had to keep my mouth shut. To say something would have meant the end of my work here in the museum, which is my life,' he told me as we walked through the corridors of the museum.

I told him I had seen the BBC film about the looting and wondered what he thought of it. He threw me a sharp look and offered me a seat in his comfortable office. He explained that they had filmed it soon after the end of the war. There was still much confusion. For Iraqis there was deep concern that the Ba'ath party structure was still in place. If he was seen to be too explicit about where much of the collection had gone, there might be repercussions for him and the staff. He explained that many items had been under the control of the staff in secret locations, but that he wasn't at liberty to say where the material was at the time the film was made in April 2003. An American officer had been put in charge of dealing with the State Board for Antiquities and Dr George told me it wasn't a good idea for him to be seen to be co-operating with the occupation authorities. Only when there was a sovereign Iraqi government, recognised by the international community, could the treasures under his control be returned. This had now happened.

I confessed my confusion. Dr George smiled. He explained that there were two classes of antiquities that had gone missing – those that were looted and those that were hidden for safe-keeping by museum staff. They were working with international agencies (particularly the Italians and Interpol) to get the stolen items returned, with some success. Thousands of other antiquities under the control of the museum staff were now back in the museum and were on display. I believed his explanation. Others didn't. The Americans maintained a watching brief on Dr George for two years without committing themselves to endorse him. They were wary of him in a senior position. They were worried that as a former Ba'ath party member he was tainted by the past and could be dangerous in the future.

It wasn't until 2005 that the authorities finally confirmed Dr George as director of the Iraq Museum, implicitly exonerating him of any wrongdoing. It was another instance of the coalition authorities taking an inordinate amount of time to come to terms with the subtleties of the Iraqi system. Their edict of May 2003 to exclude all senior members of the Ba'ath party from the public services had caused untold damage across the country. It led to the disbandment of the army and the police force and had denuded government departments of thousands of able people. The policy had been dictated in the early days of the takeover in 2003 by Washington in co-operation with the exile Iraqis – including Ahmed Chalabi of the Iraqi National Congress – who were powerful at that time. In theory, it was a useful tool to rid the country of the Ba'ath plague, but in reality it had devastated the state infrastructure.

In the euphoria of their easy victory, the coalition authorities had looked back in history to find precedents for cleansing what they regarded as an evil system. The de-Nazification of Germany after the Second World War was the precedent they chose. The decree that no senior member of the Ba'ath party could hold office in the new

Iraq was a clumsy policy that set the country back at least two years following the takeover.

The Ba'ath party was intrinsic to life in Iraq before the war. The party was organised like a secret society, except of course that it wasn't secret. Small groups of individuals numbering up to ten were grouped together in the smallest unit of the party, the *Halaq*. This group was most often a neighbourhood unit in a suburb or village, but it could also be a cell of doctors in a hospital, or the members of a football team. The *Halaq* was in turn grouped together with other *Halaqs* into a unit known as a *Firqah*. Groups of *Firqahs* were grouped together into divisions. These divisions had their own hierarchy and controlled regional functions such as political education and intelligence gathering. Often they functioned like a parallel government, side by side with mayors and local councils. There was no doubt about who was in charge. The party had the final say on everything, and within the party the Revolutionary Command Council (RCC) was the supreme body. The RCC was the personal plaything of the leader and he controlled all appointments. The overlap between street *Halaqs* and cells in industry, the arts, sport and administration gave the Ba'ath party an omnipotent presence.

Thousands of officials and officers had joined the Ba'ath party for advancement, even though their commitment to the organisation was questionable. It was a simple rule in the old Iraq that no one could advance in the public services, the police or army without being a member. When looking for a job in a hospital, school or factory, the first question to be asked was, 'What is your *Halaq*?' From this the employer could extract all the necessary information. Not belonging to the party wasn't an option for anyone serious about functioning in the old Iraq. Virtually everyone in the professions had joined the party early on in their careers, even though they may have harboured a deep hatred of the regime and its leader.

Weeding out the true believers from the opportunists would have taken time and considerable subtlety, neither of which were in great supply in 2003.

With the difficult business of Donny George's culpability in the looting out of the way, I was now able to concentrate on the key questions about the state of the Iraq Museum. David had been a little uneasy in the early part of the interview, but I touched him on the leg and winked at him at this point. The difficult bit was over. Tea was brought in and the conversation started to flow.

Dr George explained that about 10,000 items had been stolen from the collection in a three-day period from 10–12 April 2003. The looting at the Iraq Museum happened in the context of a collapse in law and order in Baghdad. Looters attacked government departments and offices and stripped them bare. The pictures of the looting were shown across the world, as was the comment of a senior US officer that the crowds were merely 'letting off steam'. Many government offices were subsequently set on fire. The Iraq Museum was spared the flames but, arguably, the damage caused to the institution was much more profound.

In advance of the war, Dr George explained that he and the teams had evacuated much of the contents of the museum. Some was stored in the Central Bank of Iraq in the densely populated downtown area, where it had been boxed up and locked in a hidden part of the basement, at a level below the stocks of cash the looters were seeking. The stash here included many portable treasures that the institution was renowned for, including thousands of cylinder seals, cuneiform artefacts dating as far back as 4000 BC, and items of gold and silver. They were locked in sturdy cases behind at least five levels of robust security doors and grills. The looters breached four of them in their frenzied attempt to get at the treasure, but were unsuccessful. The greatest damage done to the collection at the Central Bank happened as a result of the collapse of the electrical system, which caused the pumps that kept the basements dry to fail. Because the building was so close to the river Tigris, its lower levels were below the water table and the basement gradually filled with water.

Other artefacts were hidden in the basement of the museum on the other side of the river, and about a quarter of these were stolen. The thousands of items taken away by museum staff for safe-keeping and hidden around Baghdad were untouched and have since been returned. The greatest damage had been done in the exhibition areas of the museum. Many of the items there were too large or too fragile to be transported. Looters broke in and smashed the display cases, grabbing anything they could find. They destroyed priceless effigies and statues and wrecked whole exhibition floors, perhaps out of frustration, finding the items in the cases too heavy or large to transport. There were marks where looters had tried to prize the massive friezes from Nineveh from the wall. No lasting damage was done here. There is some evidence that the thieves were working to order, taking the more valuable artefacts while leaving others. Forty large pieces, including the 5,000-year-old Lady of Warka mask, were spirited away.

'There is a big market for antiquities in Switzerland, Holland, London and the United States. Many of these collectors are unscrupulous and will pay anything to get these items. The Italian Caribinieri stopped a consignment of 700 items at customs and returned them to us. They were all stolen from the display cases in the museum. We have had many successes like this, but there is a long way to go yet,' Dr George said.

Part of the problem is the size of many of the objects. The cylinder seals that are the key legacy of the Sumerian civilisation are usually tiny pieces, often smaller than a tea cup. The seals bear inscriptions that were etched in reverse, so that when the cylinder is rolled over wet clay, the writing appears. The inscription usually refers to trade or a legal agreement, but many of the seals also carry the laws and customs of the ancient Sumerians, making them crucial for the understanding of one of the world's earliest civilisations.

The task of reforming the collection and detailing exactly what had gone missing was immense and is ongoing. Estimates of the losses ranged from more than 50,000 in the earliest days following the looting to a more realistic 10,000 in 2006. The items started to come back soon after the museum staff returned to work in May 2003. Occasionally large consignments of more than 100 artefacts would turn up from Jordanian or Syrian customs, seized at the borders. The Italian authorities were particularly vigilant and returned thousands of exhibits. Some of the items displayed minor damage, often crude attempts to erase the museum catalogue number imprinted on each exhibit. Even in 2004, the items were being returned at a rate of around ten per week. Many artefacts were brought back by Iraqis who had found them discarded around Baghdad and recognised the museum markings.

Most of the larger and more easily identifiable treasures came back in the first weeks after the catastrophe, including the signature piece of the museum, the Lady of Warka.

Dr George and his staff had made huge progress in reconstituting the museum building. After the international outcry following the looting, money had begun to pour into the institution from a number of sources. The US State Department gave $2 million, while private institutions such as the Packard Humanities Institute of California paid for crucial information technology improvements. Work was going on in all parts of the museum. Security was being dramatically upgraded. A new air conditioning system was being installed and Dr George was delighted to show me their new website. It was on the internet that Dr George said the world could see the treasures of the museum. While Baghdad was dangerous and out of bounds for foreigners, interested people overseas could visit the 'virtual' Iraq Museum on the web.

Matters had also improved dramatically for the staff. Their wages were now paid every month and they had received increases equivalent to multiples of their previous salaries. Dr George told me that his own salary was now $3,000 per month, whereas before he earned less than $100. His new-found wealth didn't stop him from criticising the Americans.

'They came and got rid of the old system without putting anything else in place. They left a void. Here in the museum we are working well, but outside there is chaos,' he said. By 2006, three museum employees had fallen victim to the lawlessness – an archaeologist, an accountant and a driver.

After our interview was over, our cameraman, Michael Cassidy, started to film the galleries and David and I had time to wander around the empty, echoing chambers filled with such beauty and bounty. David took me to the Assyrian Hall, the largest and most impressive of the exhibition spaces in the museum. This space escaped any damage in 2003 and looked just as impressive as it had when I first visited in 1999. David walked over and stroked the giant winged bull, the spirit-god that was displayed prominently by the Assyrians as a talisman at the entrance to important buildings and districts. David assured me that the winged bull had protected the Assyrian galleries from the looters – a rare polytheistic reference from such a devout Christian.

The square-jawed Assyrians depicted in the enormous friezes that ran the length of the gallery were shown as almost identical warriors marching home from battle, laden down with the spoils of war. Other friezes showed delegations of priests paying obeisance to the emperor. David moved close to one of the giant noblemen on the relief and joked, pointing to the gentleman in the sculpture, 'Look, it's my great-grandfather.'

As an Assyrian, David felt a close affinity to these ancestors. 'We were here first,' he said, almost plaintively, 'long, long before the Arabs.'

It would be difficult not to feel deep pride in the presence of such ancient and wonderful art, particularly if one could follow an unbroken connection of 2,700 years. David maintained that he could trace his family back into antiquity and began to do so. After half an hour of grandfathers and great-grandfathers and great-great-great-great-great-grandfathers, I asked him to stop. 'I believe you,' I said, and we laughed.

The word 'terrible' is invariably tagged onto any description of the Assyrian takeover of power in ancient Mesopotamia. In the eighth century BC, Tiglath-Pileser III ruthlessly subjugated the area and imposed a harsh regimen on his new underlings. The Assyrians in their turn were ousted from power as part of the endless waves of invasion and conquest that characterised Mesopotamia. But unlike other defeated peoples, the Assyrians didn't flee and remained until the Christian era, when the vast majority converted to the new religion. How pure they remained as a race is an issue of some debate among academics.

They held fast to Christianity through the turbulent Muslim Arab conquest of the region and were tolerated in the Islamic heartlands. As Christians, they were described (like the other significant minority in the Middle East, the Jews) as 'people of the book'. In other words, they were monotheistic and their roots were from the same broad tradition that gave rise to Islam. All three religions trace their basic belief systems to Abraham. The Muslim authorities tolerated Christians and Jews for the most part, although intermittent pogroms over the centuries have given many Assyrians a healthy scepticism about the intentions of their Muslim brothers.

Their former strongholds across Iraq are now vulnerable and the Christian population is falling. The heartland of the Assyrians has always been the plains around Mosul and the towns and cities of northern Iraq, particularly Kirkuk and Mosul itself. David's father remembered growing up in Kirkuk in the 1940s, when the majority in the city were Turkmen, with perhaps 20 per cent Christians, 10 per cent Kurds and a small Arab minority. Under Saddam, the Ba'ath party had pursued an Arabisation policy with the aim of incorporating all minorities into the Arab fold. The policy was cloaked in the usual Ba'ath party rhetoric but amounted to a systematic attempt to colonise the northern cities and populate them with Arabs. Today the population structure of Kirkuk is one-third Arab, one-third Kurd and one-third Turkmen, Christians of various denominations and tiny numbers of others, like the strange and wonderful Yezidis. The same pattern can be seen in all the significant urban centres of northern, non-Kurdish Iraq.

Dr George joined us in the Assyrian gallery and asked if we had everything we wanted. We had spent six hours talking and wandering around the museum and were ready to go. Dr George was relaxed. He smiled a lot. I asked him if he felt optimistic about the future.

'No,' he said and smiled again. 'The Saddam years were a nightmare. Now these are the American years. Different nightmare,' he said.

In spite of the gloomy comments, there was a jolly atmosphere in the group. Our filming had gone very well. We had hours of film of the museum and were delighted to have it for our archive should another disaster strike the institution. David and I thanked Dr George profusely for his hospitality and headed back to the Palestine Hotel. We both agreed that it was the most enjoyable day we had spent in post-war Iraq.

The paper I had on my desk looked as if it had been written in a hurry. The Iraqi journalist who had given it to me had dictated a crude translation:

> In the name of Allah, the most merciful and compassionate
>> Do not adorn yourselves as immoral women before Islam.
>
> We insist the head of this family will stand with the 'brothers of Muslims' and follow basic Muslim rules ordering the women to the wearing of the veil and following the honourable teaching of Islam. Christians must do the same. We, the Iraqis, the Muslim people will not accept any mistakes.
>
> If there is a continuation of immorality we will be forced to take the following steps:
>> 1. Killing.
>> 2. Kidnapping.
>> 3. Destroying the house with all its occupants.

The letter wasn't signed, but my journalist friend had no doubt that it was genuine.

'They're sending the letters to all Muslims in the area whose women don't cover themselves with the veil or *abaaya* and to the Christians,' he said.

I had heard about the growing practice of kidnapping and the apparently random attacks that were taking place all over Baghdad and beyond. Abu Aseel had given me some insight into the chaotic lawlessness that was overtaking the country. The official word from the coalition authorities was that there were three distinct groups responsible for the lawlessness. The first were opportunistic criminals who were involved in all manner of scams, from kidnapping to pornography. The second were the organised terrorists. The Americans, in particular, were keen to portray this group as primarily composed of foreign fighters allied to the Jordanian Abu Musab al-Zarqawi and the Osama bin Laden-linked group, al-Qaeda, in Mesopotamia. The third group, according to the Americans, was composed of former Ba'ath party activists. The picture painted was of a small, determined and highly professional group of fighters operating in isolation and targeting the public at will.

The paper in front of me seemed to point to a different type of group. This wasn't a threat from al-Qaeda, which invariably tried to garner as much publicity as possible for its activities. My journalist friend told me that those responsible were Iraqi Islamic radicals with no apparent link to foreign fighters.

'They are Salafia, but they are also Ba'ath party people, all of them Sunni. They are mixed up all together and they are trying to make al-Daura all Sunni. They want to get rid of the Shia and the Christians,' he said.

The Salafia were a group of fundamentalist Sunnis who were encouraged by Saddam Hussein in secret in the last years of his rule. In a departure from his normal secular modus operandi, he built mosques for them and gave them housing and money. In part, Saddam may have believed he was buying them off – in effect, neutralising a growing conservative trend in society. He would be able to keep an eye on them if he was their patron.

Before the war, they were, in effect, a small cadre of Sunni true believers with tenuous links to the Ba'ath party. Now my journalist friend was telling me that they had joined up with former Ba'ath people and had become more powerful. Their aim was to cleanse certain areas of rival religious groups, in this case the Shias and Christians.

David came to my room and we chatted. I fidgeted with the paper, wondering when to show it to him. He could see that I was anxious and asked if I was all right. I handed him the paper without speaking and he read it carefully. He looked at me for a moment.

'You can see the problem we have, Richard. They are giving this to all the Christians in al-Daura. My family has not received this yet, but it will happen. The Assyrian market is being cleared of families. They are told they are not Islamic enough. They are being kidnapped all the time and people are beginning to leave the area. Some are going to other parts of Baghdad and to the north, but many are leaving for Jordan and Syria,' he said.

He painted a picture of a suburb in fear. Al-Daura is one of the most strategically important areas of Baghdad. It stands as a gateway to the city from the staunchly Sunni suburbs and towns south of the capital, the so-called 'triangle of death'. It also houses a power station and the main oil refinery for Baghdad. The refinery's gas flares can be seen from many parts of the capital and it provides all the refined petroleum products for the greater Baghdad area. It is predominantly lower middle class and is one of the most mixed districts in the country. As well as a substantial

Shia minority, the district was about 10 per cent Christian. I asked David why he thought this was happening in al-Daura now. He offered a number of theories, but one stood out as being the most logical and sensible.

'The insurgents need a base in each area of the capital. They already have Adhimiya, al-Thawra, Jihad and parts of the city centre around Rashid Street and other places, but they want to control a big area with a big important factory in it. Al-Daura is the best for this. They can get rid of the Shias and the Christians and then they will have al-Daura for themselves,' he said.

David confessed that his family was becoming increasingly unsettled about the changes going on in their area. 'We discuss it all the time and many of us want to leave, but my father refuses. He says he is an Iraqi and will not leave his country,' he said. He told me the family was considering leaving without their father, who had become fearful and withdrawn in recent weeks.

'We have had the looting and the criminality, but we thought it would stop last year [2003]. Instead it has got worse and worse. I cannot see it getting any better. The police are no good. They don't know what to do and we are concerned about them as well. Many, many of them are Shia from the Badr Brigade and they will not protect the Christians,' he said.

His fear was based on an extraordinary policy pursued by the coalition authorities at the time. The new army and police service began recruiting in August 2003 and by 2004 had grown to a force of more than 50,000. It was estimated at that time that the vast majority (perhaps as high as 80 per cent) was Shia. The armed wing of the main Shia political party, the Supreme Council for the Islamic Revolution in Iraq (SCIRI), the Badr Brigade, had openly moved into the forces. The evidence was everywhere to be seen. In police stations, the images of the various Shia martyrs associated with the Badr Brigade were now openly displayed. Pictures of the murdered Shia Grand Ayatollah, al-Hakim, SCIRI's spiritual inspiration, were also displayed prominently in police and army premises.

David told me that as a small minority, the Christians were increasingly isolated. The Sunnis had the insurgents on their side and they were pushing home their advantage through acts of terror and sabotage. The Shias were responding through the police and army, with (as he viewed it) the full support of the United States and coalition forces. The Kurds were comfortable in their safe zone in the north. This left the vulnerable Christians.

They were resented by most of the other groups for one reason or another. They were spread thinly in the north and around the capital and had little recent tradition of standing up for themselves. They had no militias to protect them. In addition, Shias and Sunnis believed that the United States forces were protecting the Christians. They reasoned that the Americans were virtually all Christians and they were therefore secretly in league with the Iraqi Christians. It was a 'street' perception and it was far from the truth. The US forces were actively discouraged from showing any affinity with the Iraqi Christians because of the concern that this would isolate them and leave them vulnerable to attack by extremists. Thus, they were left on their own. It was easy to see why Christians were living in fear.

The Latin rite archbishop of Baghdad, Reverend Jean Benjamin Sleiman, identified the strange no man's land that the Christians occupied in an interview with the *Washington Post* in July 2004.

'Since the end of the war in March 2003, there is a very real freedom. But we cannot enjoy it because of general insecurity, the high level of fanaticism and the belief of some Islamic leaders that Iraqi Christians are being assimilated into coalition forces, who are perceived as Christians or even crusaders…We cannot say that there is a general Islamic persecution of Christians. Still, in the shadow of general insecurity and violence, Christians are worried,' he said.

The archbishop's sentiments were honest and hopeful. It was still possible then to portray the violence as a simple form of banditry and criminality. At that point there was little evidence of direct targeting of Christians, but within weeks that would change.

Christian women had taken to wearing the veil if they ventured outside the home. Both the Sunni purists and the Shia zealots were said to have attacked Christian women. On one occasion a Christian civil servant was said to have been doused with battery acid after rebuffing a man who had questioned her about why she wasn't wearing the veil, close to the Green Zone in the centre of the city. She survived but had terrible scars.

Then came the attacks on churches. The Chaldean Catholic Church in southern Baghdad was the first to be hit at lunchtime on Sunday, 1 August 2004. A suicide car bomber drove into the car park and waited for fifteen minutes until worshippers began to stream out at the end of Sunday mass. An enormous explosion killed twelve people and injured at least fifty more. At the Armenian church, a large explosion blew out the stained glass windows, injuring more than a dozen mass-goers. Fifteen minutes later, the nearby Assyrian church near the Karrada district was attacked by a suicide bomber. Two were killed and dozens injured. In all, there were four attacks in Baghdad and one in Mosul. The final death toll was twenty, with as many as 200 seriously injured. Baghdad's churches boarded up their windows and locked their doors. Christians could now be under no illusion that they were being targeted.

The next day the bombers posted their valedictory message on the internet, praising the bombers:

O! Believers in one God...

America didn't only occupy and invade militarily the Islamic lands but they also founded hundreds of Christianizing establishments, printing false deviated books and distributing them amongst the Muslims in an effort to strip them away of their religion and Christianize them. The Crusaders are one nation even if they differed in their ideas.

The American forces and their intelligence systems have found a safe haven and refuge amongst their brethren the grandchildren [Iraqi Christians] of monkeys and swines in Iraq.

The graceful God has enabled us on Sunday, August 01, 2004 to aim several painful blows at their dens, the dens of wickedness, corruption and Christianizing. Your striving brethren were able to blow up four cars aimed at the Churches in Karrada, Baghdad Jadida (New Baghdad) and Daura while another group of Moujahedeen hit the Churches in Mosul.

As we announce our responsibility for the bombings we tell you, the people of the Crosses: return to your senses and be aware that God's soldiers are ready for you. You have wanted a Crusade and these are its results. God is great and glory be to God and his messenger. He who has warned is excused.

The exodus began in earnest. Some Christians headed for ancestral homelands around Mosul, but many more headed for neighbouring countries. Saudi Arabia, as a Muslim state where Christian worship is outlawed, was out of the question as a safe haven. Iran was equally unattractive to Christians. Jordan, which had traditionally been a safe destination for Iraqis of all creeds, had recently tightened up its entry requirements and many Christians had difficulty entering. This left Syria as the country of choice for most of the exiting Christians. The Syrian government policy of allowing all Arabs and natives to enter and stay for at least six months had been criticised by the Americans as an open door for al-Qaeda elements to use the country as a staging post for attacks on Iraq. But whatever about the truth of that, in the case of the Christians, the Syrian welcome was salvation. While there is no official estimate of Christian numbers arriving in Syria, Church authorities believe that as many as 25,000 fled to Syria in 2004 and at least a similar number again in 2005.

David was jumpy and nervous after the August church bombings. While before he could comfort himself with the thought that everyone was suffering from the attacks in the new Iraq, now he could be in no doubt that the Christians were vulnerable. The note that had been such a chilling talisman months before was now circulating widely in all Christian areas. David's family also received a copy and it copper fastened their sense of vulnerability.

On the telephone I asked him how things were in al-Daura.

'This is a question that many of the Christians in al-Daura would like to know the answer to, Richard. They do not know. They are not going out. Certainly not the women. There is shooting all night and the attacks are becoming more and more frequent. You know, it is like living through the war all over again. Except that in the war hardly anyone died in al-Daura. Now there are many, many people dying every day. And the Americans do nothing. They are not even patrolling the streets any more. The Iraqi Army are doing this, but the Sunnis say they are kidnapping their people and taking them to secret prisons for torture. The Sunnis are now attacking all the Shias. Everyone is attacking us. It is very bad,' he told me.

⁀

As I arrived for my next visit to Baghdad in 2005, my fears for the Christians had deepened. The bombings and daily attacks were now constant. The number of incidents logged by the coalition authorities had risen to more than 100 per day and a good number of these were targeted against minorities.

I kept thinking of the Jews of Baghdad and how their numbers had collapsed in the thirty years after the founding of Israel. They had once had a leading position in Baghdad society and constituted up to 15 per cent of the population. Now there were barely twenty left in the whole city.

I passed the square where, in January 1969, nine Jews were hanged in public on trumped-up charges of 'spying for Israel'. After that the flow of emigrating Jews became a torrent as they abandoned the city that had been their home for centuries. Iraq's Jews had lived in these lands for longer than Jews had lived continuously anywhere else, including their current state.

Even though there was no direct analogy between the Jews and the Christians – the Christians, for example, have no state of their own to which they can emigrate – the parallels are disturbing.

As I arrived in the Palestine Hotel, these thoughts weighed me down. I was in a melancholy mood. Ten days of work stretched ahead. It would be difficult to do any proper reporting, so dangerous had the city become.

Early the next morning I was heading to pick up my breakfast outside the hotel. Each morning I came down and bought a boiled egg and a round of freshly made bread from the lone street seller who had managed to penetrate the tight security around the hotel. He was a friendly old man and would happily give me the egg and bread on credit if I had no cash.

I was taken aback by a sticker I saw on a suitcase: 'Jesus Saves'. The owner of the case was standing at the reception desk of the hotel. He wore a brown corduroy jacket and had a heavy salt and pepper beard. I could hear that he was American or Canadian. I waited for him to finish checking out at the desk and approached him.

'I'm from Pennsylvania and I'm here to do the Lord's work,' he said, blinking.

I asked if he was finding many people receptive to his message.

'Yeah, we're getting full houses. Lots of people are open to the word of God. It's a little difficult to get the message through, but we're getting there,' he said, picking up his suitcase and making as if to go.

I asked him the name of his organisation. He looked at me for a moment.

'You can call us "Iraq for God", because that's what we're here for,' he said before giving me a mock salute and heading for the exit.

I had heard of the arrival of American and German evangelical Christians in Iraq, but I'd thought it had an urban legend feel to it until then. Before the war, many well-meaning Christians had offered their services in Iraq as aid workers. The best-known of these were the volunteers of Voices in the Wilderness. They had confined their work to supporting the Iraqis during the international embargo. Even though they weren't an overtly evangelical group, there was an unmistakably Christian flavour to their public statements and they were regarded by the Iraqi authorities as a useful – and fairly harmless – group of Western eccentrics. They drew attention to the injustice of the sanctions imposed on Iraq but didn't engage in prosyletisation. The new Christians that arrived in Baghdad after the war were very different.

Muslims are particularly sensitive about attempts to get adherents to convert to Christianity. For Muslims, it's an offence punishable by death to convert to Christianity, so the advent of open evangelising in Baghdad had stirred the blood of the imams in the mosques. The insurgents had also issued statements warning against the practice and had followed this up with attacks on Western Christians.

Four American Baptist missionaries had been killed in March 2004. The next month, seven South Korean Presbyterians were kidnapped. Another South Korean evangelical had been captured in June 2004 and his beheading was filmed and released on the internet. The church bombings of August 2004 confirmed that the insurgents had amalgamated the native and evangelical Christians into a single enemy.

For the insurgents, the arrival of Western Protestant evangelicals was confirmation of what they'd believed all along – namely, that the war for Iraq was a Christian crusade against Islam. Soon after the conquest of Baghdad, mostly American and German born-again Christians began to openly recruit in the capital.

For the Iraqi Christians, their arrival was a triple disaster. The foreigners introduced a jazzed up version of Christianity that was in direct competition with their own solemn, ancient rite. Secondly, it gave the insurgents ammunition for their claim that Christians were behind the invasion. Thirdly, the new arrivals openly preached against the ancient Christian sects most Iraqis adhered to.

The irony of American and German Protestants competing with Iraqi Christians wasn't lost on the most senior cleric of the Chaldean Catholic Church, Patriarch Emmanuel Delly.

'They're attempting to convert poor Muslims by flashing money and smart cars. Iraq doesn't need missionaries, as our Christian churches date back long before Protestantism,' he said.

His disdain for the flashy new evangelicals is reciprocated by the newcomers, many of whom regard the Christian churches of Iraq as heretical. Their orthodox born-again philosophy decries the imagery used in Iraqi churches, particularly the veneration of the Virgin, which is a large part of the Chaldean and Assyrian tradition. In fact, the Protestants dispute virtually all the important theological precepts of Iraqi Christians. At a basic level, the evangelicals believe that only their brand of loud, brash fundamentalism offers the way to salvation. Their standard line is that everyone must be 'born again' and must make a conscious decision to accept Jesus, after which they can be baptised and enter the true Christian fold. Any other form of practice – particularly where the Virgin is honoured or the mass is celebrated – is simply not Christian. They regard the transubstantiation of the Eucharist during mass to be positively demonic.

I asked David about the evangelicals and he sighed deeply. 'You know, the churches here are the only place in the world where Jesus could come back and talk to us in his own language, Aramaic. This is the language we speak. Even Saddam outlawed us from using it, but we kept it alive. We have been here since the very beginning of the Christians, and yet these Americans come along and say that they do not think that we are proper Christians. I do not know what to think about these people. They are different and I think they will only bring more trouble to Iraq,' he said.

He also confessed his fears for the future. 'The Christians are going to go like the Jews. They used to be strong in Iraq. Even the first finance minister in Iraq after the king was a Jew, but they all left. Now there are only a handful of miserable old people living near Rashid Street, maybe twenty. They have a synagogue but they cannot make the numbers up to make a congregation. This is what is happening to the Christians. We are being attacked on all sides and there is only one way to go and that is out of the country. Believe me, Richard, this is coming very fast,' he said.

I left Baghdad after this short visit with a heavy heart and kept in touch with David by e-mail and mobile phone.

⌒

As I went about my business at the end of December 2005 in Dublin, I received an e-mail from David, enclosing a new telephone number. It had a different prefix to his previous one and I rang the number to find out if he was okay.

'I am in Aleppo in Syria. Richard, I am so relieved to be left Iraq. The situation there is now very, very bad. My mother and my two sisters came with me and we are waiting for our father, who will come soon,' he said.

A little taken aback but not in any way surprised, I asked how the journey was and what the welcome in Syria was like.

'We were very nervous to drive the road to Syria. There are so many hijackings and bombings on that road. We took a normal GMC taxi and the border guards were fine. They did not ask for any money and we entered Syria very well. The Syrian customs man even said welcome. I think he was Christian. The life here in Syria is incredible. People ask you where you are from and you say Iraq and they say, "I am sorry for what is happening there." They are really very, very nice,' he said.

I put down the phone and went outside to smoke a cigarette and a great sadness overcame me. While I was delighted that David and most of his family had escaped the dangers of Iraq, it felt like another nail in the coffin of the diverse and pluralistic Iraq I had known. The Christians were an admirable community that brought another dimension to Iraq. They were heavily involved in the arts, intellectual life and the archaeological community. Their long history had taught them the value of education, about which they were passionate. Without them, Iraq would be just another Middle Eastern community and much the poorer for that.

I spoke to David again soon after our first conversation and he confirmed that his father had joined them. They had now moved to the capital, Damascus.

'Richard, there are so many Iraqis here. It is unbelievable. They are mostly Christians, but believe me, there are many Sunnis and even some Shias. Damascus is like a little Baghdad. We have shops. We have schools. We have our churches. Everything is better,' he said.

The family had moved to the capital to be closer to the Australian embassy, where they hoped to get a sympathetic hearing for their asylum case. They were also eagerly looking forward to the visit of David's two sisters and their families. The sisters had moved to the United States soon after the Gulf War of 1991 and hadn't seen the family since. Children had been born and a grand family reunion was planned.

'Now I can start my life all over again. In Baghdad, we were just surviving. Here, I can see the future,' David said.

His sisters in the United States sent money every month, which helped with the costs of renting accommodation in Damascus. Further help came from Australia, where David's grandmother had settled in the 1970s after a mini-pogrom had occurred in her home town of Kirkuk. Along with an older brother and other more distant relations, they were sponsoring the family's attempt to emigrate to Australia. The interview at the embassy had been a terse affair. David described the official's demeanour as not friendly or helpful. I recognised the type of Western official he had met and reassured him that the man was just doing his duty, albeit in a cold, officious way.

'I can't wait to meet my family in Australia again. It is many years since I have seen them and I miss them very much,' he said.

I asked him if he intended to settle in Australia. He hesitated.

'You know, Richard, I am twenty-eight years old now and my deepest desire is to make a life for myself. I want to meet a girl and marry and have children, but I will not do this in Australia. I will come back to Baghdad when everything is quiet again and I will meet a beautiful Assyrian girl and we will get married and we will live in Baghdad, by the Tigris, and have children and be happy. This is my great hope,' he said and laughed.

All through our conversation, I could hear the Damascus traffic in the background, horns blaring. While some of the Christians would stay in Syria, many more were planning to leave the Middle East forever, like David and his family. Canada and Australia were their destinations of choice. These countries were host to large Iraqi Christian populations. Sweden, Holland, France and Britain had also been sympathetic to their plight. I asked David if any of the Christians were hoping to emigrate to the United States.

'Yes, there are some. They already have family there. But we are told the United States embassy here says they cannot give asylum to any Iraqi Christians because the government in America says there is no civil war in Iraq and therefore no need for asylum. You must be in a war to be a refugee. The Americans say we are not in a war,' he said.

There was silence for a moment. Then we both laughed.

4

THE SUNNI – MOHAMMED

December 1998

It was six o'clock, a cold, crisp morning, the first hint of winter coolness in a place I had always associated with burning sunshine. Mohammed and the driver picked me up from the Rashid Hotel as normal and we set out for Mahmoudiya, a small town one hour south of Baghdad. We drove through the desultory industrial outskirts of the city in silence. In the distance was Ctesiphon, the gigantic ruin of yet another Iraqi civilisation. I had planned to visit the great arch there on many occasions but had never got around to it. There was always something more urgent to do. Today it was a report on education.

I was always a slow starter for these early excursions and apologised to Mohammed for being so quiet and withdrawn.

'I am also not feeling great this morning, Richard,' Mohammed said.

He explained that the morning had been hurried and busy, that the children had been noisy and that he had not had time to pray properly.

'My routine is upset, but I will get over it,' he said.

We drove along without saying much. We were headed for a primary school to record a radio piece about children in Iraq and how they cope in a country under the most stringent economic and cultural sanctions ever imposed on a nation. Mahmoudiya had been chosen because Mohammed knew a woman who taught there and who spoke good English. It was a relief to leave Baghdad and the ubiquitous Ministry of Information had given us special permission to go without the presence of a minder. They trusted Mohammed, as did most people who knew him. He was our rock.

The all-girls primary school was typical of contemporary Iraq and showed all the dilapidation and neglect that characterised public institutions. It was run down and starved of investment, but the teachers were cheerful and highly motivated. They spoke of the impact of sanctions. Mohammed translated. The teachers explained that the children's diet was poor. They were lacking pulses and meat. Their ability to grow and flourish was compromised.

As I finished one interview with a particularly strident teacher, I spotted the headmistress coming across the yard. She was dressed in a dark business suit with a lime-coloured blouse and sensible shoes. Mohammed turned around and greeted her warmly and introduced me to her as Tia, an old acquaintance from university.

'You will not need me to translate. Tia has better English than I do,' he said, smiling warmly and laughing.

'You flatter me, Mohammed. My English is, how do you say? Rusty. Yes, it is rusty.' We all smiled.

Tia and Mohammed spoke to each other in Arabic. There was a light, almost flirtatious quality to their discourse. When it came to recording an interview, Tia's message was so similar to the teachers' that I began to wonder if they had not all got together before our visit to work out a line for the Western journalist. It was all standard stuff, almost pro forma. No matter what question I asked, she inevitably brought the subject back to the crisis in Iraq as a result of sanctions. There was no criticism of the regime or the bureaucracy. Sanctions were the root of all problems. I thanked her and moved on.

Mohammed explained that everyone we spoke to had to follow the party line and warned me not to expect anything unique or even personal. We went into the school building and entered a Spartan classroom adorned with pictures of the president and little else. It could have been a barracks room, so bare and devoid of colour and life were the walls. Mohammed introduced us to the girls. They demonstrated their English with great aplomb and called out, 'Saddam, Saddam is our president. We love our president' in unison. They all smiled. I looked at the English textbook. There was a picture of Saddam on every single page.

In the yard I asked Mohammed to explain the Iraqi education system while I recorded his response. Behind us the girls began filing out onto the tarmacadam and lining up in neat rows. Mohammed finished his commentary and we turned around to look at the assembly. He began to explain the format for school assembly. Teachers would make announcements and then the entire school would sing the national anthem and salute the president. It would be formal but not impressive, he suggested.

The teacher spoke at length to the pupils from a lectern as they listened dutifully. Then one of the girls walked up to the podium and blew into a tuning mouth organ. The children started to sing the anthem. Mohammed translated. The Iraqi national anthem never impressed me. It always sounded like a parody and this time it seemed even more jumpy and musically incoherent than I remembered it to be. It ended abruptly.

The headmistress Tia marched out into the yard, behind the children and walked straight up to the podium. All the girls watched her. She raised an AK-47 Kalashnikov rifle above her head, shouted something and let off a deafening salvo of shots. I jumped with fright and looked at Mohammed for guidance. Smoke floated over the heads of the children as the smell of cordite assaulted my nose. What was she doing, firing an AK-47 in a school playground? The blood seemed to drain from Mohammed's face. His eyes stood out. I wasn't sure if he was angry or shocked.

The headmistress spoke again and raised the rifle once more for a repeat performance. The noise caused a sharp ringing in my ears, so I turned the recorder off and headed for the gate and the car, shocked and speechless after the unexpected military tattoo.

'What the fuck was that all about, Mohammed? You're not trying to tell me they do that every day,' I said later in the car.

'What can I tell you, Richard? I have heard that they do this at the end of the school year, but only in some schools where the Ba'ath are strong. How could they do this in the middle of a school for young girls? It is shocking, and this is from Tia. I cannot believe it. That she could become like that. She is a clever girl and now she is shooting guns off over the heads of the children. It is really unbelievable,' he said, his voice tailing off. 'Real bullets, real bullets,' he muttered, clearly distressed by the event.

As we drove back to Baghdad I nodded off and woke up as we crossed the bridge over the Tigris. Mohammed looked agitated and worried.

'Is it because of the sanctions that we are like this, or is this our real character, as Iraqis? Are we savages? Are we violent animals? Ready to shoot and brutalise the children at the drop of a hat?' he said, his hand shielding his eyes as if he was ashamed of something. 'This is not the way I was brought up, Richard. This is not the way we are meant to behave. It is savage and ugly,' he said, looking at me directly, his eyes red and moist, his voice heavy with emotion.

When we got over it, we dubbed it a 'Tia moment'. If someone did something that was uniquely Iraqi and simultaneously strange, Mohammed would look at me and whisper, 'Tia moment'. When he brought me to the mass wedding of two hundred couples being married Moonie-style by the Ba'ath party at Uday Hussein's hunting lodge, he raised his eyebrows, looked around and said, 'Tia moment'.

When we were spirited away unexpectedly one afternoon, dumped on a parade ground at a military academy in the middle of nowhere and forced to watch hundreds of soldiers in balaclavas kicking each other to bits as they displayed their martial arts skills, it was a 'Tia moment'.

When a ministry official was reprimanding me for one of my reports and he whipped himself into a frenzy of nationalist outrage, banging the table repeatedly as documents fell off and scattered on the ground, it was a 'Tia moment'.

When I realised that the man who collected the fees for the ministry didn't have a single fingernail on his hands, it was a 'Tia moment'.

A 'Tia moment' could be funny, sad, grotesque, shock-ing, pitiful, moving or revolting. Mohammed could see them coming and he would alert me in advance.

⌒

Mohammed never adopted the common practice among Iraqi men of growing a moustache. The 1980s and 1990s was a time of cultural isolation for Iraq. The fashion for facial hair had died out in most of the rest of the world, but in Baghdad, virtually every male sported one class of mous-tache or other. The wearing of beards was a different matter. That could imply religious devotion beyond what was acceptable, but moustaches were positively encouraged. It was a small sign of the independence that Mohammed displayed by being openly clean shaven and, while it wasn't unique, it differentiated him from others. During my many visits to Iraq, I noticed that the tiny number of men that were clean shaven were almost always of the same class and background – middle-class men who had travelled and who were invariably Anglophile or Francophile.

It was also obvious that the wearing of a moustache was a homage to Saddam, part of the cult that surrounded him. 'The president wears a moustache,' so the logic went, 'so I must, too.' In a society controlled by a tiny clique which was geographically confined to one province (indeed, one town, Tikrit), others found they had to copy the style of the ruling elite in the hope of advancement. Not so with Mohammed. Although I knew in my heart that he despised Saddam, we never had to say it out loud. It was an understanding that dared not speak its name, part of Mohammed's quiet dignity that inspired respect from those around him.

In many ways he was a typical member of the Iraqi middle class from the pre-war, pre-sanctions days when money was plentiful and Iraq – a development success story emerging from Third World poverty – used at least some of its money wisely. There was universal free health care of increasingly high quality and universal provision for education. Bright pupils found no financial impediment to further their education at home or abroad. The GDP per capita exceeded that of Spain in the late 1970s, and in 1980 its income per head surpassed that of the Republic of Ireland. This time of plenty was a distant memory now.

Mohammed had studied in Baghdad and received his degree in English literature before winning a scholarship to travel to Britain in 1982 to study translation at Heriot-Watt University in Edinburgh, Scotland and a further, more specialised course at York, England. He travelled on a full scholarship with airfare, fees and a handsome stipend paid by the Iraqi government. He had to visit the Iraqi Embassy in London occasionally to pick up his payments, journeys he enjoyed because they allowed him to indulge his passion for books and literature. He would scour the bookshops of Tottenham Court Road and pick up books and journals unavailable for reasons of logistics or censorship in Iraq. It was a magical time of freedom and intellectual development where he was free to mix and talk to people from many backgrounds and nationalities.

The embassy staff would use this as an opportunity to check up on him, to make sure he wasn't mixing in dissident circles or becoming contaminated with revolutionary ideas. Their concern was exclusively centred on the obsession that exile Iraqis would fall into radical Arab company in the United Kingdom and return to Iraq as a threat to the regime.

In the case of Mohammed, the internecine bickering of the Arab communities in Britain held no allure. Although he was aware of politics and new ideas, he was simply not interested. Mohammed loved Britain and delighted in its literary and cultural traditions. He enjoyed his time there so much, and I was so energised by his enthusiasm for the country, that we would spend quiet times reminiscing about favourite streets and buildings and institutions.

After his return to Baghdad, Mohammed worked on an English-language newspaper, the *Observer* – the only one in Iraq at that time – where he met his future wife, Samira. They were married in 1986 and eighteen months later she gave birth to a daughter, Teeba, and then to a son, Marwan, in 1989.

The glory years of easy money and state largess were drawing to a close and it was, quite possibly, the most difficult time in modern Iraq to be founding a family and making one's way in the world. Saddam, believing he had the upper hand following the chaos of the Islamic revolution in neighbouring Iran, invaded the country and catapulted Iraq into an eight-year war that brought only death and destitution. The war set Iraq back at least fifty years in its development and put in train the series of events that ultimately led to the current disaster.

Although not unaffected by the changes going on in his country, Mohammed continued to thrive. His skills were still in demand and he had no problem finding jobs and positions. His confidence was born of his own intelligence and his superior education, and as the years went on, he managed to make do in jobs which didn't pay very much while maintaining sufficient space to explore literary ideas and to prepare for his PhD, which he achieved in 1999.

He was employed by the BBC as a translator and rapidly established himself as the most indispensable member of the Baghdad bureau, of which I was the nominal chief in 1998 and 1999.

I may have paid the wages, but there was no question of who was the real power in our office. Mohammed would arrive early in the morning in his characteristically smart jacket and neatly ironed shirt with a copy of the latest novel or book he was reading tucked under his arm. At this time he had become fascinated by the work of James Joyce, the Irish author. He had read and reread the novel *Ulysses* and became obsessed with the notion of translating it into Arabic. One attempt had been made in the 1950s in Egypt, but that version wasn't regarded highly by scholars because the methodology employed was basic and glossed over many of the thorny issues presented by such a subtle and complex work.

On quiet afternoons we would sit in the office and analyse the challenges of the novel. How would one deal with the complex syntax (or the lack of syntax in places)? How would one treat the many puns and plays on words that characterise the narrative, which were specific to the English language and even specific to Dublin slang? How could one translate Molly Blooom's soliloquy, for example, pages of free-flowing stream of consciousness without any punctuation whatsoever?

Mohammed and I discussed this endlessly, even though it bored the others in the office rigid. He would often ask me to read passages out loud with a heavy Dublin accent so that he could grasp the subtlety of language and nuance. He was puzzled by a number of scenes and, while being no Joyce scholar myself, I tried to explain what I understood them to be and he weighed and judged my opinion with a true scholar's prescience.

He asked me to draw a plan of a Martello tower, the characteristic round tower where Stephen Dedulaus and Buck Mulligan lived in Sandycove in Dublin in the opening chapter. He asked me to draw a map of Dublin city and to trace the journey of the novel's hero, Leopold Bloom, through the streets of the metropolis. I was very impressed by Mohammed's even-handed approach to the main character. Even the mention of Jews in Iraq was considered dangerous, but Mohammed and I discussed Bloom's Jewishness at length.

Mohammed's interest in James Joyce and *Ulysses* was intensified as he had chosen to write his doctorate thesis on a 'semiotic approach' to translating the work into Arabic. This highly technical area of translation was his speciality and he had studied the subject in York in the early 1980s. In March 1999 he finally submitted his thesis for consideration to the University of Baghdad. By all accounts the reaction of the panel was utter bewilderment. They had little exposure to modern discussions about the different philosophies and strategies of translation.

It was another sign of the intellectual isolation of Iraq from the outside world and the university authorities had to scrabble around to reconstitute the board. The normal procedure in the Western world would be for a university to find an expert from abroad to act on the panel. This option was not open in Iraq because the sanctions regime made it impossible for universities to maintain contact with foreign institutions. Iraq was on its own.

Mohammed had come across this impediment in his own endeavour to keep up with modern scholarship on James Joyce. He had some credit left over at the British Library and applied in 1998 for copies of a Joyce publication. After a long delay the library finally replied, denying his request. He wrote about this in an article in an Iraqi publication.

'When I requested copes of the *James Joyce Quarterly* from the British Library (Boston Spa), I was prepared to

With Abu Aseel on the roof of the Ministry of Information in the hastily constructed RTÉ Baghdad 'Bureau', which served as our headquarters until the Americans bombed the building and destroyed our shack on 25 March 2003.

Abu Aseel and his son, Mohammed. Abu Aseel puts his son through the routine of loading and checking an AK47 rifle. 'The gun is no good,' Abu Aseel says, 'but there is little choice if you need to protect your family.'

David George during his brief period of freedom in Syria in 2005. Soon after, the secret police picked him up and locked him in jail. The family reserves were raided to get him out.

With Dr Mohammed Darweesh outside the BB bureau in the Ministry o Information building in Baghdad in 1998. Also pictured is Goran Wieker our Kurdish driver (left)

Azzam Alwash, the pioneering campaigner for the Marsh Arabs. Azzam gave up his comfortable life in California to return to his native Iraq with the aim of promoting a project to return the marshes to their original condition. His 'Eden Again' project is one of the few positive developments since 2003.

With Azzam Alwash in Nasiriya at a feast given by a local sheikh. Wherever Azzam went, his enthusiasm made him the centre of attention.

It is easy to romanticise the Marsh Arab way of life. It is harsh and difficult and lacks many of the comforts of modern life. But many are returning to an ancient way of life in preference to the chaos of modern Iraq.

Allowed to fish again, the Marsh Arabs are moving back into their historic domain in small numbers. They were the only people to spontaneously offer thanks to the Americans for overthrowing Saddam.

Hajji Abu-Sami takes his youngest daughter from the arms of his wife, Oum Sami, outside their makeshift home in the southern marshes. Like hundreds of thousands of others, they dream of a traditional life in the marshes, but are realistic about the challenges.

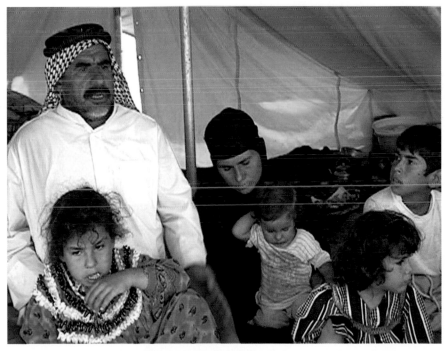

Hajji Abu-Sami with Oum Sami and family inside their tent on the southern marshes.

With Captain St John Price (left) on a British military helicopter travelling from Basrah to Um Qasr. St John was shy of the camera and careful about what information he allowed to get out.

After following the money trail through the Baghdad night, Sergeant John Marshall finds the film used by forgers. 'They're using the money to buy arms and fund the insurgency,' he said.

Corporal Rachel Looney riding shotgun on a Humvee military vehicle in Baghdad through the night. All she wants is to get home without injury. Almost three thousand coalition soldiers have been killed in Iraq. Tens of thousands have been maimed.

An insurgent from Fallujah talks about his hatred for Americans and pledges to destroy the US military operations in Baghdad.

Private Wayne 'Papa' Wiley. every group has its joker and Papa is the morale booster of the 18th Military Police unit while they try to help the Iraqi police in Baghdad.

Tom van Torre, our cameraman from Brussels, during our long trip
to the south of Iraq in 2003.

Not a great place to break down! As the insurgency gathered pace in 2003,
travelling around Iraq became a terrifying ordeal. RTÉ producer
Janet Traynor looks on with some concern as we try to fix a
burst tyre on the road south of Hilla.

pay for them through credit coupons bought when I was resident in Britain. I was shocked and depressed by the brusque reply: "We cannot process your application because of sanctions imposed by our government on your country." They also said, "Don't send any further requests until sanctions are lifted.""

The obstinacy of the institution wasn't the main issue under question here, but its sanity. The UN regime had been instigated to prevent the Iraqi authorities getting their hands on material, physical or intellectual, which could be used in military programmes to create weapons of mass destruction. How the work of James Joyce and the arcane scholarship surrounding it could have any military use was a question we asked on many occasions.

I decided to write about the issue and sent an article to *The Independent* of London and *The Irish Times*, both of which published the piece prominently under the sub-heading 'A Joyce Scholar in Baghdad'. Academics in the West were outraged by the notion that literary scholarship could be censured by government agencies. They wrote letters to both newspapers in protest.

Stephen Joyce, the author's grandson and the family member who most jealously guards the Joyce legacy, wrote to me asking if there was anything he could do for Mohammed. As it happened, there was. A Joyce symposium was planned for June 2000 in London and I asked if he would fund Mohammed's trip and invite him to the conference. This would also offer Mohammed the opportunity to travel to Dublin to see the streets where the novel was set and to enjoy the atmosphere of Joyce's hometown and mine also. Stephen Joyce had no hesitation in agreeing.

Mohammed was beside himself with excitement over the invitation and we discussed the possibilities that the trip offered.

'There is only one problem, Richard. What will I do with my family when I am going away? I am very afraid that something will happen to them. Who knows when the Americans will strike again?' he said.

I tried to reassure him that the Americans never struck out of the blue. Their campaigns were clearly choreographed in advance and they usually built up to a crescendo, finally resulting in military action. This was the pattern we had witnessed in the past and there was no reason to think that it would change. He would have plenty of notice of a rise in tensions in advance of any military action. In all likelihood it would take months, allowing him time to cancel his trip if he felt that was necessary. I urged him to take up this once-in-a-lifetime offer in the strongest possible terms. It didn't take long to convince him and he returned to the excitable state of before. After years of isolation, he would at last be able to rejoin the mainstream academic world. What a prospect!

⌒

It is impossible to understand Mohammed Darweesh without knowing where he came from. His hometown of Mosul is the most extraordinary city in Iraq and its sons and daughters cherish it very warmly. Mohammed is entranced by Mosul, by its history, its extraordinary religious and ethnic diversity and its stunning location as a bridgehead on the river Tigris. Mosul has Whirling Dervishes; Christians who speak the same language as Christ; Yazidi worshippers of a divine entity that others say is the devil; Kurdish, Shia and Sunni Muslims; Arab Sunni Muslims; Catholic and Chaldean Christians; Turcomens who originate from central Asia; and many other small sub-groups and mini-communities.

The accretion of culture that occurred over centuries has produced a distinctly 'Mosul' view of the world. It is an urbane, liberal outlook on life. Mohammed Darweesh is the embodiment of the best of these values.

Mosul sits at the crossroads of a number of ancient worlds and civilisations. On its outskirts are the extraordinary ruins of Nineveh, which became capital of the ancient Assyrian kingdom under the reign of King Sargon of Akkad from 2371 BC until its collapse in 612 BC.

Mohammed's eyes brightened when he told me of the treasure from Nineveh held in the Iraq Museum. 'Richard, you have to go to the Iraq Museum. It is the only thing we have in the whole of Iraq that comes close to the quality of what you see in the West. It is a fine building and the grand exhibition hall holds true treasures which will make you so surprised,' he said.

He beamed with pride as he described the glories of the institution that had survived two major wars and countless coups and counter-coups. And while he admired the artefacts from other parts of Iraq that were held there, it was the former grandeur of his hometown which shone through, particularly the massive alabaster reliefs.

He carefully explained the history and described the magnificence of Khorsabad, Nineveh and Nimrud, the great cities of the Mosul plains. The region with Mosul at its heart reached its highest point deep in distant antiquity. Its achievements faded away as it was annexed to other rising civilisations and was finally taken over by the kingdoms to the south, especially when it was overrun by the Babylonians and Medes in 632 BC. It was a pattern that was to repeat itself over the subsequent centuries until the Ottomans finally exerted full control over the region.

The new conquerors coveted the lucrative trading routes that passed through the region and were among the busiest in the world at that time. The Ottomans named their new province (or vilayet) after the city.

After a long period of economic stagnation, Mosul once again took off in the nineteenth and early twentieth centuries. Mosul expanded and its importance was once again asserted, only to be undermined from 1920 onwards by the increasing importance of Kirkuk, where the discovery and exploitation of a massive oil field promised untold riches. Under British rule and subsequently the British-controlled monarchy, Mosul became an important administrative and educational centre, if something of an economic backwater.

If, at the halfway point of the twentieth century, the city was less important than it had been, then no one thought of telling the ruling elite of Mosul. They regarded themselves as a cut above other Iraqis and certainly people of more substance than the Kurds who populated most of the rest of the northern Iraq. Their superiority didn't have to be asserted. It was just so.

It was into this patrician world that Mohammed would be born. Mohammed's mother was a shy and difficult woman and her otherwise happy marriage to her husband was blighted by one salient omission – her failure to produce a male heir. The weight of family and clan pressure was felt by Mohammed's mother, who, despite her best efforts, had given birth to a girl some five years before.

The young girl was much treasured by the family, but the whisperings became louder until there were open words exchanged between uncles and Mohammed's father. This further enflamed the situation and put an intolerable burden on husband and wife. Not only were they having difficulties over the failure to conceive a male heir, but their problems were now the property of the family gossips.

Relations between the couple deteriorated and there was a real prospect of the marriage falling away. Elders within the clan intervened and patched up a temporary resolution. After three months there was again no sign of a child, and for Mohammed's mother the situation had become desperate. She turned to religion.

The interaction between Christians, Sunnis, Yazidis and Shias in Mosul was comfortable and it was not uncommon for orthodox Sunnis to casually engage in worship side by side with Chaldeans or Nestorian Christians. The mix was and still is impressive.

I had witnessed one of these crossovers when standing at the entrance to a church on a busy street before mass one Sunday evening. In the corner was a rather gaudy statue of the Virgin Mary in a grotto-style presentation reminiscent of so many shrines in the Catholic world. The Virgin in this case was clearly of Middle Eastern extraction, dark but with a straight nose, her colour the only novelty in an otherwise stereotypical scene, inspired by the apparition at Lourdes, France. Surrounding the front of the shrine were hundreds of candles, put there by the devout before going into the church for mass. Some candles had been lit hours ago and were in their final throes, no longer shining beacons but squat, round pools of soft wax. Others were pert and fresh, burning brightly, having been lit recently.

A shrouded woman (whom I recognised to be a Shia Muslim) appeared at the entrance, carrying a number of shopping bags and with three young children. She gently ushered them towards the back of the entrance hall and walked over to the Virgin. Dipping into the box of candles, she brought her hands together as if in Christian prayer and uttered words to herself before placing the lit candle gently and deliberately at the foot of Mary. She then closed her eyes in silent contemplation for a few moments and then turned, as if woken from a deep slumber, to look for her children. She gathered them up and promptly walked out of the church, her plastic bags swinging gaily as she headed for home.

I was somewhat taken aback by this event. I had never come across such intermingling of religion before. Even the simplest of mixing between Catholic and Protestant Christians was relatively unknown to me, and my Irish upbringing had taught me that mixing and religion did not go easily together.

I turned to the priest I had come to interview and inquired if this was an unusual event.

'It happens every day. The Shia women here have a particular devotion to the Blessed Virgin and they come and say the Hail Mary in the hope of being blessed by God,' he said.

'The Hail Mary?' I asked, incredulous.

'Yes, they have a great faith in the Virgin, and if you stay here long enough you'll see many hundreds of the Shia women arriving here. But not the men. They are not involved in this,' he said.

This was, perhaps, a very localised custom, but it seemed to me indicative of the overlapping histories of the Christians, Muslims and others in Iraq over the centuries.

However, it wasn't all one-way traffic. Christians of all denominations, for example, were given relatively free access to the ancient site of the Prophet Younis Mosque on the left bank of the river Tigris, just outside Mosul.

Prophet Younis features in the Qu'ran, but he is also a significant figure in the Christian and Jewish tradition as Jonah, the prophet who, by disobeying God's command, caused a storm to rage which resulted in him being thrown into the sea and swallowed by a whale. His repentance while inside the whale resulted in his salvation and his remains are kept within what is now a mosque, along with a prominently displayed whale bone said to have come from the creature that swallowed the saint.

The site of the Prophet Younis Mosque has a fascinating history. Excavations have shown that it was originally an Assyrian temple to the ancient Babylonian gods, then a centre of fire worship for the Zoroastrian tradition. Subsequently it became a Christian monastery, then a church until finally it was taken over by Muslims and used as a mosque.

Such overlapping reigns and religions make certain things possible in Mosul that would be unthinkable in more monocultural parts of Iraq, particularly the south, where Shia Muslims dominate by as much as 98 per cent.

So it was no surprise that Mohammed's mother turned in desperation to the Dervishes of Mosul for help. They are part of the centuries-old Muslim sect of Sufism which was brought to this part of Iraq by the Ottomans, for whom it was virtually a state religion. Named after the founder Mevlana, the members of the Mevlevi order differ from orthodox Muslims in a number of crucial respects, principally in their extraordinary rituals involving dancing, circling and the lavish use of music and chanting.

The Dervishes had something of a reputation in Mosul for hereticism and the most conservative Sunni Muslims would have had nothing to do with them, principally because of their extraordinary system of worship. The Dervish desire for 'closeness to God' and the deep spiritual and mystical nature of their exploration of man's relationship with the unknown is in stark contrast with the public nature of standard confessional Islam. Even though their ceremonies are highly physical set pieces,

Dervishism is fundamentally a mystical branch of Islam where a deep oneness with God is the central aim.

Much of orthodox Sunni Islam is concerned with behaviour, and laws governing the relationship between followers and Allah and the inner life isn't explored to any great degree. Orthodox Sunni Muslims have a positive abhorrence of mysticism and speculation, which the more radical sects regard as blasphemous.

As an order, the Mevlevi Dervishes share much of the poetic and spiritual journey of the Sufi tradition within Islam. They also eschew luxurious living in favour of extreme poverty and humility.

Orthodox Sunni Muslims elsewhere regard the incantation of non-Qu'ranic prayers and poems in the prophet's name and particularly the use of music in a religious ceremony as decadent. Among the puritanical Wahhabi sect – the dominant ideology in Saudi Arabia and within the al-Qaeda organisation – Sufism or Dervishism are regarded as evil. Listening to adherents of these extreme doctrines, it would be easy to conclude that they regard what they believe to be deviants from the literalist movement in Islam to be worse than the godless ways of non-believers.

While such extreme Muslim views certainly existed in Mosul at this time, they did not constitute a large proportion, and certainly not a majority, of the Muslim city dwellers.

In Mosul, familiarity had not brought contempt in relation to Dervishism, but accommodation. However liberal that attitude might have been in the abstract, attending a Dervish ceremony would have been quite another matter for a Sunni Muslim, particularly a woman. It speaks poignantly of the pressure she lived under and the desperation of her situation that Mohammed's mother would consider going to the monastery in the dead of night for help.

Mohammed's mother made her way through the impossibly complicated central streets and alleyways of Mosul and moved across courtyards and squares, through tunnels and up stairways with ease and familiarity. Mohammed's description of her journey through the city reminded me of the movement of a gazelle through the high plains, jumping over rocks, moving onto ledges in a surefooted way, testimony to years of familiarity.

She didn't tell her husband and went alone and eventually ended her journey at the Mevlevihanc, the cloister or monastery of the Dervishes. Ushered into the women's room, she was to witness the strange and wonderful ceremony called the Sema (whirling dance) that dates back to the thirteenth century and is little changed today.

The twelve Semazens (monks of the Sema, the monks who dance or whirl) stand around in a wide circle with their arms crossed, ready to begin their ritual. They wear black cloaks to symbolise the tomb to which all will be consigned in time. Underneath they wear white skirts that run from the neck to the floor, which are revealed in all their drama when the black cloaks are discarded.

In the centre is the Sheikh, the leader or overseer of the ritual, through whom divine grace will flow. The arms of the Semazens are unfolded and the right hand opens up to the heavens in prayer while the left hand of the Dervish is facing down to the earth. The Dervish has thus created a connection between the celestial world and the earth, through which divine blessing can symbolically flow.

By turning his body to the left or right, but not moving his feet, the Dervish can observe all around him, thereby becoming more and more the centre of the universe. The first musical part of the ceremony is the singing of the Nat-I-Serif, a long poem dedicated to the prophet Mohammed. Then follows the call of the drum summoning the

Dervishes to wake up and enter the state of high spirituality that is calling them.

Then the monks start the Sultan Veled Walk, whereby they slowly process past each other, bowing in salutation until they enter the core of the Sema ritual itself, the four salutes. At this point the music begins to pick up pace. From its gentle start on the zitar and drums, it moves towards a sequence of minor peaks through the first two movements, each lasting half an hour until it finds a rhapsodic natural crescendo in the swirling and frenetically unrestrained movement of the third salute.

After this the Sheikh enters the circle and literally becomes the centre of their universe, the sun to their revolving planets. At this point exhaustion has become a factor for the Whirling Dervishes and they are close to the state they are trying to achieve, a kind of spiritual trance, which they believe to be a higher state of being and closer to God. All the while, the music is following their movements, leading them on sometimes, while at other parts of the ritual the music lags behind the whirling figures and allows their frenzied whirling to take centre stage, reaching a stunning crescendo.

At the end of all of this the monks recite a section of the Qu'ran, greet each other by clasping hands and joyously kissing the back of the hand of their greeter. The music continues as the ceremony is wound down and the faithful break for a meal and more music and conversation.

What a shock this must have been for a quiet, orthodox Sunni Muslim woman. Mohammed's mother stayed for the whole ceremony, which lasted more than three hours. If the aim was to mesmerise, then it had certainly worked and she approached the Sheikh with trepidation. He greeted her kindly and listened attentively to her problem. He asked her if her husband had come with her. She told him he hadn't and explained the tensions and difficulties that had arisen between them as a result of the lack of a boy child.

The Sheikh listened and nodded and sighed and acknowledged. He then asked her to wait and he disappeared into one of the ante-rooms off the hall, returning some minutes later with an object carefully wrapped in paper. He asked her not to open it until she arrived home and to put the item under her bed. He then waited a moment for her to offer a gift. She gladly produced a dinar coin and pressed it into the hand of the Sheikh. He humbly bowed his head and wished her good fortune and asked her to come back when the son was born. '*Inshallah*,' God willing, she replied.

Three months later, Mohammed's mother felt the first stirrings of a baby inside her and a local doctor confirmed that she was indeed pregnant. When he was born she named him Mohammed Darweesh, Mohammed of the Dervish, in honour of the holy man who had answered her family's yearnings.

It was the summer of 1955 and the insular worlds of the people of Mosul and the nation as a whole were on the cusp of major change. Mohammed would be born into a very different country from the one of settled confidence that his father and mother had known.

Oil production was beginning to produce a significant amount of money for the treasury of Baghdad and development projects were being initiated all over the kingdom. The ancient nation that had stagnated for centuries was about to take off in a most unexpected and unpredictable way and the consequences for Mohammed's generation would be far reaching and profound.

Within three years of Mohammed's birth, a coup by a combination of disgruntled army officers, nationalist-minded radicals and communists had removed the hated king, twenty-three-year-old Faisal II. He was shot in the head at the royal palace in Baghdad on the morning of 14 July 1958. His distant cousin Abd al-Ilah, who had acted as Regent for much of the previous twenty years and was considered by most Iraqis to be the power behind the throne following the accession of Faisal II, was also slain on the same day.

The two were shot by a young officer as they emerged from the palace, even though both were holding copies of the Qu'ran over their head as a plea for mercy from the army and the mob that had assembled. In Iraq's short line of British-imposed monarchs, Faisal II was the third and the last.

Baghdad legend has it that the young lieutenant who opened fire on the two men, Abdul Sattar al-Abosi, was posted to Basrah, where he suffered severe mental problems and was visited every night by the ghost of the murdered monarch, who pleaded to know why the officer had killed him. Lieutenant al-Abosi subsequently committed suicide.

Back on the streets of the main cities, few expressed any sadness for the loss of the hated king. There was huge popular approval of the demise of the monarchy, which was seen by many Iraqis as lazy and anachronistic. Hundreds of thousands of people lined the streets of Baghdad to welcome the new republic and its herald, Colonel Abdul Salem Arif.

These events marked the beginning of Iraq's modern history. No longer a vassal nation of the Ottomans or the British or their stooge monarchy, Iraq's destiny was now more in its own hands than at any time since it had stood at the centre of the Islamic world from the ninth to thirteenth centuries. The revolutionary ideas of Nasserism

(Arab nationalism), socialism and communism captured the imagination of a restless population.

But the manner of the change in power, the violence of the coup and, more particularly, the secretive nature of the coup conspiracy set in train a pattern that Iraq would follow until Saddam Hussein seized power in 1979. Intrigue, violence and plotting became the route to power in Iraq and every government that assumed power subsequently used this method. Arguably, the overthrow of Saddam Hussein by United States and British forces in 2003 also followed the pattern, the main difference being that it was organised from outside the country.

Within months of the 1958 putsch, rioting and internecine strife between the different political factions in Mosul and in the southern city of Kirkuk had left thousands of people dead. Coups were followed by purges of one group by another and political instability was the order of the day. Some of Mohammed's family moved to the capital to insulate themselves from the political ferment in Mosul.

Mohammed would turn to me on a regular basis and bemoan the violent past of Iraq. 'Every time they come to power with great ideas and ideals and every time they turn out to be worse than the last one. More greedy, more vain, more stupid,' he said.

Then he would look around him to make sure no one was in earshot. 'This one is more stupid, vain and greedy than all the others put together,' he would say

⌒

So this was Baghdad, ancient citadel of the caliphs and Abbasid dynasties, the city that controlled much of the known world for more than 300 years. And yet it looked like a run-down American suburb constructed in haste in the 1970s. I asked Mohammed if he would take me to an old part of the city to show me some of this ancient heritage. Mohammed dismissed such thoughts with a wave of the hand.

'You think that it is like Edinburgh or Paris, with a medieval quarter and old buildings?' he asked, raising an eyebrow.

'Yes,' I replied, 'there must be something to see, to look at. You know, old buildings from the Ottoman period, ancient mosques, something.'

But Mohammed assured me that no such coherent district existed in Baghdad. There were bits and pieces here and there. 'Not much worth looking at' was his summation.

He explained that as the oil money began to flow in the late 1960s and early 1970s, the city council of Baghdad prepared plans to clear what they regarded as the slums which crowded many of the older parts of the city. 'Slums', it soon became clear, meant anything that was more than twenty years old. Buildings and whole areas of the city were torn down in an orgy of destruction. The rebuilding exercise was done in the name of progress, as it often is in such cases, removing unsanitary, crowded and dangerous buildings and rehousing people in purpose-built regimented modern houses and apartments controlled by the city council or the state.

Money was no object in this exercise. As the treasury of the Iraqi government swelled with unheard-of billions of dollars, all of it the result of the rising price of oil, money was made available for all manner of 'social improvements'. It is worth remembering that at the time the Iraqi dinar was a strong and desirable currency, worth three United States dollars per dinar. Money rules when it comes to construction, and there were many with a vested interest in knocking buildings down and building new ones. The headlong rush to what the Iraqis saw as 'progress' precluded any acknowledgment of their rich architectural past. The past was a different place; they were poorer then. 'Who cares? Pull it down' was the dominant attitude, according to Mohammed.

Baghdad was a mere village when, in 762 AD, the spiritual head of the Islamic world decided to shift his capital from the warring city of Kufa in order to rid himself of the disputes that had begun to tear the young religion apart. Caliph Jaffar al-Mansour, the inheritor of the Abbasid dynasty, chose Baghdad because of its strategic value at a crossroad for trade and commerce as well as for the beauty and relative isolation of its location on the banks of the Tigris River. Primarily, though, he chose Baghdad because it was a new start, far from the bickering that characterised the centres of Islamic civilisation at the time. Baghdad was also closer to the Persian territories that had been grumbling about being ruled by distant aristocrats. It would be a capital without the tension and arguments of the previous capitals at Basrah, Medina and Damascus and so he named it Madinat as-Salam, 'the city of peace'. However, the old name stuck.

Abbasid caliphs were direct inheritors of the mantle of leadership in orthodox Islam because they were all descended from the Prophet Mohammed's paternal uncle, and among Sunni Muslims (the overwhelming majority of Muslims at that time and since) their authority wasn't questioned. However, Islam was still a very young religion and there was considerable argument and debate about its practices and direction, giving rise to the difficulties at Kufa.

The court of Caliph al-Mansour was by all accounts a wonder to behold. He built palaces and gardens, libraries and schools as the dynasty profited from taxes on the trade that passed along its roads and up and down the rivers. Baghdad grew and flourished.

It was during the reign of Caliph Harun ar Rashid (786–809 AD) that the high point of Baghdad civilisation was reached. The caliph loved poetry and mathematics and was said to shower poets in pearls and jewels as a sign of approval. The caliph's palace and court, which formed the original core of the city, had now expanded and Baghdad was a large city of perhaps half a million people, spreading across the Tigris River from the original settlement. It was Baghdad that produced *The Thousand and One Nights* (the *Arabian Nights*), the cycle of stories that captured the imagination of the West when it was republished in the nineteenth century.

At this point, the caliph controlled an empire that stretched from Anatolia (present-day Turkey) and Afghanistan in the east all the way to Spain in the west, with significant influence beyond that point. While Europe was in the middle of its Dark Age, the Islamic countries were developing civilisation to new heights. In Baghdad, scholars and mathematicians pushed the boundaries of the known universe. Because many of their religious ceremonies were dependent on the lunar calendar, the caliphs founded schools of astronomy which delved into ancient studies of the cosmos and moved far beyond their intended purpose. This was, perhaps, the highest achievement of this 500-year civilisation.

But the huge cultural achievement of Baghdad couldn't last. By the twelfth century, the Abbasid dynasty's influence on the rest of the Muslim world had diminished. Other rival centres of learning and power arose. But even if the empire had passed its peak, Baghdad was still the most developed and the richest city on the planet at that time.

Others had designs on the wealth of the Abbasid dynasty, and the main challenge to its authority came from the steppes of Mongolia. An army of Mongols under the leadership of Hulagu marched on Baghdad and demanded the surrender of the caliph. How ridiculous it must have seemed to Mustasim, the caliph – uncivilised, pagan Mongol horsemen from a remote and primitive land had come to threaten the most developed state the world had known.

Caliph Mustasim's confidence was misplaced. Whatever about their lack of high manners and civilisation, the Mongols were fearsome warriors and quickly overran Baghdad, butchering hundreds of thousands of its inhabitants. They collected the treasures in piles and sacked the libraries. So many books were thrown into the Tigris that it was said a horseman could ride across the river using the piles of books as a ford. It was the end of the Abbasid dynasty and Islam would never have a centralised focus like it again. The mantle of leadership of the Muslim world shifted over the centuries to Medina, Cairo and Damascus.

Further destruction of what was left of Baghdad happened under the fratricidal campaign of the Mongol Timur-leng in 1401, who demanded his soldiers bring him the heads of every human in Baghdad. He reportedly constructed vast pyramids of skulls as a monument to his ferocity.

Baghdad's high point was now a mere historical footnote. Wilfred Thesiger, the great writer on Arabia, puts it most succinctly:

Arab nomads, from the desert beyond the Euphrates, drifted into the country and grazed their herds on mounds which were once the palaces of kings. Whereas the original Arabs had settled in flourishing cities and towns and had been gradually absorbed into the native population, these new immigrants, with their black tents, their herds of camels and flocks of sheep and goats, divided up the land into grazing grounds. A system of government based on urban life was replaced by the tribal law of the tents. (Wilfred Thesiger, *The Marsh Arabs*, pp. 96–7)

So it was no surprise that almost nothing of the magnificence of Caliph al-Mansour nor none of the glory of Caliph Harun ar-Rashid survived. But Baghdad did revive over the centuries, albeit at a much lower key than under the Abbasids. Under the Ottomans, the city became the capital of their province in the centre of Iraq. This brought a measure of development and rebuilding and I was sure that some remnants of this period must remain in Baghdad. It would be hidden and difficult to find, and the only person I knew in Baghdad who could help me to uncover it was Mohammed Darweesh.

It was only some time later that I realised that remnants of the 'old world' did exist in tiny pockets across the city. In the centre of the city were two distinct areas that contained as much as 90 per cent of Baghdad's building heritage: the markets area around Rashid Street, near the Al Mustansiriyah school, and the old Jewish area of Al Hasafae, near the river Tigris.

At last, here was some irregularity in the streetscape and urban layout. Decades of accumulated development overlapped on centuries of opportunistic building as the river banks were stabilised and flood controls made more effective. Diversity of styles and street layout distinguish both areas, which are terribly run down. In a city where the guiding aesthetic of architecture is a kind of square-jawed 1970s brutalism, these small districts provided a welcome break from the tedium of straight lines. Much of what remains today is from the late Ottoman period and a good deal from the British period, together roughly dating from the end of the nineteenth century until the 1950s.

I eventually prevailed on Mohammed to go with me on a long walk around the old Jewish area east of Sa'adoun Street on the pretext of buying a watch. At that time Baghdad was completely safe for foreigners and walking in the streets was a pleasant experience. People would nod and salute in an old-fashioned manner, acknowledging the presence of a foreigner. Occasionally people would come up to me, bow slightly and say 'welcome'. I would touch my breast with an open hand and reply '*Shoukran*' (thank you in Arabic).

I found the watch I wanted and we stopped for a fruit juice at a small shop. Mohammed informed me that the idea of wandering around the streets of Baghdad aimlessly looking at buildings was not a common practice and would be viewed in a very negative light by the authorities.

'The Big Guy has eyes and ears everywhere and they will report us to the ministry, who will ask lots of questions,' he said.

'Then we'll tell them the truth, Mohammed. I'm interested in old Baghdad and you were showing me some of the older streets and buildings,' I said.

'As you wish,' was Mohammed's reply.

We left the juice bar and wandered into the labyrinth of alleys and lanes between Sa'adoun Street and the river. Ancient houses with elaborate but sturdy wooden doors fronted onto the street. Behind most of the façades was a courtyard, which in previous times would have featured a small fountain or fruit tree. Now most sported heaps of rubbish, washing lines or shacks.

Many of the houses had their original front doors now coloured with the cheapest paint of the day. Thick and stout with elaborate hinging and brass keyholes and enormous knockers, they were minor works of art as well as being artefacts of a by-gone age. The door surrounds were made with sandstone and were very similar in appearance to the material used in Jerusalem for most stone building. Tellingly, there was a gap at the apex of all the surrounds where considerable violence had been used to prize a symbol or jewel from its setting.

'That's where the Jewish star of David was hacked out from,' Mohammed informed me, clearly unhappy at this vandalism of a unique piece of Baghdad heritage. The area had been a thriving Jewish district for centuries.

Above the front door and running the width of the house was the covered balcony containing the salon, the formal talking room, fronting onto the street with intricately carved wooden screens. This feature – called *shenashil* – was particularly delightful, being vernacular. It conjured up images of cool afternoons in ancient times as a group or a couple sat overlooking the street but screened from it, conversing or possibly cavorting in secret. One could easily imagine a scene from *The Thousand and One Nights* with the Caliph Harun ar-Rashid and his rakish chief poet wandering through the back streets.

This flight of fancy didn't last long, as children poured out of the houses to inspect the strange foreigner poking around their neighbourhood. They were in turn followed by black-clad women of uncertain vintage who shooed them away as they looked me over. I smiled and bowed slightly in my customary way. The women didn't return my greeting, which was a surprise.

Mohammed was beginning to feel uneasy and asked if I would mind moving on, as we were attracting too much attention at the top of the street. I obliged and we walked purposefully towards the river past some dull 1980s offices before re-entering the magical world of ancient Baghdad 100 metres or so from the corniche.

I was admiring one section of stunning *shenashil* – a five-metre-long screen depicting flowers of an astonishing variety and detail – when a woman in a black *abaaya* approached. As was often the case, one could not make out her age. She could have just as easily been seventeen or seventy.

'Mister. I very nice. Come. Come,' she implored.

I smiled a vacant smile, not knowing what she wanted. 'Thank you very much, madam. I'm with my friend Mohammed here. Mohammed!' I shouted ahead to Mohammed, who was in conversation with a vendor at the junction with the river road.

Mohammed looked back and in an instant summed up the situation. At this point the woman opened up her *abaaya* to display a bright white bra against her dark skin. It was such a strange sight in the centre of Baghdad that I was momentarily mesmerised by the view of so much female flesh.

'You like. You like,' she kept saying, at which point Mohammed arrived and in horror started to chastise the woman, while I looked on askance.

He took me forcibly by the arm and moved towards the river, all the time calling and gesticulating to the woman, who had by now restored herself to modesty.

Mohammed then let loose a torrent of abuse about Sa'adoun Street and how filthy and depraved it had become as we headed back to the office in the gloomy Ministry of Information building across the Tigris.

'It all started during the Iran–Iraq War. At the beginning of the war, Saddam gave the families of the dead gifts. Big presents – cars, televisions, houses even – but as the war went on and hundreds and thousands of men died, it all ran out. Some families kicked out the widows and kept the presents. Widows were left destitute and they turned to prostitution. Their children are now turning to the same thing. I never saw this before the Iran–Iraq War,' he said. 'This place has really gone downhill in the last few years and all because...' he hesitated and looked around to make sure no one was listening, 'of the Big Man. I remember a time when the centre of Baghdad was clean and nice. Then came the wars and the invasions. Everything has fallen away since then,' he said.

Mohammed explained to me the significance of the thousands of ramshackle orange and white taxis that plied their trade on the streets of Baghdad and the other towns and cities of Iraq. After the death of a young man in combat during the Iran–Iraq War (1980–88), the family of the deceased were given these vehicles as gifts from the government to make up for the loss of earnings as a result of the death of the family member.

At the start of the conflict, when Iraq was in the ascendant, government officials would arrive with a note for the head of the family, entitling them to pick up a free car from a garage with the government concession for this purpose. Initially this could be a European car, an Audi or a Peugeot or some such modern vehicle. The families of some well-known heroes received Mercedes cars, but it didn't take long for the largesse to run out.

As the news from the battlegrounds in southern Iran got worse, so the generosity began to subside. Instead of brand new European cars, the bereaved had to make do with cheaper and less sophisticated models. Brazilian-made Volkswagen Passats were imported by the hundreds to fill the vacuum. These models were universally orange and white, the colour of all official taxis in Iraq.

Such generosity from the government wasn't unusual in the early 1980s in the Middle East. The high price of oil and the OPEC cartel's stranglehold on the supply of this resource brought billions of dollars into the treasuries of the corrupt governments of the region and they lavished money on pet projects. The extended families of these feudal elites benefited disproportionably from the windfall. Obscure princelets in Saudi Arabia and in the United Arab Emirates suddenly found themselves billionaires.

However, true to their nomadic Bedouin roots, the ruling families had to spread at least some of the money outside the immediate governing clique in order to maintain their position at the top of the pile. Hence, in Saudi Arabia, upon marriage, citizens of the kingdom were given houses as a gratuity.

President Saddam Hussein of Iraq, while not a hereditary ruler, mimicked his neighbours. He liked to portray himself as a feudal master, lording it over a nation of grateful subjects. Arguably, Saddam's largesse was more enlightened than that of the dynastic states. He gave his citizens a universal free health care system of high quality and invested heavily in the education system. He also handed out high-value gifts to favoured members of his regime and to prominent members of civil society.

One example of this was the gift of a brand new Mercedes 300 SL to the professor of Plastic and Reconstructive Surgery at Baghdad University, Dr Ala Bashir, in 1982 for his work in helping thousands of soldiers to recovery during the Iran–Iraq War.

Dr Bashir was a wealthy plastic surgeon and also a part-time artist who had found his way into the confidence of Saddam Hussein. He had no real need for the extravagant gift from the president, but he would have been foolish to refuse it. At least he didn't have to use the vehicle to make a living, as was the case for so many others.

As compensation for the death of a loved one, the taxis quickly became almost useless. The avalanche of new vehicles, combined with the dramatic economic collapse caused by the cost of the war with Iran and the general downturn in the revenues to the state, meant that business for the thousands of new taxis was very thin on the ground.

Nidal Aseel Tawfeeq was one of those affected. I met him at the taxi rank outside the Al-Rasheed Hotel in central Baghdad in 1999, and as he drove me to my appointment with the Greek chargé d'affaires in the Mansour district of the city, he told me his family's story.

In his late fifties, Nidal told me of the loss of his son, Marwan, in the war with Iran in 1984. This was one of the worst episodes of that terrible conflict, with Iranian troops occupying Iraqi soil and moving ever closer to a total takeover of the southern capital, Basrah.

The news of his death on the front line near the town of Qurna, adjacent to the Iranian border, came as a shock to the family, as they had been led to believe that he was stationed further north, near the city of Kut. The news was delivered by two junior officers from the Ministry of Defence who promised that the family would receive compensation for the loss of their son in the form of a new vehicle to enable them to replace the lost income.

'The same thing was happening all over Baghdad. Thousands of our sons were lost in the war and the families had the new car and they went to the streets to earn the living as a taxi driver,' he said.

The taxi business provided a very modest living up to the end of the 1980s. Only the high state subsidy on petrol enabled the owners of the taxis to scratch a wage, such was the volume of compensation cars on the road and the competition for custom.

'Everything collapsed when we went into Kuwait. Business stopped. The foreigners stopped coming to Baghdad and many Iraqis stole cars from Kuwait, so there was no need for all the taxis. *Wala*, we nearly starved during that time, my friend,' Nidal told me.

The car he was driving was the same one he received from the government, a 1984 vintage Brazilian-made Volkswagen Passat. Fifteen years later the car was still on the road, but only just. It was battered and bruised. The exterior had the appearance of the kind of stock car used by enthusiasts in Europe. The interior was threadbare and had no seatbelts. The speedometer didn't work and as far as I could make out, none of the instruments functioned to any degree.

'The car is still good?' I inquired.

'*Inshallah*,' he replied (if God wills).

My conversation with Nidal was replicated dozens of times during my visits over the years, and each time the pattern was the same: children died, compensation followed but the ruinous state of the economy and the constant wars with neighbours and foreign powers negated any positive effect of the government's generosity.

⌒

Mohammed constantly scolded me for giving money to the orphans and street urchins that inhabited the area around the Ministry of Information, where we had our office. I would always hand over a 250 dinar note (worth around ten US cents) to one of the children when arriving at or leaving the office.

Mohammed told me that many of the children found themselves on the street through no fault of their own. Their fathers and mothers had been killed or injured in the Iran–Iraq War or in the subsequent conflict following the invasion of Kuwait. Their condition was wretched. They wore rags. They appeared to be malnourished and some showed the signs of substance abuse – some were clearly sniffing glue or other solvents, while others were drinking *arak*, the strong Arab alcoholic drink fermented from the flesh of coconuts.

'Please, don't give them any money. It just encourages them to live on the streets and to stay away from government orphanages and the ones in the mosque,' Mohammed said.

His logic was typical of the middle classes in most cities around the world. Giving beggars money acts as an incentive to keep them on the streets. They should be taken in hand and brought under the strict control of the social services.

'But Mohammed, what about the Islamic obligation of *zakat*?' I asked, referring to the exhortation in the Qu'ran to give generously to the needy in society. The Qu'ran specifically warns Muslims that they will never attain piety until they spend something of what they love. How much should they give? 'Whatever ye spend that is good, is for parents and kindred and orphans and those in want and for wayfarers. And whatever ye do that is good – Allah knoweth it well', states surah 2, v. 215.

Mohammed didn't seem pleased by my probings, which were a little provocative and tongue-in-cheek.

'I pay *zakat* at the mosque and they provide food for the hungry and shelter for the homeless families. It is better for the mosque to do it than I,' he said.

His disapproval didn't stop me handing over the notes to the young children on the streets. As a visiting foreigner there was little I could do to improve the situation of Iraqi society as a whole and the small dribs and drabs handed out to the destitute seemed to me the minimum I could be expected to contribute. Mohammed continued to disapprove, but he did so in his mild and characteristically gentle way.

There was very little work to do in the BBC office in Baghdad at that time. Apart from a busy period at the end of 1998, when the United States launched 200 Tomahawk cruise missiles on the country in the campaign dubbed Desert Fox, the appetite for news about Iraq was low. When I would call the news desk in London to propose a story, the answer was invariably negative. They were happy to have me there in case of an emergency, but their interest in the humdrum events of daily life was minimal. In fairness to some editors, there was an appetite for stories about the effect of sanctions on the population, but for others there was a weariness in hearing more bad news from Iraq. It was almost a case of 'what? More stories about the effect of sanctions? We had that last month.' During one eight-week period from March until May 1999 I filed only two stories.

The lack of challenging work and the draw of a family in Dublin made life difficult in Baghdad. Mohammed and I discussed the situation on a number of occasions and his advice was always the same: I should look after family first and then worry about my career. It was sound advice and I took it. In 1999 I decided to leave the Middle East and the BBC and return to my home country.

When the time came for Mohammed's trip to Europe, I found myself in Zimbabwe covering the crisis there for my new employer, RTÉ, the Irish national broadcaster. I was disappointed that I would be unable to meet him, but Stephen Joyce had made arrangements for him to stay in London and to travel to Dublin under his own steam. The conference in London was a great success. Mohammed was greeted enthusiastically by the other academics and delivered a paper derived from his thesis on translating Joyce's epic novel into Arabic.

The Dublin leg of the visit didn't work out as well. I felt guilty that my absence had created difficulties for Mohammed. He had no one to show him around the city, and while it was undoubtedly a positive thing to be out of Iraq and away from the oppression of the state there, he didn't get as much out of his trip to Joyce's homeland as I had hoped.

In the meantime, Mohammed received his PhD from the University of Baghdad and would forevermore be known as Dr Mohammed.

It was more than a year before I saw Dr Mohammed again, in 2001. I again expressed regret at not being in Dublin when he came the previous year.

'Richard, you have no need to apologise to me about this. It was a magical visit for me and I enjoyed it enormously. Dublin was wet and busy. Just like in *Ulysses*,' he said and offered me a copy of *Gilgamesh*, Iraq's national English-language literary journal, named after the epic poem of ancient Mesopotamia. There, on page twenty-three, was Mohammed's report of his trip.

> After eight hours, I found myself at Heathrow Terminal Three. I handed my passport to the passenger control officer who carefully examined it, looked up at me and asked a series of routine questions such as: how long will you stay in the UK? Where are you going to stay? What is the purpose of your visit? I patiently told him that I had written a Ph.D. thesis on translating Joyce's *Ulysses* into Arabic and I was invited to the Joyce conference to submit a paper on the subject. He knitted his eyebrows unbelievably and said: 'You better translate it into English before Arabic. I tried to read it several times in my youth, but could not finish the first chapter!'

The visit to Europe had reconnected Mohammed to his peers in the Joyce industry. After years of isolation, he felt part of the world again. He was asked to present papers at other conferences and to attend seminars in other countries. He was flattered and delighted with the sudden upsurge in interest, but circumstances in Iraq made it difficult for him to contemplate leaving his family, even for the briefest of visits abroad.

For all his interest in literature and the arts, Mohammed was also a citizen of Iraq and a husband and father. In this context he wasn't someone to close himself off from events of the day. As the war drew closer in 2002 and 2003 I noticed a distinct and disturbing change in Mohammed's attitude. Where before he had been a friend of the West, and of Britain in particular, now he raged against the imperialistic attitude of the big powers.

'Do they think we will all lie down and be colonised by the Americans? It will not happen. Even if Saddam goes, the Iraqis won't be colonised,' he told me in November 2002, as the prospect of war seemed inevitable.

Mohammed had never expressed any support for the Sunni elite or the clique from Saddam's home region of Tikrit that controlled the government, but the prospect of the Americans installing a government which would be constituted mainly of exile politicians – Shia politicians at that – filled him with horror. Like most of the middle class he couldn't conceive of an Iraq run by the majority community, the Shia.

For Mohammed, the Shia were the threatening hordes of the south. The middle class understood all too well that the Shia harboured deep resentment over the fact that Iraq had been controlled by the Sunnis for generations, be it the Ottomans, the British-mandated monarchy or the Ba'ath party.

The only occasion I remember Mohammed losing his temper was over a colleague, a Sunni Muslim who had worked at the heart of government. After a long argument in the office over the disappearance of some money, our colleague went home. Mohammed believed the colleague had taken the money. He couldn't abide the idea of such dishonesty and worked himself into a lather over it.

'He calls himself a Muslim. How can he do that? He drinks whiskey and comes into the office hung over. I know he's really a bloody Shia in his heart,' Mohammed said.

I was deeply shocked and said as much to Mohammed, who later apologised. He explained that he had lost his temper and said things he didn't mean to say, but his comments about our colleague's Shia background stuck in my mind. I wondered if all Sunnis harboured a deep prejudice against Shias. If asked, they would deny it, but there was surely something there.

The prospect of the centuries-old order being overturned as a result of an American and British invasion struck deep fear in the hearts of Sunni Muslims like Mohammed. It gives an indication of how fearful others closer to the apparatus of the Ba'ath party must have felt. They owed everything to the Sunni ascendancy and stood to lose out from any major change. They would resist it ferociously.

Days before the war in March 2003 I met Mohammed again, to pass on a gift. I had heard from another colleague that Mohammed had become very interested in another Irish writer, the playwright, novelist and essayist Samuel Beckett. I wasn't surprised by his new interest. If ever an author chimed with the times, then Beckett was that man. I handed over the biography I had purchased for him after a warm embrace and an elaborate Arab greeting.

We joked about waiting for Godot and how long we would have to wait before the Americans would arrive in Baghdad. It was a rare moment of levity in an otherwise gloomy conversation. Mohammed looked haggard and tired and had aged considerably in the previous nine months. He looked like he carried the weight of the world on his shoulders.

He confided in me that he had acquired a gun. 'It is for the lawless time after the current guy goes,' he said.

I was shocked that Mohammed of all people would acquire a weapon. It would be difficult to find a more gentle and non-violent person than Mohammed, and yet the fear of the upcoming fighting forced him to take this course of action.

We embraced warmly and I tried to make another joke about Godot and Beckett.

'I'm afraid this time, Richard, it will be more like *Krapp's Last Tape* than *Waiting For Godot*,' and with that Mohammed headed for home to look after his family.

⌒

After the war I was anxious to follow up on all my Iraqi friends, to make sure they had survived the fighting and to find out how they were faring in the new Iraq. I met Mohammed only once after the war. I had missed the opportunity to visit him on two occasions following the end of the conflict because of work pressure, but in March 2004 I was determined to find him. The BBC had taken a house close to the Palestine Hotel, on the riverbank.

The once-charming street had been closed at both ends by massive concrete blast barriers to prevent suicide bombers from attacking the media offices. The French Ambassador's residence was also located there, offering further security. I approached the building purposefully and was stopped at the side entrance by a young female producer who demanded to know who I was and what I was doing at the office. She was clearly very stressed and anxious about being in Baghdad.

I began to explain to the impatient woman that I had come to see my old friend Dr Mohammed Darweesh and went on to mention that I had worked for the BBC in Baghdad during the late 1990s. She eased off a little at this point, although the tensions of life in Baghdad were etched in her face. Although the BBC quarters had a strong collegiality, there was no disguising the bunker mentality that was inevitable from that style of living. Producers and reporters lived behind barriers and their work was difficult and dangerous. It gave them little satisfaction. Most wanted to be out and about reflecting life in the city, but they couldn't leave the compound because of the dangers.

Mohammed appeared and rescued me from the anxious producer. We embraced warmly again, exchanging three kisses on the cheeks and sat down to talk over tea in the small garden. We trawled through our stories of the war and its aftermath. I noticed that Mohammed had changed the habit of a lifetime and had acquired a moustache. It made his face look totally different from before and somehow less distinguished. It was clearly a form of camouflage, a protection from the insurgents. In a city where barbers were being routinely assassinated (because they engaged in the un-Islamic practice of shaving beards) by religious fanatics, it was better to fit in. Standing out in any way had become extremely dangerous.

The irony of this gentle man who had survived without facial hair during the entire reign of Saddam Hussein, when every male over sixteen wore a moustache, only to now sport one was difficult for me to accept, but I kept my council. It wasn't a worthy topic of conversation with so much else to come up to date on since our last meeting just before the war.

I inquired after his family (all of whom survived the war unscathed) and he inquired of mine. I asked him how he was coping with the situation and the pervasive sense of danger and violence.

'What can we do?' he said. His tone had changed and he was decidedly more gloomy than I remembered. He told me he was afraid coming to work each day and that when he was at work he feared the journey home. On his way home he worried about his family. Would they have survived the day? Would his daughter have made it home from school? Would the kidnappers that were running rampant around Baghdad find his son or daughter or wife? Would he be the next victim to turn up in the river or be dumped on a rubbish heap? There were many questions and behind them was an all-consuming fear of this new, unrecognisable country.

'Believe me, it is like a really frightening nightmare but I am awake all the time,' he said.

I asked him if he still found time to read.

'Reading is a thing of the past, Richard,' he said. 'I would love to sit down at night and read a novel or prepare a paper, but I am too worried. I am too nervous to read.'

5

FROM THE MISTY SOUTH

September 2003

It didn't look promising. The al-Janoob Hotel was a truly
awful dump. It was a big concrete box, plonked by the side
of the Euphrates River. The gloomy corridor leading to
my room was illuminated by a single light bulb, like all the
public areas of the hotel, giving the lobby and other areas
a gloomy twilight feel at all times of the day and night. The
only clean bit of my room was the metre-wide section of
the bed covered by fresh sheets. Everything else was caked
in filth and dust.

The hotel had another name in the 1980s. Under
Saddam it had been named al-Anfal, after the campaign
initiated by his cousin Ali Hassan al-Majid (Chemical Ali)
to destroy the Kurdish population of northern Iraq after
they had taken up arms against Baghdad. The name was a
warning as well as a calculated insult to the Shias of
Nasiriya. Ali Hassan al-Majid had also unleashed his
forces on the tribes of the south after the 1991 Shia

uprising, crushing their challenge to Saddam. Nasiriya had been one of the main centres of the revolt and the name of the crumbling hotel beside the Euphrates River stood as a reminder to the Shias of what could happen to them if they disobeyed the powers in the north.

We were in Nasiriya to record interviews and film sequences for a documentary looking at the state of Iraq six months after the end of the war. Our documentary project was a wide-ranging one and our ostensible object in Nasiriya was to talk to Shia leaders. We had many people to meet in Nasiriya and interviews to record, but at the back of my mind all the time was the hope that we would learn something about the Marsh Arabs. We wanted to be the first journalists to document the return of life to the marshes.

Our guide was to be the charming and passionate advocate of the Ma'adan (Marsh Arab) way of life, Azzam Alwash. I had concerns about Azzam. He sounded too good to be true. He was American-educated and had abandoned his highly successful engineering practice in California to come to post-war Iraq to help re-establish the marshes and the culture of its people. He was powerfully built, handsome, spoke English with a west coast twang and his Arabic was distinctively that of a southern Shia.

He smiled a lot and when he did his extensive salt and pepper gray beard would open up to show a fine set of American-maintained teeth. He had the energy and drive of a New York business executive, but he was Iraqi and could deal with the humblest soft drink vendor on an equal basis. He seemed to motivate everyone around him, and Iraqis in particular were dazzled and inspired by his energy. The only question that remained was, 'is this man a hopeless dreamer or someone who really will get something done?'

We had heard rumours that something was stirring in the marshes, that thousands were returning. Our trip had been very gloomy up to then. Everywhere we went in Iraq there was evidence that the country was slipping backwards into chaos and civil war. Violence was beginning to reach catastrophic proportions in Baghdad and around the Sunni Triangle. The Jordanian embassy had been destroyed in an audacious suicide attack. The United Nations compound had been wrecked by a suicide bomb only weeks before. This put an end to the international mission that had showed some promise in bringing together the disparate elements of the Iraqi body politic.

Outside the capital and the Sunni Triangle, government was almost non-existent and the hoped-for revival of the economy hadn't transpired. A visit to the marshes seemed an interesting way to illustrate one of the few positive aspects of the change in regime in Iraq.

Ever since I had read Wilfred Thesiger's book on the Marsh Arabs, I had been fascinated by them. They were a people who lived on water in the driest region on earth. Their customs and practices were as old as civilisation itself. To meet them would be a journalistic coup and a fulfilment of a personal goal.

I was, however, under no illusions about what remained. We had acquired footage and photographs that graphically depicted the catastrophe that had occurred in the marshes. Where before there was a vast watery marsh inhabited by 300,000 people, now the photographs showed wide expanses of calico flatness, devoid of any evidence of human occupation. One photograph showed the Saddam Canal, a drainage project named after the president. It was taken by an American airman in 1997 from the cockpit of an airplane patrolling the no-fly zone below the 33rd parallel. The channel was two kilometres wide and full of water. On either side as far as the eye could see stretched a parched wasteland. It wasn't sand, though it was the colour of sand. It was hard to believe that water and vegetation and people had occupied this area since the dawn of human civilisation.

Even the ebullient Azzam was sceptical about what we would find. 'Mother Nature has been dealt a cruel blow in the marshes, so don't expect much if we ever get there,' he told me days before in Baghdad.

As we busied ourselves in Nasiriya, concentrating our filming on post-war rebuilding initiatives and gathering views on the new Iraq, we tried our best to find out what was happening in the marshes. I was hopeful that our contacts with the al-Issa clan who lived south of Nasiriya would prove useful. At one stage the al-Issa had been a powerful tribe in the marshes and their influence had been extensive in the reedlands north-east of Nasiriya in the distant past. Like many of the tribes in the area, they had always included some families that adopted a sedentary lifestyle over the centuries. The settled al-Issa had occupied a large tract of land near the 'spit and sawdust' town of Suq-as-Shuyuk (the market of the sheikh) on the edge of the previously extensive marshlands. Whatever was left of the marsh-dwelling element of the clan had given up their ancient lifestyle and settled permanently here sometime during the 1990s.

They proved to know nothing of any use about the Ma'adan and even regarded them with contempt.

'The marshes. It's all gone and the people there are all in Baghdad. You will find nothing there,' an elder told me. 'It is good that it is all gone. My father came from the marshes and he could not read or write. He didn't even know the holy Qu'ran. A terrible place.'

Their dismissal of the Marsh Arabs was odd and all the more surprising because it appeared to be a form of self-loathing. They had left the lifestyle of the marshes behind them and looked back only in anger. They still lived near the water but were no longer of it.

Back at the al-Janoob Hotel in Nasiriya, I related my gloomy findings to Azzam. He didn't seem put out by the information, as he had heard more optimistic noises from others in Nasiriya. Rumour had it that fifty kilometres east of Suq-as-Shuyuk, a large group of Ma'adan had reoccupied the marshes. It was a rumour, but it was all we had to go on. That was the extent of the information we had gathered after a few days in the main city of the middle marshes. We were short of hard information.

Azzam stroked his beard and waved his arm extravagantly. 'If they are there, we will find them. It might take a while, but we'll get there in the end. Don't you worry,' he said.

My trust in Azzam had begun to build over these days. He clearly was an idealistic individual, but his ease in dealing with people added to his credibility. His commitment was never in question, but he did work to a different timetable than the rest of us. His work and life passion was the Ma'adan. He had no problem devoting days to search for them. It was all part of a long-term programme. Success or failure wouldn't be determined by a single visit to the region.

I, on the other hand, was a journalist under severe time pressure with a looming deadline on a long form documentary film. Journalism, particularly television journalism, has become so time sensitive and risk averse that the idea of heading off in search of an obscure tribe without a predictable outcome would be regarded as madness. Our team had a meeting that evening where we weighed up the pros and cons of the trip. All credit to our producer, Janet Traynor, who agreed to the wild goose chase.

As we ate our meal in the shabby dining room of the hotel, Azzam came alive with his stories of the marshes. As a child in Basrah, he had been taken out by his father to see the life of the Ma'adan and described a magical world little changed from the one detailed in Wilfred Thesiger's seminal work, *The Marsh Arabs*.

According to Azzam, even as late as the 1980s, the southern marshes were populated by a fiercely independent, roguish community who lived on floating islands made from compacted reeds and vegetation. Some lived on dykes or banks of earth above the water line. They greeted strangers in massive cathedral-like guesthouses called *mudheefs*, also made from reeds. Their rough hunting, fishing and farming way of life and its autonomy entranced the young Azzam. He loved their rice paddies and their *mudheefs* and he was entranced by their lifestyle. The contrast between his own modern way of life in Basrah and the timelessness of the Ma'adan became a point of fascination for him.

'If there is even the slightest chance that we will find them, we must try,' he implored.

We were now under his spell and it was agreed, amid some excitement, to make the arrangements to depart at dawn.

Before leaving we had one of those unpleasant experiences that have become a defining reality in the new Iraq. Late that night there was an urgent knocking at my door. I opened it to find our film producer, Janet, terrified. Janet is extremely good looking and has long, cascading red hair – Iraqis would stare in astonishment at her. Iraqis assumed that I was the boss and she the assistant. On at least two occasions, Iraqi men were shocked to hear that Janet was in charge of the budget. They would have understood her better if they had asked about her background. Janet comes from the Irish badlands, the Cooley Mountains on the frontier between the Republic and Northern Ireland, a tough place by any standard.

Moments before she knocked on my door, an Iraqi night porter had gained access to her room and attempted to assault her. She managed to fight him off and escape. The porter was still there, standing at the end of the dark hallway, leering in a grotesque fashion. It was like something out of a badly acted movie. I went as if to challenge him and he turned and headed off to his office downstairs.

It was a reminder of the dangers for a woman on her own in small-town Iraq and further evidence of the collapse of authority in the wake of the defeat of Saddam. Such an occurrence would have been unthinkable in the old Iraq. This was the city where Jessica Lynch, the US army private, was cared for by medical staff after being injured at the beginning of the war. Even though she was an enemy fighter, the Iraqi medical team looked after her and even assigned her a private room in the state hospital. She was unharmed and protected by police and security officers for the duration of her stay in Iraq – contrary to the sensationalist reporting of her situation in the United States. Such chivalry at a time of war was unusual. It had completely disappeared by October 2003.

Janet stayed in my room that night, and when morning came we were happy to leave the al-Janoob Hotel behind forever, but not before reporting the porter to the manager and receiving assurances that he would be disciplined.

Arriving at Suq-as-Shuyuk, Azzam immediately began working the streets. The town was ramshackle and dusty and clogged with traffic. We stayed in the GMC, trying not to attract too much attention. Azzam arrived back with confirmation that some Ma'adan had moved back to an area fifty kilometres inland, on the fringes of what had previously been the central marshes.

He then went to the local authority offices to negotiate our passage into the district. The talks lasted two hours and we were eventually given permission to go but strictly on condition that we took three policemen and an official with us. The official had taken part in the Shia uprising of 1991 and had hidden in the marshes for three years thereafter. We agreed to the security contingent, albeit reluctantly.

Two policemen came in the GMC with us and I questioned them about the Marsh Arabs. They weren't very impressed. 'Criminals and rascals' was their verdict on them. The policemen, both city dwellers from Nasiriya, regarded their posting in Suq-as-Shuyuk as a disaster, like a step back into the pre-industrial world.

'They don't like us and we don't like them. They are always stealing and shooting their guns and we are always looking for them. This is the way it is,' one told me with a shrug of his shoulders.

Azzam tried to turn their minds, gently and patiently explaining the history of the Ma'adan and detailing something of the oppression they had suffered. While they expressed interest and even asked some questions, their opinions were built on rock-hard prejudice. Our two policemen were polite, but it was clear that they weren't about to change their attitude to the Ma'adan. It was easy to see that they would be gone from the area at the first opportunity.

It was difficult to reconcile modern-day Suq-as-Shuyuk with the town described by Wilfred Thesiger in *The Marsh Arabs*. He had visited in 1954 during one of the worst floods of recent history, when half the town was underwater. Then, Suq, as it is known locally, was a thriving commercial centre for the Ma'adan, with its own self-contained industries of boat building, matt weaving and merchanting. The bounty of the marshes provided the mainstay of the economy of the town. It was also the administrative centre for a wide area, providing governmental, policing and educational facilities for up to 100,000 Ma'adan. The Marsh Arabs may have regarded the urban people of the town with suspicion and disdain, but it was their economic lifeline to the outside world.

Today, Suq is a tattered shadow of its former self. Run down and neglected, its outskirts are host to thousands of refugees who live in appalling poverty, as bad as anything one would find in the more war-torn countries of Africa. The tents and shacks of large families were situated metres away from murky open streams of sewage and poisoned water. Barefoot children splashed in the muck while women carried water from standpipes miles away. There wasn't a tree in sight and nowhere did the residents bother to plant vegetable gardens. Even though they had been there for years, this was still a temporary settlement as far as the residents were concerned.

Virtually all of the residents of Suq were Ma'adan, their pitiful conditions today testimony to one of the late twentieth century's most brutal attempts at cultural genocide. As late as the 1980s the marshes of southern Iraq retained virtually all its cultural capital intact. The 300,000–500,000 people who regarded themselves as Ma'adan had coped with the advent of modernity and managed to survive the Ottoman, British, Royal Hashemite and finally Ba'athist regimes up to that point. Although there is some evidence that there was a drift to the towns, there was still a critical mass of people in the marshes to ensure continuity.

The cultural practices and lifestyle of the people stretch back far into the ancient past, to a time before the building of the pyramids of Giza and the growth of Baghdad, Damascus and the other cities in the Fertile Crescent. The Ma'adan can trace a direct cultural lineage dating back as far as the Sumerians, the first people we know to have codified language and written down law. They had adopted Islam and incorporated the Arabs and their language, but some other aspects of their tribal life predated the advent of Mohammed and his followers. The blood of many different races, cultures and tribes has mixed in the reedbeds of southern Iraq.

In less than a decade, Saddam managed to achieve what every other modern ruler of Iraq had failed to, namely the annihilation of the marshes and the destruction of the culture of the people. The first cracks began to appear during the Iran–Iraq War of 1980–88, when deserters from the Iraqi army found a safe haven in the vastness of this watery region. They realised that the army couldn't follow them. Within a few hundred metres the pursuers would become hopelessly lost in the labyrinth of streams and the vastness of the high reeds. They could rely on no help from the Ma'adan, who regarded all authority with a deep mistrust. They gave succour to the deserters and in some cases the runaways stayed and married into the Marsh Arab clans.

The fact that the Marsh Arabs were Shia and the pursuers of the deserters were Sunni Muslims, fighting a war against the self-confessed Shia republic of Iran, was another factor. As the fighting intensified, Iran saw the military usefulness of the marsh region and used the area to launch military forays behind Iraqi lines. Saddam and his military elite realised they had a major problem in the marshes. The region was permeable and it was conceivable that the Iranians could infiltrate the area in large numbers and push their offensives hundreds of kilometres north near the town of Kut, ever closer to the Sunni heartlands, using the marshes as cover. It was impossible to seal such a large and topographically complex area.

Struggling to find a coherent strategy to deal with the threat, Saddam ordered the systematic mining of the al-Huwaizah marshes which straddle the Iranian border. Floating mines were sown by the thousand. Saddam mobilised elite elements of the army to deal with the rearguard danger and placed a number of battle groups – amounting to a division – at strategic intervals to deter a large-scale invasion. He built straight embankments deep into the heart of the marshes and placed troops there. The strategy was partially successful.

Punitive raids against the Ma'adan were conducted on a small scale. Villages were burned and tribes attacked. Those Marsh Arabs that were accessible were harassed and arrested at will. The campaign lasted until the end of the war in 1988. At that point Saddam had managed to contain the threat from the marshes without ever being in control of the vast wilderness.

However, much worse was to come. Saddam's invasion of Kuwait sparked a new crisis for the Marsh Arabs. Yet again their loyalty was to be tested as hundreds of thousands of soldiers descended on southern Iraq. The fighting itself didn't impinge much on the life of the Ma'adan. The aftermath, however, convinced Saddam that the marshes had to be obliterated.

As his armies retreated from Kuwait under fire from the international coalition, Saddam was horrified to find that soldiers were again deserting in large numbers. Soldiers emboldened by the defeat of the dictator in Kuwait found the courage to denounce him in the settlements of the south.

They found refuge in the marshes, where the tribes welcomed them and supported their argument with the Ba'ath government. As the whole of the Shia south rose up against Saddam, the Ma'adan were at the forefront of the short-lived revolt. They sheltered the rebels and ran arms for the leaders, capturing and killing a significant number of Saddam loyalists. Like virtually all the Shia, they were convinced that the Americans supported their revolt and would aid them if Saddam were to attack them with heavy weapons.

All that seemed some way off during those heady few months in 1991. The Ma'adan controlled the marshes and with the city-based rebels created a no-go area for the Ba'ath government in the south. There was no sign of a counter offensive from Baghdad, where Saddam was coping with the fallout from his ignominious retreat out of Kuwait.

But it was only a matter of time before Saddam got his revenge. The backlash, when it came, was truly shocking. Tens of thousands were killed as the government used its remaining helicopters and heavy weaponry to prize control of the south back from the rebels. As Saddam's cousin Ali Hassan al-Majid masterminded the recapture of the towns and cities, the punitive raids on the marshes soon intensified. Many were killed on the spot. Whole villages were slaughtered, their bodies buried in makeshift mass graves far from roads or settlements.

In late 1991, Saddam reached into the archives and dusted down his copy of a document prepared by the imperial authorities. When Iraq was a British colony, plans had been developed to use the water from Iraq's two rivers for irrigation and agriculture. The British plan of 1948 envisaged the creation of a third river equidistant between the Tigris and Euphrates to deliver water for agriculture to boost the food supply. This new agricultural zone would lie north of the marshes just below Babylon.

The logic was that it was wasteful for water to be spilling into a vast, unproductive marsh when it could be more usefully employed growing vegetables for profit. The British had been impressed with the resourcefulness of Iraqi farmers and believed the project would help wean the country off colonial subsidies.

If there was a distinctively British colonial character to the plan as it was first envisaged, then there was a distinctively Ba'athist quality to the implementation decades later. The nature of the undertaking had changed from a development project to a punitive strike at the heart of a perceived internal enemy. Whereas before the sole purpose of the drainage system was to provide irrigation, now the only purpose was to take water out of the marshes and deliver it to the sea.

Saddam devoted a third of Iraqi GDP in 1991 and 1992 to the drainage projects, and on 7 December 1992, the renamed Saddam River (originally the Third River) project was officially inaugurated. The water began to flow down the massive canal, reaching the sea through the Basrah canal, depriving the marshes of their lifeblood. The project was cloaked in Ba'athist propaganda. It would create an 'agricultural paradise' and 'new living space'. Some suspected that Saddam hoped to transplant Sunni Arabs there in the hope of creating a bulwark against the restive Shias of the south. But it was just more empty rhetoric. Almost none of the promised agricultural development took place. No towns were created. Whereas the planning documents showed thousands of hectares of lush market gardens, the reality would be much more bleak. The channel did what it was intended to do – drain the central marshes.

But the Saddam River project was only the first of dozens of similar initiatives across the south that aimed to destroy the ecosystem. In 1993 and 1994 the Al-Qadisiya River, Umm al-Ma'arik (Mother of All Battles) River, Taj al-Ma'arik (Crown of All Battles) River and the al-'Izz (Prosperity) River projects were all completed. Dams were also constructed to stop any backflow from the newly constructed canals.

The remaining wetlands were divided into polders after the construction of yet more dykes and dams. Residual water was left to evaporate. Gradually the massive programme of works had their effect. Even though the flow of the Tigris and Euphrates had been strong, residents on the marshes noticed a fall in water levels in 1993 and a further, more dramatic drying in 1994. By 1995 the marsh system as a whole was breaking down.

In areas the marshes dried up completely, leaving only small, stagnant pools of dark, lifeless water. Areas of reed growth became isolated from each other and fish stocks began to collapse. The rice fields cultivated by the Ma'adan for centuries lost their freshwater flow and dried up, causing a food crisis.

Meanwhile, Saddam was attacking the Ma'adan. Columns of troops launched raids deep into the former wetlands, killing at will. The Ma'adan were marshalled into the towns and villages on the fringes of the former marshes and dumped on reservations. The remaining rebels in the marshlands scampered between isolated pockets of reeds in an ever more desperate battle for survival. By 1998 the job was completed. The marshes were destroyed. What had been a watery garden capable of supporting up to half a million people was rapidly turning into a salt-encrusted, wind-blown desert.

Something of Saddam's attitude to the Marsh Arabs can be gleaned from the memoir of his former personal doctor, Dr Ala Bashir. Writing in his memoir, *The Insider*, he quotes Saddam on the subject in 1991 – the only known quotes from the former president on the subject:

> The Marsh Arabs. They are not real Arabs… They arrived with their huge buffaloes from India because the Abbasid Arabs needed manpower. That was twelve hundred and fifty years ago and they haven't developed since. They are not like other Arabs. They have no moral standards… You can't trust the Marsh Arabs. They lie and steal and have no pride. They don't live like civilised people. And as for their women – they have no principles. They're quite immoral – no, indecent. (Ala Bashir, *The Insider: Trapped in Saddam's Brutal Regime*, Abacus, 2005)

The dehumanising that must take place before genocide is clearly evident here. If you are going to annihilate a people, they must be demonised first. It helps if the enemy is foreign or originally foreign (even if the supposed 'foreignness' of the Ma'adan was a fabrication). They must be backward. They must be immoral and untrustworthy, liars and thieves. If they are sexually suspect, this helps as well. All of which makes it much easier to deal with them harshly or destroy them altogether.

Saddam was helped by the isolation of the country at the time. Much of the murder and destruction happened as if behind closed doors because of the sanctions imposed on the country by the international community. Iraq had moved off the radar of Western news organisations. Finding accurate information was difficult. But the United Nations received many reports of brutality and its rapparteur passed them on dutifully to the UN assembly in New York. UN members huffed and puffed but did very little.

The best-quality reports on the tragedy were done by non-governmental organisations (NGOs). Human Rights Watch described one incident from August 1992 involving 2,500 villagers that was particularly chilling:

The victims, among them women and children, were rounded up in the marshes of al-Chibayish (west of al-Qurna) together with captured fighters of the opposition SCIRI. According to testimony obtained by Human Rights Watch, including that of a survivor, they were taken to an army camp in northern Iraq, where they were executed over a period of about two weeks. (Human Rights Watch, *The Iraqi Government Assault on the Marsh Arabs*, January 2003)

By the late 1990s the Ma'adan had been chased out of their homelands or killed. They lived as beggars and refugees in the towns around central Iraq. Many had been transported to the Sunni heartland near Baghdad, where their marginal existence meant they presented no threat to the government. The rebels were either dead or neutralised.

The former marshes were wind-blown, salt-encrusted wastelands. Only a tiny fragment remained in the eastern part of the al-Huwaizah marsh – that part mined by Saddam in the 1980s. Ironically, that small oasis owed its precarious survival to the streams that flowed from the Kabil mountain range across the border in Iran – water that Saddam had no control over.

Whether it is described as genocide, ethnocide or even ecocide, the effect was the same – a once proud and admirable people, the way of life and the land they inhabited were now gone. They were banished to an alien urban landscape and a lifestyle they neither liked nor admired.

The evidence of this was plain to see as we headed out of Suq on our quest to see if anything had been salvaged. The squalid settlements were devoid of vegetation and the only living plants we saw were a few bulrushes in the river Euphrates near Suq. Along the roads were the stumps of previously flourishing date palms, long since decapitated.

Azzam explained some of the crucial ecological issues to us as we drove towards our destination. The giant reed that is the keystone plant species of the marshes (*Phragmites australis*) has a potentially long dormancy period. The reed can survive for up to ten years without moisture before it dies off forever. The reed is the defining plant of the marshes, and without it there is little hope of regeneration for the people or the wildlife. Azzam explained that the biggest question about the reflooding of the marshes concerned the giant reeds. If they had gone past their dormancy period and died off, then the whole wetlands restoration project would be a pipe dream.

Some had suggested the possibility of a large-scale project to tackle this eventuality. It was suggested that reeds could be cultivated in a scientific manner and replanted in the marshes to 'give nature a helping hand'. Azzam said that although the project had some merit, it would need a well-organised and properly funded government to push it through. In the context of the chaos we witnessed in the country in 2003, it didn't seem likely.

A secondary consideration was the salinity of the water and land. The reeds are a freshwater plant, although they can thrive in mildly saline waterways. The drying of the reed beds had drawn salt crystals to the surface. This was a natural occurrence and had happened in many areas in the past. The problem now was the scale of the salination. Vast swathes of ground were ten centimetres thick with salt. Water pouring over the surface would quickly become like sea water, Azzam explained, potentially poisoning plants. Other possible problems could include the migration of sea creatures into the area, potentially upsetting what had been a very delicate ecosystem.

In addition to their ecological importance, the reeds are the economic lifeline for the people, providing fodder for animals and the base material for shelter and enclosure. Virtually every domestic implement was dependent on the reeds, and even if it wasn't made directly from reeds, it was the income generated by the selling of reeds that enabled the Ma'adan to buy other goods. Without the reeds, the marshes could never hope to return to life.

Azzam had heard of another area far to the east where a dyke had been broken in May 2003 and where a limited amount of water had spilled into a former marsh area. To date there had been no return of vegetation. In that case the salinity of the water wasn't the problem, rather, the reeds appeared to have simply gone beyond the point of recovery. This worried him. Left to its own devices, it would take decades, perhaps even centuries for such a wetland to reform itself.

After leaving the main tarmac road thirty kilometres out from Suq, we travelled along a rutted dirt road constructed on top of a levee that contained the Euphrates River to our left. After an hour or so we spotted some fishermen in the distance and slowed down to ask them for directions and information.

They approached us warily in their long *dhows*, similar to ones I had seen pictured in Wilfred Thesiger's book. They were Ma'adan who lived outside Suq. They told us that they settled in the town in 1996 after their section of the central marshes was drained and attacked by Saddam. They were forbidden to fish or to leave Suq after that and complained of a terrible life in the town. Many left in the hope of finding work in Baghdad or towns further north. After the fall of Saddam in April, they bought boats and now they fished the waterway and sold the produce in Suq, where there was a keen demand for fish. They used simple nets while dragging fishing lines behind the boat as they moved along. They complained that the fishing had become difficult because of the influx of others seeking out the same quarry.

'Some are coming from Nasiriya and others are even coming from al-Samawah. They use bombs to kill the fish. It is terrible,' one of them told Azzam.

One of them raised a line of fish a metre long. On it were small barbles and some medium-sized carp and other fish I couldn't identify. In all they weighed about five kilograms – a reasonable, if not excessive, return for a morning's fishing. They told us they intended to return to the marshes at some stage in the future, but the older members of the clan and the women were reluctant to go back. They had become used to the town and its comforts and were worried about the isolation of the marshes.

They had plenty of information to impart on the return that was gathering pace. They reported that many hundreds had abandoned Suq and headed for their ancestral places. Little had been heard of them since. One told us that a sub-chief from an important tribe had moved back in early May and was still in the marshes, close to the road, ten kilometres further along the embankment on the right, perpendicular to the road we were travelling on. They had no specific information on the sub-chief, but no one had seen him for some time.

'He is dead or he is well. It is one thing or the other,' one of the fishermen told Azzam with a smile.

We thanked them, politely declined their offer of free fish and drove on.

After half an hour we arrived at the area described by the fishermen. The levee had been breached and a twenty-metre-wide channel had been opened, through which water was flowing at a prodigious rate into the flatlands to our right. We left one of the policemen with our vehicles and followed the direction of the waterway for about a kilometre.

Ahead we could see green and soon we came upon the first of the returned family groups. They lived in tents but had already made a start in constructing an enormous *mudheef*, the characteristic architecture of the Ma'adan. Five-metre-long reeds had been anchored in the ground in rows opposite each other and five metres apart. They were brought up to meet in the middle, creating a giant arch. That was as far as they had got in the construction. The next phase would be to secure the reeds in the middle with ropes (traditionally made from worked reeds) and then cover them with huge woven mats. The resulting building has a strongly classical appearance and looks very like the ancient buildings carved into the red rock at Petra in Jordan.

This group of Ma'adan were shy and motioned us to follow the water until we came to the point where the waterway spilled out into the marshes, where we would find the sub-chief of the clan, Hajji Abu-Sami. He would speak for them, they told us.

We hurried along, Azzam's excitement building as we went. He pointed out the damage to the surrounding countryside caused by the drying up of the soil. A surreal blue plain to our left was a noxious salt deposit, he explained. He picked a green plant and cursed it. This was the type of desert scrub vegetation that was taking over in many parts of the former marsh.

'*Phragmites australis*,' he proclaimed, looking ahead and pointing to the reed growth in the channel we were following. Ahead we could see what appeared to be another settlement. Azzam motioned for us to stay while he went to negotiate with the sub-chief, otherwise known as the headman or even the Sheikh.

A day on the marshes has always been governed by the sun. As it rises in the morning, much of the work of the day is done, before the heat becomes unbearable. Temperatures of more than fifty degrees centigrade are the norm in the summer months, and even in winter the open nature of the wetlands and the concentrating glare from the water keeps temperature at intolerable levels. At eleven o'clock, it was already at least forty degrees centigrade and we were beginning to struggle with the heat, mopping our brows and drinking water, looking every bit like the white colonists of old.

In the distance Azzam appeared, waving enthusiastically, beckoning us forward. We gathered our equipment and marched down to the place where Hajji Abu-Sami had established his camp. He greeted us warmly and showed us around his makeshift settlement. He had pitched camp at the point where the narrow ten-metre-wide channel leading from the Euphrates spread out and spilled into the marshes. From the settlement it was possible to see on one side as far back as the Euphrates and on the other the horizon. It was strategically well positioned.

All around were the signs of new life. There was a family of water buffalo, a handful of cattle, a scattering of goats and sheep and everywhere the sense that life was returning to the marshes. The family slept in a large canvas tent. Behind this was a corral for the animals, a store for food and grain and a primitive latrine. Surrounding the whole was a fence of giant reeds, robustly tied together and swaying gently in the wind. Most of all, there was shelter from the sun.

We settled down for an intimate talk while Oum Sami (his wife) prepared tea and coffee. There were four young children, who watched us carefully. The impression I gained was that they had already got used to their life of isolation on the marshes. Certainly there were few white Westerners like us near the marshes. We giggled as they sat motionless, their eyes following our every move. They were particularly fascinated by Janet's red hair. The youngest girl ventured over after a few minutes and touched Janet's hair. She smiled a charming, toothless smile.

Hajji Abu-Sami began by welcoming us warmly to the marshes. He praised George W. Bush for liberating Iraq from Saddam, the first and only time I had heard this sentiment spontaneously offered by an Iraqi.

'The blessings of God on Mr Bush and all the Americans. They have given us back our home. *Al hamdillilah*,' he said.

He explained that his clan was a sub-group of the al bu Mohammed tribe and previously occupied the marshes south of Chubayish. They migrated to other places during times of need, but they regarded Chubayish as their ancestral home. During the Iran–Iraq War they were forced to move further into the central marshes to evade the shelling and strafing that came from Iraqi forces. They escaped the worst excesses of that campaign, the isolation of their location aiding them. After the war they resumed their semi-nomadic lifestyle while occasionally supplementing it with paid work near Suq.

He explained that his brothers had occasionally worked on drainage projects near Suq – ironically, the very canals that eventually linked up and drained the lifeblood of the marshes. As he spoke, Hajji Abu-Sami would occasionally take a corner of his headscarf, the *keffiya*, and daub his eyes or wipe his nose to emphasise a point. It was a theatrical gesture, although I had to stifle a laugh when he took his scarf and blew his nose into it.

After the invasion of Kuwait in 1990, Hajji Abu-Sami explained that the previously closed world of the Ma'adan began to change as never before. While in the past they regarded the government and the urban people as little more than a nuisance, now they had to take notice of them in earnest.

'Strangers from the cities appeared on the marshes and asked for our protection. They were soldiers who had run away from the army and we gave them shelter,' he said.

After the war more and more deserters arrived in the marshes, pleading for help from the tribes. In most cases, he explained, this was given, although he laughed and added that some were just robbed and sent on their way by the more unruly natives of the marshes. At this time the marshes were awash with money and guns and booty looted from Kuwait. But it wasn't long before it all began to sour.

'There was a lot of fighting between the newcomers. Then there was a lot of fighting between different people in the marshes. They were also attacking the towns of Suq, Qurnah and Nasiriya. They killed all the Ba'ath people there and threw their bodies in the river. Our people did a lot of killing,' he said with some relish.

The backlash was swift, he explained. Initially airplanes bombed and shot anything that moved on the open water. That stopped after a few weeks and there was relative peace for about three weeks. Then the helicopters appeared. His eyes widened as he described how the heli-copters would hover for an extended time in the same place and then unannounced would let loose a salvo of shots, fire shooting from their guns.

Abu-Sami's family hid in the marshes while this went on, expecting things would calm down after a few weeks, when they could again resume their lives. But the attacks went on and on for months and then the water started to dry up.

Soldiers began to appear in different parts of the marshes and those they didn't kill were rounded up and marched off to an unknown destination. Hajji Abu-Sami explained that he had a wife and family to move – 'not this one,' he gestured towards Oum Sami, his second wife, in a slightly dismissive manner – and it was slow and difficult. It was also impossible to find enough to eat because of the disruption. They couldn't fish any more and their rice paddies had died through lack of care.

There was constant shelling of settlements and villages. One day he marched his family and their livestock towards the army post on the old road to Suq-as-Shuyuk. Many others were doing the same and they were all gathered up, their livestock was shot and they were put on trucks and transported to Baghdad. The loss of their buffaloes and sheep was a big blow. Marsh Arabs (in common with most nomads) count their wealth in livestock. Hajji Abu-Sami and his family were dumped on the outskirts of the vast Shia slum called Saddam City (now renamed al-Sadr City).

'It was terrible. We had to keep moving. Some people got jobs. Others worked as servants and many were poor. We were in Baghdad but they did not let us stay and settle down. A curse on them,' he said.

Oum Sami added her own observations. 'It was very difficult and very tiring. We barely survived. Sometimes we had something to eat and at other times we had nothing at all. I was always worried about the children. What will I feed them tomorrow? They refused us food from the government. They told us to go to the registered place. But we couldn't go back there because we were not allowed near. A curse on them all,' she said.

And so their miserable life in Baghdad began. It was difficult to make out exactly what year all of this took place, but it appears that the family was one of the last to leave the marshes, perhaps as late as 1997.

In late 2002 Hajji Abu-Sami and his family moved south again. Under the pretext of needing to get back to Suq to vote in the presidential elections, Hajji rented a car from another Ma'adan family and settled among friends in a small village near Suq. It seems that Hajji and his wife had a good inkling that change was on the way and wanted to be in place to take advantage of the opportunities that arose. There was some harassment from the Ba'ath party members who visited the site after the elections, but for the most part they were ignored. Their main aim was to stay in the south, far away from the alien world of Baghdad.

When the invasion started in March 2003, all the Ma'adan were nervous. They heard about the battles raging in Nasiriya from refugees who flooded into Suq. They told tales of the ousting of Saddam's people in the city and the fighting by the Feddeyin Saddam. It appears that all the Shia in the south had the same opinion. They were waiting for cast iron assurances that the Americans wouldn't abandon them this time. The memories of what they regarded as the broken promises of 1991 were still fresh in their minds.

Those assurances never came, but as the second week of the war drew to a close, Ba'ath party members and loyalists were attacked in Suq and killed. Those that survived, fled. The news travelled fast around the refugee camps. The town was now under the control of tribal elders, while representatives of the Shia political parties in exile in Iran made themselves known after decades of secret membership.

Hajji and his wife petitioned the tribal elders to allow them to move back to their home area, deep in the former marshes. The elders refused, saying they were making plans to blow up the embankments that prevented the water from finding its way into the marshes. Hajji volunteered to help.

On 6 April, as the American forces were capturing Baghdad and 1,000 kilometres to the north-west I was on my way through the western desert to Amman, a large group of Ma'adan assembled all the explosive power they could find on the banks of the Euphrates River. They had artillery shells, landmines and tank rounds. The flow of the river had been swollen by the release of water from the main drainage canal back into river – apparently a spontaneous act by Ministry of Irrigation employees who controlled the gates and locks. They were sympathetic to the Marsh Arabs.

They chose a point on the river where a deep (but empty) gorge ran off into the former reed beds so that the water would flow straight for a while before opening out. Hajji described the event with relish. They all gathered and waited.

'There was a big bang and then another bang and another. The ground shook and some of it fell back down. Everybody cheered and fired rifles in the air. No water came yet. Then they brought a digging machine from Suq and pushed away some of the soil and a trickle of water came out. *Hamdillilah.* We celebrated,' he said.

The next day Hajji and his wife and children left their temporary settlement and made their way out to the breach in the river. They were astonished to see a strong flow of water from the river up the canal and out into the wilderness.

'We were happy, very happy. It is better to be here than there in Baghdad. *Hamdillilah.* This is a blessed place. In Baghdad no one cares about you. Here, even the beggars have enough to eat,' Oum Sami said.

At this point the youngest child, a boy of no more than nine months, crawled over and reached for his mother. Oum Sami smiled at him and cradled him before parting the middle of her *abaaya* and offering the child a pert breast. She nursed the child while chatting away amiably to us. It was another sign that the Ma'adan were different from other Arabs. It would be inconceivable for a mother to feed a child so openly and naturally in any Arab country. A woman's life in many of these ultra-traditional societies is hemmed in and governed by a plethora of petty rules and taboos that stifle female initiative and imagination. The Ma'adan had plenty of rules for their womenfolk, but their lifestyle seemed to take the edge off the more prurient ones.

Oum Sami had no problem interrupting her husband and even contradicting him if she felt it necessary. The couple seemed at ease with each other in a way that was difficult to pin down. As a second wife, one detected the tensions normal in polygamous societies – competition for food and resources between two families and the petty jealousies that characterise this type of system. Hajji's only other mention of his first family was a vague reference to sons in Baghdad. Oum Sami looked at him sharply on that occasion. Their return to the marshes had clearly worked for them and the acquisition of livestock brought stability and more nutrition for the children.

I also suspected that the move had brought unexpected dividends for Oum Sami. She was now the uncontested matriarch of the family. Her sojourn in Baghdad and Suq had automatically brought a lessening in her status. Living under the patronage of bigger families in both places meant that she'd had to pay obeisance to stronger, more established women. Constantly asking for favours and food inevitably brings lower esteem and, perhaps more importantly, lower self-esteem. The marshes were her salvation.

In the months since they had come home, they reported all sorts of changes in the marshes. Most importantly, the reeds had begun to grow again. There was now enough reed growth in the immediate vicinity of their camp to keep the buffalo family and all the cows fed all the time. For taller reeds, used in bedding and for mending the enclosure, they would head out in their *tarada* (long canoe) and cut massive bundles in parts of the marshes where growth was strong.

The buffaloes lolled about, doing their own thing. If they felt warm or were irritated by the flies and mosquitoes, they awkwardly hoofed over to the water and slipped silently into the murky brown stream, tiny eddies and whirlpools appearing in their wake. They looked at home there, moving freely and snorting every few minutes. The calves were only six months old, but already they had mastered the art of entering and leaving the water. They dove below the surface every now and then, appearing metres away in a great flourish with a loud whoosh.

The animals were domesticated but not as docile as cattle, and Oum Sami warned us to be careful, particularly near the young bull. He stood aloof from the others, and when he entered the water, he swam alone. One of the older boys, dressed only in a tattered pair of shorts, joined the maternal group of buffaloes in the water for a short time and was accepted. He clung onto the matriarch's neck while she swam along, all the while talking to and cajoling her.

The animals made little noise. They came and went more or less as they pleased. Their mutual dependence was total. The Ma'adan relied on the beasts for milk and income. Ultimately, the capital of the family was tied up in the buffaloes, which were valuable. The buffaloes couldn't survive in the wild without the care and feeding of the family. It was a truly symbiotic relationship.

Sitting on a bundle of reeds and watching the world go by, I looked to the sky and saw all sorts of birds. One caught my attention. It was hovering over the moving water at a height of about ten metres. As the sun was still high in the sky, it was difficult to make out the species, silhouetted as it was against a bright blue background, but it soon dove and came out with a small fish before flying off. Immediately after this I noticed another bird doing exactly the same. Azzam came over to me and pointed to the sky.

'Pied kingfishers,' he said, pointing out that there was a queue of birds waiting for access to a stretch of the river that was teeming with fish. It looked like the airspace around a busy airport, with birds waiting their turn to hunt for the fish. It was a wondrous sight.

Hajji offered us a ride through the marshes in his *tarada*, which he expertly manoeuvred up to the bank. On stepping into the *tarada* I was amazed to see how unstable the canoe could be. The slightest tip on either side of the vessel sent it rolling in an alarming fashion, almost to the point of capsizing. Hajji offered advice on keeping the boat stable while confidently poling the *tarada* off into the reed beds.

We had to sit low in the *tarada*, so low that I could barely see over the sides of the vessel. Any attempt at moving my legs or arms by even the tiniest margin caused the boat to sway. Eventually I found a position that was both comfortable and gave me a clear view of the surroundings. Within moments we were far away from the sounds of human voices and the only noises to be heard were the lapping of water, the splashing of fish breaking the surface and the constant chirping of birds near and far. Hajji half sang, half recited a poem to the wetlands, so laced with local references and words that our translator was baffled.

'Something about the sky and the fish and relaxing in the water, I think,' came the translation. We laughed.

Even though he poled like a gondolier, Hajji was no swashbuckling Italian boatman. He moved us along with a grunt while jabbering away to himself amiably. Our translator didn't know what to make of it all. It seemed that Hajji had two languages – conventional Arabic for the interview and for dealing with outsiders and his own dialect for the marshes. We floated along for hours, marvelling at the new life. We punted up narrow gorges and around islands. We manoeuvred through dense growth, lost in a world of water and gently swaying reeds.

Hajji pointed out a mound with what appeared to be extensive ruins and explained, in Arabic, that they were from the Sumerian time – a reminder of the antiquity of marshes and their communities.

Azzam was still talking when we arrived back. The man was so full of energy and enthusiasm that he put the rest of us to shame. He was raving about the size of the reeds and wondering aloud how they could be so tall after such a short time.

'It is only five months since the water came back and the reeds are more than three metres in places. It's justice, isn't it? Regardless of what Saddam did to prevent Mother Nature from doing her thing, Mother Nature came back. As hard as he tried, he did not end up killing the civilisation itself,' he said.

We could see small fish all over the marshes and this excited Azzam even more.

'This is very encouraging. The fish are back, using the marshes as their spawning grounds. Small fish will grow and mature and they are the food for next year. I never thought it could happen so quick,' he said.

We speculated that perhaps the water table in this section of the marshes was high enough to allow some of the reed clumps to survive the general draining and so bounce back with such vigour. Azzam offered the possibility that the same thing had happened with the fish – isolated stands of water maintained small populations that exploded when the waters flowed again. Perhaps the waters in this section of the marshes never became too saline and its sweetness promoted growth.

Azzam stroked his beard, deep in thought. He shook his head. 'The absence of data is a real issue. We have little or no idea about what is happening here or in the other reflooded areas. The water here seems good, but in other places I hear it's brackish. We really don't know. We need research teams out there taking samples and doing the basic work,' he said.

After a while, a number of fishermen with their boats came towards us. They had been fishing in the marsh area but, like all the others we met, still lived in the settlements towards Suq. They greeted us with a friendly handshake and showed us their catch. They complained bitterly about the size of the fish and how little they would have to sell at the market.

We nodded in sympathy. They pulled up their boats and made off for the road. They would be back in the morning. Hajji Abu-Sami waved them off and then cursed them.

'Liars!' he told us. 'They say that but they sell the fish for a lot of money in Suq. Then they tell me they have nothing to give me for keeping their *tarada*s safe. A curse on them,' he said with a flourish and a wry smile.

It now appeared that Hajji Abu-Sami's role on the marshes was more substantial than I had previously thought. He was a senior tribesman, but he also appeared to control access to the marshes by holding the bridgehead where the water spills out into the plains. In effect, all who wanted to enter the marshes had to pay Hajji a fee which was really a tax, although, of course, it was never described as such. I asked him about this and he gave me the impression that the fee was voluntary, a small contribution for keeping an eye out and helping with the *taradas*.

'What if they won't pay you?' I asked with a smile.

'This way, my friend,' he said, walking off to the enclosure where the reeds were stored.

He toppled a stack of reeds two metres high and showed me a brand new Kalashnikov rifle, sitting neatly in a clear plastic wrapping, and laughed uproariously. I joined in, but my laugh was more nervous than his.

Up till then my view of the Ma'adan had been a rather naïve version of the eighteenth-century notion of the 'noble savage' – a people heroically fighting against the elements, struggling manfully against the capriciousness of nature. It doesn't take long for such romantic musings to be scuppered when cold reality displaces starry-eyed idealism.

The lifestyle of the Ma'adan has never been an easy one. Even while he praised and mythologised their civilisation, the great champion of the Ma'adan, Wilfred Thesiger, was aware of the difficulties the Marsh Arabs faced. He spent a significant part of his seven-year sojourn (1951–58) in the marshes ministering to a people whose health was pitifully poor. Even though he was without medical training, his solid understanding of science enabled him to save the lives of hundreds of Ma'adan. Life for the average Ma'adan was hard and brutally short. Illnesses and disease were common and the feuding nature of the tribal system gave rise to arguments and vendettas that would make the Cosa Nostra blush.

The very waters that enabled the marshes to function were the source of many ailments. Dysentery and water-borne epidemics ravaged the marshes through the ages, even up to the 1980s. Infant mortality was high and young children died from the simplest of health complications, chiefly diarrhoea. Without access to health care or education of any sort, the Marsh Arabs' life expectancy and life outcomes were virtually unchanged from antiquity. This was still the case even when the rest of the country and the greater region were enjoying an unprecedented improvement in quality of life brought about by the oil boom.

There is reasonable anecdotal evidence that the population of the marshes was on the decline in the 1970s as younger Ma'adan migrated to the towns in search of education and work. The lack of improvement in their lives on the marshes pushed them out, while the oil-based boom in the rest of Iraq was a strong factor in attracting them into urban life.

Oum Sami reflected the general view of many Marsh Arabs. She wanted the traditional lifestyle of the Ma'adan, but she was determined that there should be some modern improvements.

'There should be schools for the children and we must have electricity and water. This is the message for the new government. We want our children to have the good things of the world as well as the old things,' she said.

I looked around and wondered. Here we were in the middle of nowhere, hours from the nearest hospital or school. I didn't think it possible for such services to be brought into the heart of the marshes, at least not in a conventional manner. Azzam, however, had been talking extensively to Hajji and outlined another possibility to me.

At the point where the Ma'adan had broken the dam, there was a supply of electricity, stretching along the road on top of the levee.

'In time, you can imagine a compromise lifestyle where the children and others in the family will live close to a nodal point where services will be provided and the rest of the family will live deeper in the marshes. It's not impossible, but it depends on the will of the government to do its part,' he said.

Oum Sami was enthusiastic about this possibility. 'This is my idea. Yes. The best of the two worlds,' she said.

I had my doubts. The administration in Baghdad was primitive and I felt sure that the Marsh Arabs were a very low priority.

The desire to leave behind the worst aspects of the previous life reassured me that the Ma'adan themselves weren't being unrealistic about the return to the marshes. Even to my amateur eye, it was clear that the marsh was only at the very early stages of re-establishing itself. The biodiversity that characterised the vast region was nowhere near what it had been in the past or may be in the future. The vast range of mammals, birds and fish that the Ma'adan relied on for food was struggling to regain a foothold in the newly flooded plains.

Before their destruction, the marshes boasted an impressive range of mammals, ranging from the Mesopotamian fallow deer to the striped hyena to the smooth-coated otter. Ma'adan who spoke to Thesiger in the 1950s remembered a time when lions roamed the area, before the widespread introduction of the rifle killed them off. The endemic gazelle was also hunted to virtual extinction by the same method.

Bird species survived the onslaught of the gun only to be hit by another man-made disaster. The endemic birds of the marshes suffered a catastrophic drop in numbers when the marshes were drained. Only remnant populations of Basrah reed warblers and Iraq babblers remain. The data on countless other species, such as the Euphrates softshell turtle and the Mesopotamian gerbil, does not exist.

The millions of birds that used the marshes as a temporary wintering ground have also been decimated and the health or otherwise of their population is unknown. The fate of other animals, such as the grey wolf, wild cat and boar, which roam between the mountainous regions of Iran and the marsh, is also not documented.

Azzam had the feeling that there were remnant populations of virtually all the animals and birds of the region in pockets scattered around the vast region. His most urgent task was to try to quantify their numbers. He had managed to attract funding from a number of sources, chiefly the Italian overseas aid programme and USAID. The money would be used for a range of important studies aimed at gauging the viability of reflooding the marshes, led by European and American scientists. An important aspect of the project would be the valuable training it would offer to Iraqis. 'Capacity building', as it is called, was desperately needed.

These studies started in earnest in 2004 and the first results were published in the international journal, *Science*, in February 2005. Using local and international expertise, scientists assessed the hydrology of the area to see if there is enough water available to sustain the marsh ecosystem. None of the studies so far have conclusively proven that there is enough water available. This question is all the more complicated and sensitive because of the transnational nature of the rivers that flow through Iraq.

The river Tigris rises in the Armenian plateau in Turkey and is 1,840 kilometres long. Its sister, the

Euphrates River, originates in springs in the highlands of eastern Turkey and is 2,700 kilometres long. In both cases, the rivers are Iraqi for much of their passage. However, most of the water originates in Turkey – 52 per cent in the case of the Tigris, and up to 98 per cent for the Euphrates.

An added complication is that the water originates in Turkey's most backward and undeveloped region, an area of endemic unemployment and outward migration. To address this, successive Turkish governments planned to use the water from the two rivers for development. The GAP project envisages the building of twenty-two dams and nineteen hydro-electric power stations on the rivers in Turkey. Using massive tunnels cut through the mountains, the Turkish government aims to open up 1.7 million hectares of land for agriculture.

The Ataturk Dam alone has the capacity to absorb more than a year's flow of the Euphrates River and, if fully utilised, could reduce the current flow of the river to a trickle before it even reaches Iraq. Similar projects on the Tigris would have a dramatic, if less catastrophic, effect.

Simultaneously, Iran is in the final stages of implementing a water management strategy on the Karkheh River that rises in the Zargos Mountains and helps to sustain the Huwaizah marsh in eastern Iraq. In addition to hydro power and water for irrigation, Iran is planning to sell much of this sweet mountain water to Kuwait, using an elaborate pipeline via the Persian Gulf.

It all adds up to a dramatic increase in the competition for water resources in the Tigris and Euphrates river valleys. In the rush for big developments and infrastructure in the region, one wonders where the Marsh Arabs will find a voice.

Our time in the marshes had come to an end and we made our preparations to leave. It is customary in Iraq to leave a gift upon departure, and I scrambled around trying to find some token of our appreciation for Hajji and Oum Sami's hospitality. I found a silver card case with my employer's stamp: RTÉ. It was the type of case one would give to colleagues after a business meeting and was quite out of place in the context, but I had little else to offer, so I approached Azzam to ask for his advice. He laughed when I showed him the case and said it would be perfect.

'The Ma'adan love trinkets and will treasure it, but make sure you put a $20 note in it as well. They love money even more,' he said.

I passed on the gift to Hajji, who immediately handed it over to Oum Sami. She smiled broadly, opened it and laughed out loud. She then picked up the baby and did an impromptu jig with the infant in her arms. We all laughed and headed back to the vehicles, Hajji's blessings ringing out as we trudged along the embankment. He was back in lyrical mode, calling out praises and blessings to us.

As we drove back to Nasiriya I closed my eyes and enjoyed the bittersweet feelings that our time on the marshes evoked. The joy of meeting people for whom the war had brought some benefits was tempered by the reali-sation of the difficulties ahead. More than any other people I had met in Iraq, the Marsh Arabs have a fighting chance. Without a malevolent central government, their lifestyle could be easily recreated, if only the water keeps flowing.

Back in ramshackle Nasiriya, I asked Azzam if he thought the marshes could be saved. He looked at me, stroked his beard and smiled another one of his perfect smiles.

'We will get thirty, maybe forty per cent of it back. But it will not be exactly as it was before. My worry is that the young ones have lost their connection with the land. There are no maps telling you which way to go on the marshes, but the mothers and the fathers know. The transference of those skills from one generation to the next has been stopped and that is the challenge from the cultural point of view. We can do things there, but it will take time. The overarching question is about water. Will neighbouring countries take too much? Will there be enough left for the Marsh Arabs? I don't know. That is a question above my pay grade,' he said.

6

THE BRITS

May 2006

The beautiful fifteenth-century barbican sits at the top of a small hill in an out-of-the-way part of the garrison city of Colchester, the oldest city in Britain. The town itself seems unaware of the serious business that goes on in the range of ugly buildings that stand behind the pretty fragment of previous splendour. The stone gate hides a gloomy range of military buildings, many of them former warehouses, that host the most important court martial in Britain. For such a significant military court, I had expected more security. I thought the place would be bristling with armed guards and sniffer dogs, but after a cursory nod from the unarmed guard at the gate, I wandered up to the court enjoying the sun of late spring and marvelled at the view of the town from the elevated position.

On the left were tennis courts and a further run of single-storey buildings. The neat sign on the grass identified them as the Officers Club, Colchester Garrison – leisure for the lords of the army.

Under the sober and kindly direction of the Judge Advocate General Michael Hunter, four soldiers were charged with manslaughter. They were Sergeant Carle Selman of the Coldstream Guards; Lance Corporal James Cook; Guardsman Joseph McCleary; and Guardsman Martin McGing of the Irish Guards. Their victim was an Iraqi boy, eighteen-year-old Ahmed Jabber Kareem, killed on 8 May 2003 amidst the chaotic looting that engulfed Iraq after the short-lived war of the previous month.

The British were newly arrived in Iraq and the looting that had started in Baghdad soon after the war ended had now spread to Basrah with a vengeance, stretching their meagre resources to the limit. Almost everything about the tragic event spoke of the uneasy relationship between the British and the Iraqis, then and now. The British spoke no Arabic and couldn't understand the Iraqis. The Iraqis believed the British were in Iraq with ulterior motives, namely, to steal their oil. When they arrived, the British expected to be greeted with cheering and flowers strewn at their feet. The Iraqis expected the foreigners to rebuild their shattered country within months. Neither happened. Expectations were unrealistic on both sides.

Iraq is the latest in a long line of British interventions in far-off countries and their army is accustomed to rapid deployment. The British military is a disciplined force with a high reputation for effectiveness in urban conflict. The reputation arises from its long association with Northern Ireland where, it must be said, not everyone agrees that they have acted in a disciplined military fashion. However, in military circles worldwide, the British are believed to operate to the highest standards with great effectiveness. Other armies, notably the United

States' forces, envy the British their light touch in handling civilian/military interfaces. The Americans did virtually no training for this type of work before they deployed to Iraq. In retrospect, it now appears that they deliberately didn't prepare for a long, drawn-out urban conflict because they expected to be gone within weeks or months. The British were much better prepared.

The British assumed control over the region, but their understanding of authority was very different from that of the Iraqis. The southern Iraqis' only exposure to authority stems from the rule of Saddam Hussein. His brutal suppression of Shia consciousness in the south is the stuff of legend. The Shias lived in a state where, although they composed the majority, they were treated like the 'enemy within'. They were preyed upon like a persecuted minority. They were treated by the predominantly Sunni government as a kind of third column – dangerous and potentially seditious. The army and special units were the forces used by Saddam to keep them down. In addition to this, you can add a thirty-year-long legacy of deliberate underinvestment and deprivation, which is plain for all to see in the region. The only investment in the south for decades had been in the road system. The aim here was to create infrastructure to ferry the military in and out. Hospitals were pitifully badly off. Schools – even by Iraq's low standards – were starved of funding. All of this was deliberate, the result of detailed government policy. The strange relationship between Iraqis from the south and any type of uniformed authority must be understood in this context.

Ahmed Kareem and his three friends were out looting in Basrah when they encountered the British soldiers. They were robbing anything they could find and had targeted a workshop where they believed they could steal some objects to sell at the market in the city. The British apprehended them and after a while, the thieves were released or released themselves and went into the Shatt-al-Basrah waterway. Most of the robbers swam across the waterway, but Ahmed Kareem couldn't swim and he got into difficulties before drowning. The British left the scene at around this time. His bloated body was fished out of the canal some days later. So much for the uncontested facts of the case.

The court martial heard wildly different versions of what happened and who was responsible. The prosecution case was that the soldiers roughed up the thieves and humiliated them before sending them towards the waterway under threat of further violence. Getting them wet was seen as a form of mild humiliation. When he saw Ahmed Kareem getting into difficulties in the water, one soldier made as if to strip off his clothes to go and help, but the others ordered him back into their armoured vehicle. It sped off, leaving the struggling Iraqi to a certain death. This, the prosecution argued, was an unlawful killing, not as grave as murder but certainly manslaughter.

The four soldiers disputed this version of events. They denied the charges and rejected the allegations that they had beaten up the looters. In fact, they rebutted virtually every aspect of the prosecution case and were confident they could work the court martial in their favour.

Martin McGing sat beside his voluble Queens' Counsel Jerry Hayes as his lawyer deployed all the tricks of the barrister in a courtroom. Guardsman McGing was immaculately decked out in his formal Irish Guards uniform, the crease in his trousers sharp enough to peel an orange, his buttons shining in the light, his peaked cap lying sheer on his forehead, almost obscuring his eyes. He didn't move or utter a word during the hours of the cross-examination of witnesses conducted by his counsel. He was a picture of military discipline and decorum. His barrister played the barrister role perfectly, too.

The key prosecution witness, Mohammed Hanoun, sat uneasily on the stand as Mr Hayes tutted and sighed loudly and brought to bear all the skills of the combative barrister. Mr Hanoun wore casual brown trousers and a bright cotton sweatshirt. He was timid in the court and raised his eyes only to look at the judge or address the barrister. He had been one of the looters and he had been the one who told Ahmed Kareem's father about the death of his son.

Mr Hayes: 'I put it to you that in 2003, the people responsible for keeping the thin line between order and anarchy in Basrah were the British Army.'

Mr Hanoun: 'No. The British opened up the companies.'

Mr Hayes: 'Are you saying that the British Army encouraged the looting?'

Mr Hanoun: 'No. They didn't say it. But they opened up the companies so that people would be looting and would not oppose their entry.'

Mr Hayes: 'That is a lie.'

Mr Hanoun: 'No!'

Mr Hayes: 'Are you telling the court that you would have done anything for money at that time?'

Mr Hanoun: 'Yes.'

Mr Hayes shook his head and sighed theatrically. He had alleged the witness was a liar and then established that the young man from Basrah would do anything for money. He touched his client gently on the shoulder, as if to say, 'Don't worry, son, we're getting there.' The defence of his client was going very well. He resumed his former stance and brought Mr Hanoun back to the day of the death, when Ahmed Kareem had disappeared in the water.

Mr Hayes: 'You didn't ask for help to find poor Ahmed, did you?'

Mr Hanoun: 'No. I only made a complaint.'

Mr Hayes: 'Your interest was in trying to milk the British taxpayer for compensation, wasn't it?'

Mr Hanoun: 'Not that. No, no.'

Mr Hayes: 'Did you go to Ahmed's funeral?'

Mr Hanoun: 'No. I didn't know his family or his house.'

Mohammed Hanoun had been on the witness stand for four days and the tension was beginning to show. He started off his testimony in a confident and purposeful manner. Now, after hours of forensic cross-examination, his demeanour had changed. He was slumped in his chair. His answers were becoming more truculent and he was clearly insulted by some of the insinuations of the defending barristers. It was easy to see that the ordeal was a form of mental torture for the young man. Everything had to be done four times – once for each of the accused. He had to admit four times that he was a thief. He was alleged to be a liar four times over four days. The same evidence was churned over and over and re-presented as the translator struggled to keep up with the pace of events. It was all becoming too much for a young man, far from home in a strange town among strangers.

He began to preface answers with references such as: 'As I told you before…', 'I told the other man that…' and 'If you would only believe what I have already told you…'.

His reactions spoke volumes about the Iraqi experience of law and authority. Law and authority came from above and it was dispensed to those below. If someone killed another person and a third person had witnessed the event, then the police would arrest the witness and detain him in jail until the day of the trial – however long that may take. Innocent parties were treated as harshly as perpetrators under Saddam's bizarre system, so it was no surprise that the witnesses became sullen and stressed under questioning.

I had seen it many times in Baghdad and other parts of the country. Someone in authority would question a citizen. The person being questioned would immediately become quiet, fearful and monosyllabic. Admitting to anything could prove fatal, and the only response was to deny or to call for mercy. The consequences for family members could also be profound.

Above and beyond individual experience was the changing cultural perspective on law and order all over Iraq in the days following the invasion. Videos looted from intelligence agencies and from Ba'ath party offices soon after the war began circulating. Every market had stalls selling video CDs of these events. At the thieves' market in Baghdad I had seen one stall where the films were categorised into sections. There were separate sections for Ba'ath party torture, the Shia uprising, prisoner execution from the Iran–Iraq War, etc. They showed extraordinarily cruel interrogations of suspects. Many dated from the uprising in 1991 and showed detainees being systematically tortured and violated in the most shocking ways. They were confirmation of what everyone had believed for many years, although much of what went on was hidden and took place behind closed doors. These films were watched across the country with a kind of horrified fascination.

As Mohammed Hanoun's questioning continued, these videos were at the back of my mind. Although there was obviously no torture or ill-treatment involved, Mohammed acted as if there was at least the threat of some sort hanging over him. He grew sullen and with-drawn. He was merely fitting into the pattern that Iraqis have learned when dealing with men in uniform. It was a pitiful sight.

And so the trial continued, with Iraqi witnesses making a poor show of defending their evidence and the skilled barristers driving a 'coach and four' through their testimony.

During coffee breaks outside the courtroom, some of the barristers and the defendants and their families made no secret of the fact that they believed the case was a farce.

'Do any of these fuckers tell the truth?' one person said to me.

'Pork pies for lunch,' his colleague responded.

A lawyer claimed one of the witnesses was incapable of telling the truth. 'He's a lying cunt. I don't think there ever was a body. I don't think there was even a death. It was all invented to get compensation and to come to Britain on a jolly. A day at Colchester Zoo and an afternoon outing to Mersea Island and they get a hundred pounds a day expenses,' he said with a dismissive wave of his hand.

The defence teams were in a good mood and it came as little surprise when the military jury arrived in with their verdict of not guilty and Judge Advocate Michael Hunter dismissed all the charges against the soldiers.

The Military Police authorities had failed to present a plausible case against the men. Perhaps it was an impossible thing to do. Gathering evidence in a chaotic war zone where people are traumatised by decades of conflict and presenting it in the calm, dull world of suburban Colchester is a tall order. Too tall for the prosecutors in this case.

After days of bewildering delays and endless false starts, we finally arrived at Basrah International Airport at five in the morning, tired and irritated. Our first flight from Brize Norton air base was cancelled and we were told that we would leave from another airfield, the American base in the UK, Fairfield. The second flight was abandoned because of a faulty undercarriage in the chartered jet. When that was fixed we were ordered to be ready to depart at five o'clock in the morning. When we arrived at the military airfield we were told that we would not be leaving until the following day.

The next day we turned up at five o'clock in the morning only to be told that the flight would depart at midday. We finally left at six o'clock that evening. As we took off from Fairfield military airport, I could see a squadron of United States B-52 bombers parked at the far end of the airfield and was reminded of the television images during the war of these behemoths taking off with their cargo of airborne missiles and bombs. Exactly six hours after their departure from the UK, the bombs would fall on Baghdad. It could be timed to the minute, which is more than could be said for our own departure.

The 400 soldiers on the jumbo jet with us seemed unfazed by the delays. They were being deployed into a war zone. A couple of days here or there made no difference to them. But my cameraman, Michael Cassidy, and I were furious. If it were a commercial flight, we would be compensated and pampered, but in the military, such notions are regarded as ludicrous.

'No point, mate,' one soldier told me as he saw my rage growing. 'You'll get there when you get there. You've got the right time and the wrong time and army time. You're in army time, mate. Get used to it.'

The soldiers moved around by order and there was no dissent in the ranks. How could there be? They were soldiers, after all. While we openly fumed at our treatment – the plane diverted to Germany and then to the United Arab Emirates – the troops looked on with a mixture of bemusement and contempt. We were acting like spoiled children. Civilians don't understand the 'army way'.

I was beginning to learn the first lesson of the British military. As a soldier, your time is virtually worthless. You are owned by the military. They have bought your life. They will feed you and pay you and look after you and they will use you as they see fit. But the civilian concept of 'time is money' counts for little in the theatre of war. Personnel are a resource to be deployed when the military deems it necessary. There is little room for individualism. You will do what you are told to do.

The Basrah airport terminal rises from the desert as the ziggurats of antiquity would have done in ancient times. It was yet another folly from the Saddam days. Built with no care for expense, its runways seem suspiciously long and wide for a civilian airport. As we arrived, the huge terminal building was unlit and ghostly as the cold desert night gave way to the first orange glimmer of Basrah's famously searing sun. The terminal was out of the same school of brutalist architecture that is found all over Iraq – press F11 for Ba'ath party offices, press F12 for airport terminal. There were a few soldiers moving around purposefully, but we couldn't find anyone to direct us to our rendezvous point. Would our liaison officer from the British Army know that we had been so delayed? Would all our carefully organised appointments be scuppered?

We were to be embedded with the British forces in southern Iraq for two weeks. Our itinerary included visits to the British Navy operation in the port city of Um Qasr, patrols with soldiers in the city of Basrah, a visit to the British-controlled garrison in Baghdad, a day at Basrah prison, a day at a police station and a briefing at the British consulate in Basrah. It promised to be a varied and interesting trip, albeit under the control of the British military, which had the last word on everything we did and controlled our movements.

Iraq had become so dangerous by the end of 2005 that I had resigned myself to never be able to work there unilaterally again. Simply turning up and operating as a normal journalist had become impossible. Talking to people on the streets, making friends, visiting hospitals and offices, following tenuous leads – all were mere memories now. Even meeting my Iraqi friends had become difficult. With the increase in attacks on all foreigners and the ever-present threat of kidnapping by insurgents or bandits, movement in Iraq could only be achieved by military convoy. There were still significant dangers in travelling this way – as the scores of British dead proved – but at least it offered the prospect of prompt medical and evacuation facilities, if the need arose.

I had been opposed to the whole business of embedding with coalition forces from the beginning of the conflict. The process seemed to me to compromise the fundamental independence of the journalist. The embedding contract allows the military to censor the reports of the reporter. A basic clause forbids the journalist from identifying his location and from commenting on crucial aspects of the development of the conflict.

When I saw the reports of embedded journalists from 2003 I was unimpressed by another aspect of the embedding process. There was an unquestioning, almost naïve quality to them. Journalists would quote the military commander as if his word was incontestable fact. This was understandable, given the fact that the journalists were living and eating with combat units, dependent on them for their very survival. What surprised me most was the way the reporters and soldiers appeared to be the best of friends. This was, of course, one of the great successes of the war from the military management perspective. From a journalistic point of view, it was much less satisfactory.

However, like many journalists faced with the choice of either reporting under 'embed' rules and not reporting at all, I chose the former. I was aware that it would severely limit my ability to meet and befriend Iraqis. That would put them in danger, so I justified the trip to myself on the basis that the British were another actor on the Iraqi stage and their opinions and experiences needed to be reported in the same way as everyone else's. One couldn't understand Iraq without coming to terms with them. If being embedded with them was the only way to do this, then so be it. I would 'embed', but I was determined not to be 'in bed'.

And so we made our way out of the gloomy interior of Basrah International Airport into the growing brightness of daylight. There, standing in front of a spanking new Land Rover, was Captain James St John Price, the officer from the UK Ministry of Defence press office who would become our guide, censor and friend during the trip.

'Richard. Good to meet you. I had almost given up on you. Good flight?' he laughed.

He was short, good looking, bespectacled and tanned and spoke with the unmistakable confidence and clipped tones of the British upper middle class. I have always tried not to classify people according to their background, but with some it is inevitable. St John (pronounced 'sin-jin') Price was one such person.

'I've juggled the programme. We've lost a couple of legs but we'll be able to walk again. We're almost back on track,' he said.

On meeting him the confidence and assurance of generations was communicated. Everything from his former regiment (Blues and Royals) to his shoes (leather brogues), from his accent (pure Sandhurst) to his attitude to Tony Blair (past his sell-by date) screamed his background at you.

I had made friends with many wealthy Britons of this class over the years. I invariably found them interesting and entertaining, but there was an abiding strangeness about them that I had always struggled to overcome. Their unshakable self-confidence bordered on arrogance. Inevitably, it was a façade treatment – a badge of culture they wore unconsciously. It rarely penetrated to the core of the personality. But it was unmistakably the product of a successful country, albeit only recently revived courtesy of a grocer's daughter from Grantham and a left-wing barrister from northern England.

There was something faintly comic about St John Price. His efficiency was impressive. As a captain, soldiers who had information to pass on would salute him and address him as 'sir'. I found this amusing, partly because he looked so young, his face boyish and charming. He would invariably thank them politely and invite them to 'crack on'. This soon became our motto. If it was coming close to lunchtime, I would ask Michael Cassidy if it was time to 'crack on for lunch'. He would reply that he had been waiting to 'crack on' for lunch for some time and it was about time we 'cracked on'.

St John Price was mostly unaware that we made fun of him behind his back or that many of his colleagues saw him as an upper-middle-class adventurer who would leave the army and go back to his private fortune. The lack of awareness was one of his many charms. He wasn't judgmental and took people as he found them. If this gave him a Basil Fawlty-like persona at times, so be it.

If he had known that all of this was sloshing around my mind as if in a wave machine, then St John would probably have dismissed it. That was his way. It wasn't relevant to the task in hand and as such wasn't worthy of wasting much time over. In his self-contained, self-confident manner, he would have seen these as my perceptions, my problems, my baggage. Even though he was young, he had a lot of experience. His father was 'in business' and he had travelled the world. He had come across 'my type' before and knew how to deal with me.

St John brought us to the tent city that would become our home for the duration of the visit. It was very well equipped with sturdy canvas tents that had their own air-conditioning supply. It was close to the camp food hall, another elaborate canvas structure, known as the mess. He showed us the ropes. Breakfast was served between seven and nine each morning and was recommended. Dehydration was an ever-present worry because of the soaring daytime temperatures and he urged us to take drinks on regularly. Vast stocks of bottled water were available at all times. Lunch was served in the middle of the day and the highlight of the food service was dinner that was prepared by an army of highly skilled Sri Lankan chefs. St John said they conjured up some of the finest food in the world from very little.

'These guys do a pukka chicken curry. Superb food. If you go to the American bases, you'll see how superior it is,' he said.

I was a little sceptical about this, but after a few days of stunning curries and fine relishes, I happily concurred. If an army marches on its stomach, then the British could be assured of the energy to sustain a marathon. As events were turning out in southern Iraq, that might be on the cards.

All of the food and supplies came in from Kuwait via the nearby border crossing at Safwan. Unlike the Americans, whose supply lines were long and vulnerable to enemy attack, the British could be assured that their food would arrive in on time.

St John then took us on a tour of the British headquarters near the airport. This was yet another Saddam-era square box updated by the British. As we went around the building I took in the various names and badges on the doors of the offices. Here was housed the intelligence agencies, military strategy groups and the operational support for the air supply corridor to Baghdad, where a further 500 British troops were based. It was compact and neat and had an air of composure and ease about it that one never found at the American offices in Baghdad. That was partly the 'British way' but also a reflection of the lower threat level that the British faced in southern Iraq. In principle, the south should have been quieter – its homogenous population should have been a key factor.

But the detail very rarely agreed with the simple head-line. Two weeks before our arrival, two soldiers from the elite British Special Air Service (SAS) in plain clothes had been captured at an Iraqi police roadblock. The versions of what happened at the checkpoint reflect the entrenched positions of both sides. The Iraqi police said the soldiers were acting suspiciously, became aggressive and were arrested and detained in a police station. The British said they were captured by police elements loyal to the radical Shia cleric Moqtada al-Sadr, whose members had infiltrated police stations all over Basrah. The British attacked the police station in order to retrieve their colleagues, demolishing a wall of the cells with a tank. The Iraqi police were furious at this action. Crowds descended on the scene and attacked the British with petrol bombs and small arms fire. Pictures of a tank commander emerging from the tank on fire were beamed around the world. The British escaped from the location and the Iraqi authorities angrily denounced them as terrorists. Co-operation between the British and the Iraqis was formally halted by the governor and the assembly. There was an angry stand-off between the two sides. So much for the sleepy backwater of Basrah.

While Baghdad and the centre of the country was being torn apart by the insurgency and the sectarian strife that began to plague the region from early 2005 onwards, the impression had been given that the south was coping just fine. The British had helped to propagate this version of events, but it was deeply misleading.

While spared the mayhem of the Sunni Triangle, the south had descended into another version of chaos. Internecine strife between the various new parties and factions created after the war fostered an instability in the south that was proving difficult to contain. Alongside this, criminal factions had begun exploiting gaps in the security infrastructure and thereby becoming stronger. Towns had slipped from the grip of the British. Suburbs had come under the control of little-understood militias and groups, headed by men virtually no one had known before.

But oversailing all of this was the malevolent presence of Iran just a few short kilometres over the Shatt-al-Arab waterway. For Iran, the south of Iraq is a zone of special strategic importance. Not only is Iraq the home of most of Shia Islam's most holy shrines, but Basrah is seen by many Iranians practically as an extension of their own country.

Iran virtually occupied the city and its hinterland for a brief period during the Iran–Iraq War of the 1980s. Iran also became home to most of the southern Iraqi dissidents following the Shia uprising of 1991. Many of the politicians who rose to power in the elections of 2005 lived in Iran for much of their later lives. The leader of the most important Shia political party, SCIRI, Mohammed Bakr al-Hakim, spent much of his adult life in Tehran. He was destined for national leadership in Iraq's new government until, in August 2004, he was assassinated in a huge bomb attack in the holy city of Najaf.

Most significantly of all, Grand Ayatollah Ali al-Sistani, the supreme leader of all Shias in Iraq and the most highly respected cleric in Shia Islam, is Iranian. His first language is Farsi – the national language of Iran – and he apparently only speaks Arabic in a halting fashion. Not that any of his Iraqi adherents would know, as his wisdom is disseminated by text only. There is no recording of the sermons of Ayatollah al-Sistani in the way there has been of all the great Shia thinkers of recent times. His sermons from Najaf – where he has lived most of his life – are read out by other leading Shia luminaries. Most southern Iraqis would be surprised and shocked to learn that their highest spiritual authority is an Iranian.

Put together, this special relationship gives solid clues as to Iran's role in the south. It is the common currency of diplomatic chit chat in Baghdad and elsewhere to acknowledge that Iran has been the biggest winner since the Ba'ath party was ousted. The political groupings it harboured – SCIRI, Dawa, elements of the Hawza, Badr Brigade – are all leading members of Iraq's elected government. Pilgrims have access to the holy shrines of Iraq. Iran can use its influence and technology to influence the insurgency in the south. Iran also has a front seat in the Iraqi war and can observe at very close quarters the tactics and modus operandi of its arch foe, the United States. And finally, Iraq is no longer a threat to Iran. 'Game, set and match to the Ayatollahs' was how one senior British officer described the situation to me.

St John was much more circumspect. When I asked him about recent British ministerial pronouncements that the Iranians were in cahoots with those attacking the forces in southern Iraq, he demurred and babbled. I asked him if they had captured any Iranians or found any Iranian made bombs they could show me or if there was any evidence whatsoever of direct involvement. He looked mildly perplexed.

'The Iranian issue has been ventilated and is not up for discussion any more, I'm afraid,' he said.

I laughed and asked who had taken it off the subjects for discussion. He didn't find that amusing and declined to be drawn any further on the issue. It was yet another one of those times when the civilian and military approach to life came in conflict.

'I'm just saying that I have nothing to add or subtract from what has been said,' he concluded.

I thought I would have better luck with a senior British diplomat based in the centre of the British zone in Basrah. I was informed before we arrived that I wouldn't be allowed to identify the person by name. This was an unattributable background briefing which I could only quote as 'diplomatic sources at the highest level'. This rule seemed absurd – there were hardly many senior diplomatic sources in Basrah – but as I agreed to it, I respected their wishes.

The rotund gentleman sitting at his desk in the spacious office in the palace complex had the confident look of the British foreign service diplomat. He wore a sober suit, cream shirt and modest tie. He had a small gap between his front teeth and short, cropped hair. He smiled warmly and I quickly began to realise that the man was from the old school – he was a Foreign and Commonwealth Office veteran rather than a plant from Blair's inner cabinet. I warmed to him immediately. He spoke reasonably good Arabic and had many years of experience in the Middle East, including a stint as ambassador to Baghdad during the rise of Saddam's regime.

He started off our discussion with an ancient Sumerian proverb: 'People never speak about what they have found, but about what they have lost.' He felt this summed up the changes in Basrah since the demise of Saddam. There had been limited progress and he acknowledged that there was a huge amount of disappointment with the slow pace of change.

When I asked him about the role of Iran, his eyebrow furrowed. 'A difficult one,' he said and smiled kindly, like an old professor explaining a complex issue to a keen student.

'I don't know any more about the planting of Iranian bombs than you have read in the newspaper. But what is clear is that political parties here have close connections with Tehran. And here's the nub of the matter. Would it do your electoral prospects much good to go out there and openly proclaim allegiance to Tehran? Would you be popular? The answer has to be no. It doesn't work politically. Every Iraqi is a nationalist at heart and everything I've heard here suggests to me that Iraqis don't like the influence of Iran in their internal affairs. But we are helped by another factor which is not taken into consideration very often. There is not one unified position in Tehran. It is riven with factions and influence groups. If there is a danger, it is that they are working out their internal conflicts by proxy here, and that would be very danger-ous,' he said.

I smiled and nodded to St John Price, who wasn't paying as rapt attention to the conversation as I was. He had closed his eyes and appeared to be nodding off.

'So any influence the Iranians may have here will be underground and nefarious,' I suggested.

'Your words, not mine,' he said and smiled knowingly. He went on to explain how much was at stake in Basrah. 'Fifty years ago, Basrah was the Dubai of the Middle East. It was a thriving city, the natural hub of the Gulf. That could happen again if the conditions were right and it could happen very quickly,' he said.

I looked sceptical. 'But Basrah is a disaster and there's no sign that the political parties have any interest in putting it right. They seem more inclined to fight their own battles than do anything for the region or the city,' I offered.

'There's truth in that. But then again, who would have thought in the 1920s or even in the 1960s that Ireland would become one of the wealthiest countries in the world? Remember that Iraq is producing just 1.6 million barrels of oil a day from the southern fields. That could easily be quadrupled if there was a relatively peaceful tran-sition. The stakes are higher in Basrah than elsewhere and the reason for that is that the potential here is higher than anywhere else in Iraq, except perhaps in Baghdad. The scope for various activities is wider, and if Basrah can regain its status as a gateway as well as a port and an oil centre, much can be achieved,' he said.

'You're a man of vision,' I said. We both laughed.

The conversation with the senior diplomat reminded me of the long history of British involvement in the Middle East and the deep institutional memory of Iraqi affairs and issues that exists, particularly in the Foreign and Commonwealth Office, Britain's ministry for foreign affairs. Not only was the diplomat on top of his brief, but his conversation was peppered with references to Iraqi history. Given encouragement, he could and would range widely over the sweep of regional history.

He comes from a long line of British Arabophiles, going back to T.E. Lawrence, Mora Dickson, Freya Stark, E.S. Stevens, Wilfred Thesiger and Gertrude Bell. Virtually all were distinguished by their upper-class or upper middle-class background and their passion for all things Arabic. Lawrence even became an honorary Arab to the Arabs. Britain's pivotal involvement in the creation of the modern Middle East also created a cadre of civil servants and entrepreneurs who understood the region, and Iraq in particular.

It was their project, after all. It was they who took the three Ottoman provinces of Basrah, Baghdad and Mosul and forged them into a single nation. While Winston Churchill railed against the huge costs of forging the new nation, his underlings got on with the slow, dull business of making it a reality. They created the police, army, public service and oil industry that sustained the country until the invasion. As late as 1960, it was still possible to cash a British domestic postal order at Baghdad Central Post Office. The legacy of the British public servant was a long and distinguished one. Many soldiers died trying to create it and are buried in the military graveyards in Baghdad or Basrah. It wouldn't be an exaggeration to say that they created Iraq.

Many have remarked on the parallel between the British social order and that of tribal societies. It was particularly on the minds of the new colonists as they supplanted the Turks after the First World War:

The old order goes. Like the country squire in England, the Sheikh is becoming an anachronism: the Latin central- izing conception is ousting the old personal ideas which were common to our Teutonic forefathers and to the Beduin of the desert... For we were fundamentally in agreement with the old order: the differences between the feudalism of the East and that of our public schools and Universities was not so great as one might think: and there were many points of contact between a tribal chieftain and the sons of English country gentlemen who ran the Empire (Freya Stark, *Baghdad Sketches*, 1937).

All of which made it more difficult to fathom the aston- ishing ignorance about Iraq among the military today. Perhaps the changing social order in both England and Iraq had something to do with the chasm between the two sides. This was at the back of my mind as I arrived back at the tented military camp near the airport. Sitting down with St John Price and a number of other officers over lunch, I asked for their opinion on the likelihood of Iraq splitting up into the three provinces that had existed before the nation state. Could Iraq revert to its shape before British colonisation? The background was informed by the intense speculation that arose in the run- up to the general elections that would provide Iraq with a government for five years. The Shias and the Kurds were in the ascendant. They had negotiated very astutely in the run-up to the referendum on passing the country's first post-Saddam constitution and had managed to insert a number of clauses allowing considerable regional auton- omy. All the talk in the Arab and Iraqi press and among the public was about the level of autonomy the provinces would enjoy and whether it amounted to a charter for a kind of loose federalism or even the ultimate break-up of the country.

St John Price looked at me blankly. I asked if he had an opinion on the subject. He shrugged his shoulders. I asked if he was following the debate and if there were any discussions or lectures from experts on the subject for the benefit of the military. The party erupted in laughter. I quickly dropped the subject. It was clear that the people involved in the day-to-day de facto running of southern Iraq were deeply uninterested in the country they were trying to administer.

I was puzzled by this, particularly as the British establishment has been so pivotal in Iraq's history. Was it simply that the army's role was purely a military function? Or was it that the general opposition to the war in Britain had in some way affected the troops? Had the British Army lost its institutional memory of Iraq? Had Britain's junior role in the coalition undermined its self-confidence in an intangible way? The answer seemed a complex mixture of these possibilities and many more. It was clear to me that while the British operations in Iraq were competent and professional, they lacked focus and their mission was unclear to the people implementing it on the ground.

St John Price didn't believe that the lack of domestic support for the war was a major factor in the minds of the British military. 'We're here to do a job and we'll leave when we are told to. It's as simple as that,' was his rather peevish response to my point.

Whatever about the debate, the reality was that the British deployment was part of a new type of military arrangement. From the Boer War to Suez to Northern Ireland, the British Army had been content in the past to invade a region on political orders and to sit there – to occupy the land. The watchtowers of the borderlands in Northern Ireland, the Martello towers on the east coast of Ireland, the citadel in Gibraltar and the forts in Cape

Town are testimony to a history of long-term occupation, mostly dating from colonial time. Basrah isn't like any of them. Basrah is a temporary set-up. It could be taken down and moved out at a month's notice.

I had the feeling that the British tradition of conquest and occupation is no longer part of the deal – no longer part of the psychology of the officers and men. This is a quick reaction force. The aim is to go in and then get out quickly. The British aren't hunkered down for a Malaya-type guerrilla war. In that conflict, the British forces successfully co-opted the Malayan police and militia to take the fight to the insurgents, and after a long and dirty conflict, they succeeded in subduing the revolt. It took hundreds of thousands of soldiers and an iron will to achieve this. Neither was on display in Iraq.

I asked St John Price when he thought we would be able to go out with the British troops on routine patrol. The British rightly prided themselves on the professional-ism of their urban operations. They also put great store in having good relations with the ordinary Iraqi public. As much as was practicable, they tried to patrol without the heavy armour favoured by the Americans. They also tried not to use body armour when walking the streets. The idea here was that this would show the Iraqis that they didn't fear them and that their intentions towards ordinary civilians were friendly. It was a masterstroke of public relations in the early part of the takeover and may have spared the British the problems encountered by the Americans in the centre of the country. The contrast between their approach and that of US soldiers in the more volatile Sunni Triangle was stark in the extreme.

However, it was difficult to know if this went beyond mere public relations. Sceptics will note that when the Queens Dragoons battle group was redeployed to the

Sunni heartlands south of Fallujah to relieve an American unit fighting in that town in 2005, they adopted American tactics. Circumstances on the ground, rather than high strategy, seemed to be the key issue.

St John Price was still equivocal about our joining a patrol. 'I'm not sure when it will happen. We have to be cautious, conservative, with civilians, because of the threat level. We're waiting for approval on that,' he said.

As the days went by I became more and more anxious about this lack of contact with Iraqis. I was keen to reflect the relationship between the Iraqis and the British, but it became more obvious as time went on that this relationship was at a low ebb. I inquired daily about the likelihood of going out on patrol and the reality slowly dawned on me that it wasn't going to happen. Not only were things difficult with the Iraqi authorities in the wake of the incident with the SAS soldiers, but the ease they had previously enjoyed in their dealings with civilians had evaporated, replaced by open hostility. One private told me that every time the British appeared within the city, they were greeted with a hail of stones and abuse. At that time it became obvious that the British had more or less given up patrolling the streets in any meaningful way. I wasn't likely to get my day out with the squaddies on roadblock duty.

Instead of travelling around in a jeep at our leisure, we were ferried everywhere by helicopter. My sense of being in Iraq at all was slipping away. I rarely met Iraqis and those I did come across were invariably wary of speaking to a foreign journalist. I was living in the world of the British military. Their connections with the outside world – Iraq – were tenuous, to say the least. I began to ask what exactly the British were doing in southern Iraq. They weren't patrolling. The Iraqis weren't co-operating with them on security matters. There was no contact at all with the newly elected authorities. Not for the first time I asked myself what 8,000 troops were doing on a daily basis.

Part of the answer came during our visit to the port city of Um Qasr. We flew down by helicopter but were unable to secure a flight back. Instead we drove back in convoy. Four armoured Land Rovers and twenty soldiers formed the core of our escort as we headed along the road to Basrah. Chatting to the soldiers in the vehicle, a picture emerged of an army hunkered down in a fortress-like situation whose only action was the movement of personnel and provisions along the roads. They spent virtually all their time looking after themselves and their bases and no time at all reaching out to the Iraqis or working with them.

This aspect of the British operations in southern Iraq highlighted a key psychological aspect of our being so closely intertwined with them. By this time, I had become friendly with St John Price and a number of other soldiers. We ate together, we slept in the same conditions and shared virtually every waking hour. Would it seem ungrateful and even churlish to bring up the obvious point that they seemed to be doing nothing for Iraq at that time? The answer is affirmative. It was difficult to bring the subject up in interviews. The sense of disappointment the interviewee would communicate when asked was palpable. This was the most insidious aspect of the business of becoming embedded. The military realised that if they became friendly with you, it would be more difficult for the journalist to ask the hard question. In my case they were correct up to a point. It was partially successful – which is all it needed to be.

The border line is marked by a double fence of razor wire and a deep ditch and runs straight as far as the eye can see. At the point where it terminated at the Gulf coast, a short wharf marked the international treaty line. It was across this unpromising-looking frontier that Iraqi troops had attacked in huge numbers in the early morning of 2 August 1990. Back then Iraq had a navy that was reasonably well equipped and battle hardened from the eight-year-long war with Iran. When the Republican Guard divisions swarmed over the Kuwaiti border near Safwan in the early hours of 2 August, naval boats transported hundreds of soldiers towards Kuwait City in a pincer movement. Reports at the time said that while the Iraqi boats were entering Kuwait harbour, huge speedboats were motoring away in the other direction carrying rich Kuwaiti families off to exile in Saudi Arabia and other Gulf states. They entered in triumph, unopposed. It was, perhaps, the Iraqi Navy's finest hour.

But the glory was short lived. The international coalition that ousted Saddam from Kuwait targeted the naval base at Um Qasr and destroyed all its facilities and sank its boats. Iraq's navy lay in ruins, much of it scuppered on the ocean bed. Hemmed in by international sanctions and under the ever-watchful eye of the United States and Britain that patrolled the skies of the southern 'no-fly zone', Iraq's navy struggled to rebuild itself. It was a navy almost without boats or weapons. Its seamen turned up for duty, but their patrolling was confined to short trips around the Fao peninsula on ageing converted fishing vessels, *dhows*. The US Navy was the power in the region and their massive floating cities held sway over the whole Persian Gulf. The ignominy of defeat was daily reinforced as US planes from the aircraft carriers in the Gulf flew low over Um Qasr to inspect Iraqi rebuilding efforts.

Um Qasr was one of the first targets of the coalition as they moved into Iraq in March 2003. After a number of false claims to have taken the port (reported as a fact countless times by journalists embedded with US forces), the Americans finally overcame resistance and secured Iraq's only deep-water port two weeks after they first announced its capture.

The rehabilitation of Iraq's navy was now under the control of the British, who showed me around their facilities at Um Qasr over a three-day visit. Their purpose was to train the Iraqi Navy up to the point where it could become a self-sustaining unit. It was an uphill struggle. Iraq's armed services under Saddam had been stripped of all initiative and were left deliberately weak so as to pose no threat to the dictator. The chain of command within the services was purposely obscure and discipline was virtually non-existent. Many in the Iraqi Navy had never been to sea and the force was poorly trained and motivated. The British inherited this shell of a naval service and were struggling to build a unit capable of defending Iraq's sea space.

Using half a dozen small boats, the British Navy tried to train a new cadre of officers and men. The results had been mixed. A large number of the newly trained seamen had simply disappeared – some deserted and others got caught up in the chaos of post-war Iraq. Some weren't able to do the job, but couldn't be dismissed without provoking a mutiny in the ranks. A small group of capable and motivated officers was slowly emerging from the training school and it was in these officers that the British placed their faith.

When I first arrived in Um Qasr, I had the idea that the very notion of an Iraqi Navy was somehow ridiculous. Iraq, after all, had only one small port and was virtually landlocked in every other direction. At the back of my mind was the old joke about the navy of Paraguay –

thousands of people, only one boat and that only used for weekend fishing by the president. It only took me a short time in the company of the British Navy to realise how foolish this attitude had been. Iraq's southern coastline had become the locus of a vast international smuggling ring. Criminals and pirates had moved into the vacuum created after the collapse of Saddam and were trading in all manner of contraband, even as they terrorised the civilian population. They also harassed commercial traffic on one of the most important shipping routes in the world. The maritime chaos affected tankers and ships as far as the Straits of Hormuz. Control of the Iraqi sector was virtually non-existent, and as the insurgency began to grow in late 2003 and early 2004, the potential threat to Iraq's economic lifelines in the Gulf intensified.

Attacks on Iraq's land-based oil facilities picked up during this time and the country was rapidly becoming almost wholly dependent on the Basrah and Khawr al-Amaya oil terminals for its export earnings. These platforms lie deep in the Gulf, some fifty kilometres out to sea. From the air they looked very unpromising, small floating concrete decks which have seen better days. Around them, huge oil tankers queue up and manoeuvre to take on oil. The dilapidated platforms have become the sole oil-exporting facility for the whole of Iraq. They are responsible for more than 95 per cent of Iraq's earnings – at least $30 billion worth of oil passes through them each year. It took a while for the importance of this to sink in. If the platforms were put out of action, Iraq would have virtually no foreign earnings at all. If insurgents were to cut the pipeline or blow up the platforms, then Iraq's economic collapse would become positively Hogarthian.

It almost happened. On the morning of 24 April 2004, three small *dhows* headed for the oil platforms. The

American marines stationed there at the time eyed them up. There appeared to be nothing to be alarmed about. Fishing boats work the waters of the Gulf intensively. But these *dhows* changed course suddenly and headed for the platforms. The marines fired warning shots. Men on the boats fired back and then, just as they neared the Basrah platform, two of the *dhows* exploded, causing damage to the facility. The platform was out of service for a couple of days, causing a loss of around $30 million in revenues and the international price of oil jumped from $33 to $40 a barrel. The attack was claimed by the Jordanian Abu Musab al-Zarqawi, an Iraqi affiliate of al-Qaeda.

The audacious operation highlighted the vulnerability of this crucial facility and sent alarm bells ringing through the nascent Iraqi government, the US Navy and the British, who were nominally in charge of the area at the time. The desire to have an effective Iraqi naval force was pushed higher up the political agenda and the British were charged with the task of speeding up the process.

With few facilities intact after the war, the British and the Americans created a trailer park city to serve as their headquarters while they trained a new naval force. Dozens of white cubicles served as the quarters for the hundreds of naval personnel. A large tent was used as the mess and there was even room for a small bar, housed in a smaller canvas structure. The bar operated the standard two-drink policy of the British armed forces. Other prefabricated structures were used for training and as offices. The whole base had a cheerfully improvised, even ramshackle appearance.

St John Price introduced me to Mica John Southworth, a captain in the British Navy. He was in his late twenties, tall, tanned and one of the most impressive young officers I had met in Iraq. He was frank and forthcoming and carried little of the cultural baggage of St John Price and his colleagues from the Blues and Royals. The naval mentality appeared to be different to the army. They took great pleasure in simple things, such as having their own bar. They were remarkably neat and tidy in their appearance and they were supremely confident in their tasks. All of this was aided by the nature of their mission, which was more focused and straightforward than that of the army and greatly helped by their dominance of the oceans. Fundamentally, though, it was a matter of culture and in this respect, too, the British Navy appeared to be different to the army.

Starved of contact with native Iraqis, I told Captain Mica John of my difficulties in meeting ordinary people. He promised to introduce me to a number of Iraqis who were working with the British, but again confirmed that UK forces were hunkered down at present because of the boycott by the regional government. Patrolling had been cut back and like all the foreign forces in southern Iraq, the navy was primarily concerned with sustaining their own forces. But because of the fact that the Iraqi Navy was so dependent on foreign support, there appeared to be a better atmosphere between the two forces and a higher level of co-operation. There may have been difficulties at a high level, but on the ground the two sides had worked out a practical arrangement.

Captain Mica John took me to the Iraqi barracks within the compound and I was surprised to find a solid, even elegant building clad in warm-coloured sandstone. It was shockingly cool after the torrid heat of the tents and caravans. He introduced me to Commander Adel Nouri, the deputy chief of the Iraqi Navy. He sat behind his desk proudly tapping on his computer, a picture of executive efficiency. Tea arrived and we settled in for a long chat.

Commander Nouri was a Christian, a rare enough creature in southern Iraq. He was a large, fit-looking man in his late forties and he also spoke English impeccably, a relic from his time at the University of Basrah. We talked about the growing sectarian tensions in the country and he bemoaned the collapse of communal harmony.

'Everywhere there are attacks, the smaller group suffers. It is really terrible. In Basrah, everything is quiet most of the time, but then there are incidents,' he said.

'What type of incidents?' I asked.

'Well, there are criminals who take advantage of the weakness of the police and attack other people,' he said.

'You mean sectarian attacks?' I offered.

'No, merely criminals. I don't think you could say that there is a lot of sectarian clashes,' he said, backtracking rapidly and catching Captain Mica John's eye.

He explained the many problems of the navy with a little more candour. The Ministry of Defence in Baghdad often failed to pay the wages of the sailors and this caused problems. It was very difficult to get decisions made at a high level. There was much political interference in the affairs of the navy. There was no budget for naval vessels and equipment. There were problems with discipline. Sailors who stepped out of line or transgressed weren't punished because the navy was trying to distinguish itself from its Saddam-era predecessor. But it had gone too far, he explained, and some of the rank and file were taking advantage of the soft approach. And so the tale of woe went on and on. Altogether it added up to a service in chronically bad shape.

'It sounds to me like the navy is barely functioning,' I said.

'That wouldn't be correct,' he said. 'We are functioning, but not at a high level. We can certainly do better.'

I asked what would happen if the British forces moved out and left the Iraqis to their own devices. There was an audible intake of breath and a shuffling of feet as Commander Nouri composed himself to answer.

'Without our British friends, it would be very difficult,' he said, again looking at Captain Mica John.

'Would there be any way of protecting the oil platforms without the British and American presence?' I asked.

'No,' was his simple and honest reply.

The interview over, we relaxed and drank some tea. It was so pleasant to be in the company of Iraqis after days with stiff British soldiers. Commander Nouri told me about the security arrangements to protect his family from insurgent attack because of his association with the British. Put at its most simple, he has told no one what he does for a living. It's a secret, although one which I'm sure many people have cracked. I mulled it over in my mind. The deputy head of the Iraqi Navy doesn't tell his neighbours what he does for a living. It seemed absurd.

He described the tensions in Basrah as 'awful'. The political parties and factions were fighting against each other and barely noticed that there was a country to run. They showed no interest in building up the bureaucracy of the state and were only intent on gaining power. If they had power, then they automatically had patronage and that would allow them to consolidate their interests. I said it sounded like he was no fan of democracy. We both laughed.

'It is not that I do not like democracy, it was more that we Iraqis were not used to exercising freedom. We are like prisoners set free from prison. We do not know what to do,' he said.

We shook hands and I wished him well and headed back into the vortex of the British military.

Later that evening as we were relaxing over our two-beer ration in the bar, I chatted with St John Price about the prospects for the British in Iraq. He continued to put his positive spin on the whole adventure and I continued to be sceptical. We changed the subject and talked about his time in Northern Ireland, where he served on two occasions. Like most British soldiers, he hated the place. It was cold and miserable and there was outright hostility from a good proportion of the population. I sympathised and agreed that the British Army's job in Northern Ireland was a difficult one. I explained that over the border in the Republic of Ireland, we had largely been insulated from the worst excesses of the 'Troubles'. He agreed and described a trip to Dublin he had made some time before. I explained that the Republic was experiencing an economic boom and that the influx of more than 100,000 foreign nationals was changing the demographics of the country in an interesting and profound way. He remarked that 100,000 was a small enough number and he wondered how they could have such an effect.

'How many people do you think are living in Ireland?' I asked.

'I don't know. About twenty million,' he replied.

Our company erupted in laughter and St John Price looked perplexed. Mica John joined in the conversation.

'It's about six million, you berk,' he told St John.

He looked a little abashed and so we moved the conversation on to more solid ground for St John. He told us about guard duty at Buckingham Palace and the privileges of being on duty at Marlborough Barracks along the Mall, which included an apartment on the Mall. The bedroom featured an ancient giant oak bed with an enormous canopy. St John explained that this was the bed where Captain James Hewitt first slept with Princess Diana. He thought this was truly fascinating and explained that it was every officer's aim to get a girl into the bed. Apparently, because it had been touched by such a revered celebrity as Princess Di, the girls were enthusiastic.

It was the day before we were due to leave and Michael Cassidy and I were very relaxed. We had survived yet another trip to Iraq. The barman decided that because we were non-military people, the two-beer rule could be relaxed and so we kicked up our heels and enjoyed a rare night of revelry.

It was almost midnight when we decided to call it a day. I looked St John Price directly in the eye and said he was doing a good job at presenting a positive picture of the state of southern Iraq.

'But it's all bullshit, isn't it? If you left here tomorrow, the whole place would collapse in a heap, wouldn't it?' I said.

'It might. But it's my job to put across the British perspective,' he answered and smiled.

'Time to crack on,' I thought and headed for my bed. We left the next morning.

7

THE YANKS

September 2001

I looked down from my hotel room on the forty-second floor, and just below the level of my window was the top of the highest spires of St Patrick's Cathedral. It was a spectacular view. Journalists don't normally stay in the New York Palace Hotel – it's way too expensive – but this wasn't a 'normal' time. Four days earlier, terrorists had smashed two planes into the World Trade Center, killing nearly 2,000 people. Hotel rooms were suddenly affordable in New York. I was drafted in to provide some back-up to our overworked correspondents and to reflect the human side of the catastrophe.

I floated around the city as if in a dream. The city had been violated and the wounds were still raw. The smell of decay permeated lower Manhattan and acrid smoke still hung over the site of the World Trade Center, waiting for the cool winds of autumn to blow it away.

New Yorkers – famously truculent and arrogant – were suddenly happy to stop and talk to an Irish reporter. They spilled their hearts out and revealed their innermost fears. In those fevered few days after the assault, virtually everyone was sure that further attacks would follow. More than one worried that New York as an entity would be undermined by the World Trade Center attacks. At times it felt like further attacks were imminent – they could happen at any moment. More than one person told me that they believed the city wouldn't recover from the trauma. People would leave in their thousands.

That wasn't the problem for the hundreds of Battery Park residents who turned up at a basketball arena in south Manhattan. Their obsession was how to get back into the apartments they had abandoned hastily on the morning of 11 September. Their homes bordered on the site of the attack and all had been damaged in one way or another as a result of the event. Even though most of the problems were due to the extraordinary amount of dust and rubble that had covered the Battery Park estate, the fear of the management company and the residents was that structural damage could have been caused to the high-rise apartment blocks as a result of the impact of the explosions. A spokesman for the management company assured the residents that they would be allowed back to their homes as soon as was practicable, but he was adamant that no one could go back until the engineers had cleared the site as safe. To the sounds of loud groans from the residents, the representative said that this was unlikely to happen in less than ten days.

The memory of the attacks was so raw that when I interviewed the Battery Park residents, one only had to mention the words 'attack' and 'Trade Center' and they were off. They would talk obsessively about exactly where they had been when they realised what was happening and what they thought of the situation now. Not a single person mentioned Osama bin Laden or al-Qaeda. After a week of reporting, this surprised me, so I made a point of asking people what they thought of bin Laden and al-Qaeda. Mostly people shrugged their shoulders and made simple comments.

'Whoever did it, they should get him. That's all,' one elegant lady told me at the entrance to Central Park.

'The death penalty would be too good for him. He needs a slow, painful death,' one Irish-American told me in a bar in the Bronx.

It was too early for reflection, too soon for asking the big question: Why? The wounds were still too fresh for serious analysis of the background to the assault, the trauma too palpable for reasoned discussion on how to find and deal with the masterminds. After the shock of the event, the response would take time, although I saw my first sign of the visceral anger that 9/11 generated just before I left the US.

At the end of my ten days in New York, I invited some friends up to my suite in the Palace for a drink. I also asked along some of the people I had met in the previous days. To my delight and surprise, most of them turned up, making a group of fifteen or so. Perhaps they were looking for an outlet, a different place to let off steam. The rooms were spacious and comfortable and I ordered snacks from room service for what was turning into a proper drinks party. There seemed to be an extraordinary number of staff on duty in the hotel, many more than was needed by the small number of residents. They called up with mixers, chips, nuts and complimentary bottles of wine. Everyone marvelled at the panoramic views of the Rockefeller Center and St Patrick's Cathedral, but the discussions returned obsessively to the assault on the World Trade Center and the new, uncertain world we all shared. One couple said they were considering relocating out of the city altogether.

'I can't see myself here in five years' time. If you want to have kids, New York is difficult anyway,' she said.

'I'm sure there will be a downturn after this, so I think we might sell up and move on to somewhere that's less of a target. Take the opportunity while it's going,' he said.

One guest had been drinking heavily. He was a doctor I had met, a friend of a friend. He was of southern European ancestry and was in bad shape over 9/11. He talked obsessively about the Arabs and Osama bin Laden. He blamed the ills of the world on them. As the evening went on and he got more and more drunk, I tried to avoid him, moving away when he came near. As the group dwindled it became more difficult to evade his attentions. He had heard I had been in Iraq and clearly wanted to collar me to talk about it, and as time went on it was obvious that he would have his way.

'Do you think he did it?' he asked.

'Who?' I asked.

'Saddam,' he replied.

'I don't think so. I think it was probably al-Qaeda and Osama bin Laden,' I offered.

'Yeah, but Saddam and bin Laden are the same. They want to destroy the US. We've got to get them before they get us,' he said.

I began to explain why I thought Saddam wasn't involved. Bin Laden was an implacable foe of Saddam's. The Iraqi dictator's biggest fear was internal dissent, and the resurgence of radical Saudi-style Wahhabi Islam in Iraq under bin Laden's patronage would be unthinkable, etc. But it was a waste of time. The doctor wasn't listening. He looked at me blankly and then waved his hand.

'I don't know anything about that. All I know is that we're going to go there and take the fucker out. He's got six months and then we're going in to rip his throat out,' he said, his bloodshot eyes standing out alarmingly.

As events unfolded, it took a year and a half.

⌒

I had become inured to some strange sights when the doors of the ancient lifts of the Palestine Hotel in Baghdad opened. Often, one would be confronted by machine-gun-toting Ghurkhas – veterans of the Ghurka regiment of the British Army. They spoke some English but were unfriendly in the extreme. When the doors opened, they would swivel to point their guns at the occupants of the lift with some menace. They guarded at least three floors of the hotel, regulating the comings and goings for the mostly American companies that occupied whole floors. There was a racist pegging order in how these guards were paid. White Americans and British were paid up to $1,000 dollars a day for such work. Europeans and white South Africans were paid around $700. Russians were paid about $500, while the Ghurkas were only worth a daily rate of $250 dollars. It may have been a small fortune for the inhabitants of an obscure misty mountain kingdom in the foothills of the Himalayas, but they looked like they resented their lower pay.

Imagine my surprise, then, when the doors parted on the twelfth floor and standing there was a giant of a man wearing a Stetson hat. 'Howdy,' he said in a deep southern baritone as he entered, and the entire elevator car erupted in laughter. He smiled and showed his perfect teeth. He was obviously used to making an entrance.

He was more than two metres tall and it was only his great height that saved the others in the lift from getting a mouthful of his ridiculously large hat. He was dressed in a beige suit and wore enormous lizard or alligator skin boots. He was a stereotype, straight out of the central casting.

I looked at him carefully, noting his clothing and manner. It was still novel for me to meet Americans in Baghdad. For as long as I had been going to Baghdad – particularly during the pre-war days – the only Americans I met were the small number of journalists allowed to cover this branch of the 'evil empire'. There was an even smaller number of people who turned up from time to time, campaigners who opposed UN sanctions and came to Baghdad to demonstrate their solidarity with the Iraqi people. The journalists were a mixed bunch, but the activists were even more diverse. They ranged from campaigners genuinely horrified by their government's policies in Iraq, to a group whose only reason for being in Baghdad seemed to be self-promotion.

Now, in late 2003, there seemed to be a huge number of Americans around the city. It was just before the insurgency made it almost impossible for white foreigners to move around Baghdad in an open way, but at this time there were Americans in the hotels, patrolling the streets, in the markets and all over the Green Zone.

When the lift finally arrived at the ground floor, I followed the Stetson man across the lobby and introduced myself to him. We shook hands and I tried to follow his heavily accented explanations of what he was doing in Baghdad. He claimed to be from Texas and said he was involved in the oil industry. I started asking questions about how the rebuilding of the sector was progressing. He put up his dinner plate-sized hand and motioned for me to stop.

'I'm here to work. I'm going to al-Amara and Nasiriya today and I'll be back in a week. If you're here then, we'll talk,' he said, smiling at the end and showing his large and uncannily perfect teeth.

We parted and I chuckled as I walked on to greet Abu Aseel for our daily meeting. 'It's not every day you come across someone like that in Baghdad,' I thought to myself.

⌒

We were told to meet the military convoy at the iconic parade ground in the centre of the Green Zone. The area is famous for its cross sword sculptures which mark the start and end of the marching strip. The huge swords are held by giant hands, allegedly modelled on those of Saddam Hussein. The sculptures have a distinctively oriental quality to them, and this is only partly achieved by the curved swords themselves. Such weapons are intrinsically linked to the Arab world and have been brandished by armies from the Middle East for centuries. However, it is also the unusual symmetry and order of the parade ground that give it such a distinctively oriental feel.

Many harbour a deep distaste for the monument, believing it to be a fascistic statement of Ba'athist power. There are plans to destroy it completely, replacing it with a series of monuments to the brutality of the Ba'athist era. The idea here is for interpretive museums and parks, designed to explain Iraq's troubled history to its citizens. Inevitably these are the designs and plans of outsiders and exiles, propagated initially by the Coalition Provision Authority (CPA). The CPA was the American appointed government of Iraq and its head was Ambassador L. Paul Bremer. It operated from June 2003 until June 2005. From its headquarters in the Green Zone, minutes from where we were waiting, the CPA produced grandiose plans for the radical overhaul of Iraqi society – almost none of which were ever implemented. The destruction of all the monuments that the Ba'athists had erected was high on their action list, even while the country descended into African-style poverty and Afghan-style violence.

In general, I found that Iraqis were fond of the monuments that had been erected in Saddam's time. As my Iraqi friends told me countless times, they wanted the things of Saddam's time but not the time itself. At a juncture when the security situation in the country was deteriorating, when there was little electricity and water and as the ranks of the unemployed swelled, there appeared to be little appetite for gesture politics of this sort.

We had made our way to the crossed swords monument on foot. As an Iraqi, Abu Aseel wasn't allowed to drive there, so he dropped us on the fringes of the Green Zone and we walked along vast, empty highways until we finally found the parade ground. Carrying heavy body armour and camera equipment, we shuffled up to the crossed swords and slumped down, dripping with sweat in the forty-degree heat.

An Iraqi guard was perched high in a strange-looking sentry box halfway down the marching strip and he approached carefully. In halting Arabic we explained that we were waiting for some American soldiers to pick us up.

'Americans coming here?' he asked.

'Yes. Military police. We are going out on patrol with the military police for the next twenty-four hours,' I replied.

He shot us a look of pure fear and returned quickly to his sentry box 500 metres away. Tom van Torre, my Belgian cameraman, and I began to play football with an empty can of Coke as the sun began to sink behind the building line. Embedded in the ground were the green helmets of Iranian soldiers captured during the Iran–Iraq War. They spilled out of giant steel mesh nets that were hung from the arms holding up the crossed swords. They were placed so that marching Iraqi soldiers trod on the captured helmets of their arch foe as they paraded in front of Saddam. Very symbolic. The dedication of the monument announced that the worst thing that could happen to a people was to fall under the dominance of another: 'The Iraqis have written in history a record of their heroism in defending their homeland. I have slain the invaders and severed their heads and I made out of their severed heads an arc of triumph. Here we are passing under the eye of God, who will protect the Iraqis from harm and who will not show any mercy to the evil ones,' it read.

The monument, like so much in Iraq, only had a tangential relationship with reality. Erected in 1985, it commemorated a war which was ongoing and in which victory over the Iranians was never assured. After years of ebb and flow on the battlefield, Saddam's forces and the Iranian army had fought each other to a standstill. The bitter foes only finally agreed to cease hostilities in 1988, when Ayatollah Khomeini famously likened the agreement to drinking a cup of poison. That was years after the monument had been created.

Some American troops were evidently less impressed by the monument, scrawling messages on the embedded helmets: 'Ha, ha. You lost', 'Iraq scum. Boil in hell' and 'This shit stinks' were some of the more choice offerings.

We smoked some more cigarettes and waited. After two hours we were getting worried. With only temperamental handheld satellite phones to use for communication, I was concerned that there had been some mix-up or problem with our appointment.

The US Army press office didn't inspire confidence. Its haphazard and apparently arbitrary approach to tasks reminded me of dozens of other large bureaucracies I had come across, but those had been mostly in Third World countries, which is hardly what one expects from the world's only true superpower. It took hours and hours of negotiations with junior bureaucrats before one was passed on to decision-makers. The junior members of the press office staff appeared to take pleasure in obfuscation and prevarication. They would take a request, shuffle over to the phone, sit down, read the piece of paper five times, pick up the phone, put it down, read the paper again and finally pick up the phone and make the call.

As we waited in the fading light of an October day, it occurred to me that it was quite conceivable that they'd simply forgot to pass on the instructions to the relevant military unit or that they'd passed on incorrect arrangements.

Every now and then a military convoy would pass along the road perpendicular to us, roaring towards one of the army compounds in another part of the Green Zone. We would wave in the hope that this group were on the look-out for us. But as the time passed, a certain note of anxiety started to take hold. Our fear was that we would be stuck in the middle of the Green Zone with no transport. We wouldn't be able to leave and our colleagues outside the fortified zone wouldn't be able to come in. Not only that, but the centrepiece of our story of life in Baghdad – life for the American soldiers here – would evaporate. What started as concern and became anxiety soon transformed into panic as the third hour of waiting passed. We phoned everyone we could think of, but nobody could help. As time moved on and the light faded, panic moved into despair and then resignation as we accepted what appeared to be the inevitable – we wouldn't get to meet the people who were effectively running Iraq. They either weren't interested in getting their message across or they weren't competent. Both were eminently believable options.

Then another convoy jetted by at speed. We waved with all the enthusiasm we could muster. The convoy stopped about half a kilometre away. They turned back and headed in our direction. We were elated.

'You guys from Irish TV?' the tall sergeant asked.

We all nearly jumped for joy and introduced ourselves to Sergeant John Marshall, who would be our guide for the duration of our time with the American military. He was tall, tanned and sported a Ba'ath party-style moustache, which I naively thought might endear him to the Iraqis. He was from Iowa, which I subsequently learned was a sleepy backwoods state famous for its steaks, strip malls, wide open plains and little else. Most of the 18th Military Police force turned out to be from this out-of-the-way state in the American midwest. I was excited. The midwest was a blank for me, but it was from this deeply republican territory that President Bush got most of his support. I thought it important to meet them – all the better to understand the Bush-supporting American mind.

We met the other members of the force, including Corporal Rachel Looney, Sergeant Michael Mahon and Private Wayne Wiley. They were initially a little frosty. I' had the impression that no one had told them they would have an Irish television team crawling all over them for twenty-four hours. But their initial coolness didn't last, and after an hour or so they relaxed with us and were extremely friendly, almost naïvely so, bearing in mind we were news journalists.

Back at their base in the centre of the Green Zone, Sergeant Marshall explained that tonight's mission was a complex and potentially dangerous one. Their Iraqi sources had given them details of a counterfeit racket that was linked to the insurgency. The gang had print-quality transparencies of the 250 Iraqi dinar note and were printing billions of them. While the notes were only partially useful in the Iraq of 2003, it was expected that a new currency would be issued soon. It would be called the 'new dinar'. The new currency would be a real one, backed by hard currency deposits and swappable one for one with the old. When that happened, the gang could potentially launder millions of dollars worth of fake notes, creating a large pool of cash to continue the insurgency.

'The bad guys need guns and weapons. They've got them. They need people. They've got plenty of them. But they also got to have money and we aim to cut out this source of finance. Simple as that,' Sergeant Marshall said.

It was the first time I had heard the term 'bad guys' from an adult and I looked at Sergeant Marshall. 'By bad guys, you mean the insurgents?' I asked.

'Yes, sir. Call them Wahhabis, insurgents, jihadis, Ba'athists or whatever. Our aim is to take them out,' he said.

At that point I couldn't figure out if Sergeant Marshall was just using simplistic terms as shorthand or whether he had an unsophisticated view of the situation in Baghdad. He had been stationed in Baghdad for six months, and like most of the Americans I met on that visit, he was a reservist. In 'real life' (as he put it, no doubt as a contrast to the 'surreal life' he was living in Iraq) he was a policeman in Iowa. Many of the other soldiers from the unit were also reservists from Iowa or neighbouring states.

The American unit was attached to a new Iraqi police station, the entrance to which was obscured by a maze of razor wire and chicanes, designed to deter suicide bomb attacks. The Iraqi police service was so new that many of the officers lacked uniforms and weapons. The idea was that the Americans would provide the might while the

Iraqi officers would provide the intelligence, language and other skills to fight the insurgents. It was a neat idea, but on the ground it was in its infancy, and in reality, the Americans provided virtually all the facilities for a hopelessly unprepared Iraqi police force.

At that time, all American operations were based on the notion that the insurgency was composed mostly of disaffected members of the former Ba'athist regime, who were organised in a cellular structure. They thought that there were a number of key individuals directing the attacks, former bigwigs in the intelligence and military structure of the country. Their idea was that if only they could crack the leadership of the organisation, its brains and its finances, then the insurgency would falter. What they saw in the Iraqi insurgency was a virtual mirror of their own military organisation. They looked through American eyes and saw not an Iraqi uprising, but a kind of reverse image of their own military machine, one which was evil in contrast to their own good, one that was black to their own white. It had leaders and middle ranks and soldiers and it was funded in an organised way. There were sinister personalities out there, plotting against the Americans. 'Decapitating the leadership' was a key aim.

This added another dimension to the discussions with the Americans. They returned constantly to notions of good and evil. These people were 'bad guys'. Others on the American side were 'good guys'. They even used the term over the military radio. They constantly told me they were in Iraq to 'do good'. At times I felt like I was listening to my six-year-old son. He had often asked if there were 'bad guys' in Iraq and if they would kill me. He would wake in the middle of the night, shaking with fear of Iraqi bad guys. It was understandable in a child, but in an adult I found it ridiculous. At this level of the American military, the conflict had been boiled down to a battle of good versus bad. This didn't square with my experience or understanding of what was going on in the country.

For days before meeting the US troops, I had been trying to make contact with members of the insurgency. It was difficult and frustrating. It goes without saying that it was too dangerous for me to go interview insurgents in person, so I was trying to find a way of gathering their views without putting our crew in danger. It appeared that the opposition to the Americans was fractured and chaotic. Through a number of well-connected Iraqi colleagues, I had built up a sketchy picture of those fighting the Americans in the city of Fallujah, fifty kilometres from Baghdad. They appeared to be highly motivated groups, many operating in isolation from each other. Their main purpose at this time was to harass the US forces and their allies in Iraq and to expel the Americans from the country.

This colleague agreed to speak to a group in Fallujah on my behalf. I was sure that he was telling the truth about his contacts with the insurgents despite his shifty nature and shockingly discoloured teeth. We communicated back and forth for a number of days. Finally I asked our intermediary to record an interview with the leader, using a camera we would provide. Initially the suggestion was turned down. Interestingly, the leader of the group cited the killing of Ahmed Shah Masood in Afghanistan by the Taliban as a reason for not allowing us to send a camera. In that case, a camera crew was setting up to interview the Afghan when the machine exploded, killing the Taliban's main enemy in Afghanistan. It was a strike of pure terrorist genius. Up to then, journalists hadn't been used in terrorist acts. Other precedents he mentioned were from the Gaza Strip, where Israeli intelligence used satellite tracking devices inserted in cameras to attack suicide bombers. There was a lull in the negotiations for a couple of days and then, out of the blue, a message came back, saying my bona fides had been confirmed by a trustworthy source in Baghdad and the leader would agree to answer questions sent.

A week later the tape arrived back. I asked an Iraqi academic colleague to watch it with me so that I could pick up some of the subtleties that might be lost in a paper translation. The leader appeared in a nondescript room with an Iraqi flag draped across a wall. His face was covered by a *keffiyeh* (Arab scarf) and he wore military-type camouflage fatigues. On the ground were various weapons, including rocket-propelled grenades, AK-47s and mortars. He spoke slowly, deliberately and confidently. He wasn't reading a script but was responding to questions I had written down.

'We are fighting the illegal occupation of our land by the United States. We have taken part in many actions against the enemy. We have killed many and will kill many more. We will not rest until every single American has left our land. We are the sons of Iraq. This is our land. The Americans say that our religion is a terrorist religion, but we say that it is the Americans who are the terrorists. They have made a big mistake by invading Iraq. We will make this their graveyard,' he said.

The intermediary asked him if he was working in league with any international elements.

'We have no contacts with al-Qaeda or with Hamas or Islamic Jihad. We share the same aims but we have not talked to or met them. In the future I do not rule out that we will co-operate with them. But as of now we are on our own, patriotic Iraqis fighting the enemy,' he said.

The intermediary asked him if he followed Saddam.

'We do not follow any person and we do not want the time of Saddam. We are fighting to destroy the Americans and their puppets in Iraq,' he said.

After hearing the translation, I was initially disappointed. I had expected something more from them, although what exactly I wasn't sure – at least something more newsworthy, sensational even.

I turned to my Iraqi colleague, who made extensive notes during the tape.

'This man is a young man, I would say no more than twenty-five. He is educated. I would say he has been to university or to higher college. I would not be surprised if he was a teacher or training to be a teacher. He speaks very well. Not in dialect. His accent is that of a man from Fallujah, but an educated man from Fallujah. It is hard to think of what else we can say. I would guess that he has been in the army. He is very comfortable talking about weapons and even picking them up. He looks like he has used them before. The religious talk is standard stuff. He is a Sunni, of course. I do not read too much into it. Everyone can talk like that. The phrases and references are banal. It has no particular religious quality to it. It is nationalism, really. That's what he is talking about,' he said.

I was flabbergasted. My colleague had painted a rounded picture of this group as a result of the fifteen-minute tape. The picture was of a strongly motivated team, led by educated men, trained (as virtually all Iraqis are) in basic military techniques. Their motivation was the expulsion of the United States and the overthrow of whatever regime was put in place by Washington. They had strong nationalistic reasoning, and while religion was a motivating force, it wasn't defining. If they were to be believed, they operated in isolation from other groups but were ready to co-operate where necessary.

If the exercise had proven anything, it was that the opposition to the coalition in Iraq was very complicated. Among the Sunni, there were groups such as this one in Fallujah. There were others operating in the central south who were more Ba'athist in character. Still others were loyal to the self-appointed al-Qaeda chief, the Jordanian Abu Musab Al-Zarqawi, some of them foreigners willing to die as martyrs. The level of overlap or co-operation between the different groups was unknown at that stage, but it was a far cry from the good guy, bad guy routine.

Back at the police station I wondered whether the forces they were fighting against were up to the task. We wandered around the building, introducing ourselves to the various key players. Most of the station was occupied by US troops, some of whom were asleep after a long, hot day shift. Everywhere one found an American, technology was close at hand: computers, handheld music systems, portable DVD players, etc. The contrast between their equipment and that of the Iraqis was stark. The largest Iraqi office was a shambolic mess, filthy and devoid of any equipment. Iraqi police officers rushed around, but there was a generally aimless feel to the office.

As we prepared to leave on our night-time operation, we were joined by a young Iraqi, Adil, who would act as the interpreter for the Americans. He was brash, reckless and difficult to like. Even the soldiers were wary of him. Aged about twenty, he was vague about his background, but it was obvious that he was a Christian and had spent some time in the United States and New Zealand.

'I've been living in New Zealand for about nine years but this is always going to be my home country. You can't change who you are,' he said.

I asked him how he came to be in Baghdad.

'Right after the coalition took over, I came home and offered myself for work. I am now working as a translator. Since I came back I have found out that this place has got a lot of trouble. There is a lot of stuff that has to be fixed up,' he said.

I asked if he was aware that many Iraqis would regard him as a traitor for working with the Americans. He exploded.

'Yeah, those Ba'athists. They don't care about anything. Why should I care about them? They are already traitors for what they did to the Iraqi people. And what about blowing up the UN? That is not the best idea for helping Iraq,' he said, dismissing me with a wave of his hand.

He had the air of a zealot about him and I put him down on my list of 'dubious characters' for the night, particularly after I spotted him secreting a gun in his rucksack.

It was dusk when we snaked our way around the razor wire chicane and headed out into the Red Zone. The capital had been divided up into zones by the American authorities. Initially there had been yellow and orange zones, areas of the city where it was possible for the coalition to operate on foot or in vehicles but with caution. However, only a few months after the takeover, the city was now divided into two. The Green Zone was the former palace complex of Saddam and was closed off to the ordinary public. It housed the CPA, embassies and the exile forces brought back to Iraq by the United States with the intention of installing them in power. Coalition forces operated freely there. The rest of Baghdad was the Red Zone.

We travelled in unarmoured Humvees, the main vehicles used by US forces in Iraq. They have taken the place of the iconic Jeep, veteran vehicle of World War II and the Korean War. Inside, they are well designed and very simply equipped and can carry up to six soldiers and their kit. In the centre of the rear compartment there is a gunner position which allows a soldier to pivot 360 degrees above the vehicle with a mounted machine gun, giving extensive cover while moving through the city. The Humvee also had a sophisticated communications system which allowed the front passenger to communicate with headquarters and gave a global position system (GPS) location to a central office. This would be useful should a rescue be necessary. Apart from these high-tech gadgets, the vehicle was very simple and robust.

But it wasn't armoured and I asked Sergeant Marshall why. He explained that the armoured Humvees were in great demand and tended to be used when travelling along the highways and in specific areas. If the MPs had to go anywhere in the Anbar province (including Fallujah or Ramadi), they would request armoured vehicles, but there weren't enough going around to use them all the time. He recommended that we place our personal body armour by our side at the doors. This would marginally help if the vehicle was shot at, but, he laughed, 'They're not going to stop a bullet from an AK-47. Only the good Lord will help you then.' I asked when they were last attacked. Again Sergeant Marshall laughed.

'Every time we go out we're shot at. How do you know you're being shot? Well, when the bullets start bouncing off the vehicle, then you know you're being attacked,' he said.

I was sure what he was saying was true, but it was also clear that Sergeant Marshall was enjoying my discomfiture. Private Wayne Wiley chipped in.

'We've been shot at. We've been mortared. We've had grenades dropped in on us. Just the other week we were going down Rashid [Rashid Street, one of the main arteries in the city, a road with a wide underpass at one junction] and some guys dropped a hand grenade in on us. It bounced out and blew up behind us,' he said.

The underpass was subsequently closed to coalition traffic and the walkway above blocked off by razor wire.

The soldiers took a particular delight in describing their close encounters with the enemy. They were lucky enough not to have lost any comrades to enemy fire yet and the near-misses reinforced their sense of comradeship and purpose. It was also clear that they enjoyed scaring us with their tales of derring-do. Ironically, we were better equipped than some of the soldiers, who lacked personal body armour. We had a full armoured jacket and helmet, whereas some of the troops only had a helmet.

A ten p.m. curfew was in place across the city, and as it approached, vehicles began to speed up and head for home. The curfew was strictly enforced and there were many tales of cars caught out late at night being attacked. The policy was not to shoot on sight, but the practice among the new police and some of the American military was to do precisely that. After all, a vehicle travelling illegally through the night in Baghdad could only be up to no good.

The 18th Military Police Brigade had a powerful sense of purpose and I was deeply impressed by this group's cohesion and sense of comradeship. In a war zone where the enemy is potentially everywhere, that communality of design is vital. Without it, the American casualty list in Iraq would have been a multiple of what it was.

As we neared our first target premises, I began to realise that we were in a familiar part of Baghdad, close to the river near the Jadiriya bridge in a comfortable middle-class district called Karrada. This was a favoured suburb for businesspeople and wealthy public servants and was mixed and, in places, charming. It was also home to some of the best restaurants and the only decent bakery in Baghdad prior to the war.

The target of the operation was a family said to have been deeply involved in the counterfeiting operation. They weren't the kingpins, but they owned the print shop where the currency was being printed.

The Iraqi currency, the dinar, has been through as many traumas as the country itself. While in the 1970s it was a valuable currency because of the avalanche of cash generated by the oil crises, since then the dinar has steadily lost value. From a peak where a single dinar was worth three dollars, the currency has steadily lost its worth. When I first visited in 1998, the dinar was running at about 300 to the dollar. In 1999 it fell to around 500. By 2001 it was worth less than 1,000 to the dollar and by 2003 a dollar could buy more than 2,500 dinars. It was so worthless that in 2000 Saddam started printing 250 dinar bills on the cheapest of paper. These bills looked as if they had been photocopied. They were crudely printed and the serial numbers weren't sequential. Most Iraqis thought they were part of some scam perpetrated by Uday, Saddam's despised son who had a hand in virtually every fraud in the country.

As the currency wasn't highly regarded, Iraqis played a complicated game of buying dollars and holding them until they absolutely had to have dinars. Then they would exchange them. If there was a period (and there were many) when there was a temporary shortage of dinars, then people would sell dollars and only buy them back again when they thought the time was right. The whole population, it seemed, had become expert currency speculators.

But the scam being targeted by the Americans was of a different order. Because of the crudeness of the dinar notes, they were easily replicated. With the right equipment, it was easy to print money and the prospect of the currency change accelerated the fraud.

We arrived at the house in Karrada and it was surrounded. The family was clearly comfortable. The house was well built and had two cars in the driveway. Sergeant Marshall's assistant emerged from his Humvee carrying a giant mallet. The Iraqi police officers started shouting through the gates, calling on the occupants to emerge and give themselves up. There was no response. The mallet man swung into action and in a few seconds the sturdy gate was reduced to scrap. The soldiers and police flooded into the house. We followed.

Inside the family had gathered in the parlour. They looked fearful. Adil arrived and started to talk to them, aggressively. He had now acquired an M6 rifle, the standard-issue weapon of US troops. One of the MPs touched him on the shoulder and said, 'Easy, big man, easy.'

An extensive search of the house was underway. The main reception rooms were studies of Iraqi bourgeois kitsch: plastic flowers, formal portraits of the family, ceremonial gun hung on the wall. The dark living room was dominated by a giant widescreen television, hopelessly out of scale in the room, but it still occupied pride of place in the centre of the room.

Private Wiley guarded the door and pivoted on the spot, pointing his gun alternately out the door and up the stairwell. With his thick glasses and scrunched-up face, he looked comic – although he carried his gun menacingly enough.

After about an hour, Sergeant Marshall emerged into the hallway carrying a huge wad of notes. Simultaneously, an Iraqi policeman produced a massive haul of 250 denomination notes. All of the dinars were still in massive sheets, each one containing forty-eight notes. Even though the currency was worth little, each sheet was worth six dollars. There were thousands of them, and when the new currency was issued, they would be converted into real money, backed by dollar deposits.

The father of the house was arrested. He was a gentle-looking, mild-mannered man of around sixty years and he only seemed mildly perturbed at the intrusion. The Iraqi police interrogated him on the spot. He answered their questions sceptically. His wife fetched his heart medication, some fruit and a bottle of water and he was handcuffed and taken out to one of the waiting vehicles.

Another, younger man, dressed in a *dishdasha*, was also apprehended. He was clearly terrified by the appearance of the Americans in the house and was more willing to supply information. The Iraqi police questioned him closely for a few minutes, and while they never laid a finger on him, their stance and approach was aggressive and threatening. He agreed to take us to the print shop.

We headed off into the night. It was well after ten o'clock and cars were racing across the city to make it to their destination. There was almost panic in the eyes of some motorists as they saw our convoy. Many would screech to a halt as they spotted us. They were fearful that the Humvees would open fire on them, as had happened on countless occasions since the end of the war. The Americans had a reputation among Iraqis as being trigger-happy and stories of families killed at US army roadblocks were legion. The biggest fear among my Iraqi friends was to be stuck behind an American convoy and to have one's innocent manoeuvres misinterpreted by the gunners riding shotgun on the turrets of the Humvees. This would almost certainly lead to an attack by the Americans and certain death.

From the vantage of the Humvees, however, it was easy to see how the situation looks completely different.

Assailed, as they are, by all manner of attacks, the Americans travelled at a heightened state of alert, not to say paranoia. Baghdad driving, at the best of times, is erratic. Drivers switch lanes and swerve off the main drag with no notice. If you're the gunner on top of a vulnerable Humvee that had been attacked by insurgents on many occasions, these actions weren't the charming, chaotic behaviour of passionate Orientals, but the sinister precursors to another suicide mission. It was no surprise that soldiers let loose as they did.

But on this occasion our gunner, Corporal Rachel Looney, held her fire and we proceeded to the old market area of the city without major incident.

It was a shock to find the markets devoid of any life, Ottoman-era buildings shuttered up with not a soul to be seen. The streetlights weren't working and the scene was only illuminated by the flames of burning rubbish which was piled up at the end of every day and burned. It smouldered through the night. We eventually found ourselves in a once charming but now run-down street with many alleyways and lanes leading off into densely populated tenements. To the left stood what was once a fine municipal building. Judging by the stonework and the fine detailing, I reckoned it was an early-nineteenth-century Ottoman house, effectively a home and office in one, a common enough occurrence at that time. It was five storeys high and its sandstone classical façade was still intact.

The soldiers deployed across the street in defensive formation, covering as many vantage points as they could. One team of three stayed in the centre of the road covering the parapet roof of the six-storey buildings which overlooked the area of operation.

Donning our full body armour, we waited at the side of the street, taking in the atmosphere and noting the way the soldiers were conducting themselves. The Humvee that was originally ahead of us revved its engines and swung around in a short arc, heading straight for the fortified steel doors of a nondescript warehouse-like building fifty metres in front of us. The vehicle crashed through the doors and reversed quickly. Soldiers and Iraqi police officers streamed through the broken doors and swarmed over what turned out to be a printing works.

I entered the building with Adil, the interpreter, who had transformed himself into a battle-ready soldier. I asked him if he enjoyed the work.

'I love it. These guys, they're scum,' he said, gesturing to the Iraqis who were arrested. 'They're up to something, I can assure you of that. We've just gotta find out what it is. We're just trying to help the Iraqis. Some people don't want to be helped, but we're just doing it for the innocent people. These guys, they're not innocent.' He struck his open hand with a clenched fist.

His mini-homilies were a mixture of the innocent and the sinister. He was clearly enjoying his job as helper of the Americans, but the film crew regarded him as a potential danger. He swaggered around each location as if he was the boss, swinging his AK-47 with abandon and talking all the time. To us it seemed that a young and clearly irresponsible individual was being given free reign to do what he liked. This was confirmed when he knelt down at the entrance to the building and aimed his rifle to the outside and called out 'pow, pow', as would a child.

As the team searched the building, I wandered outside to chat to the troops. Sergeant Michael Mahon was keeping an eye on the rooftops and was a calming, stable force in the platoon. He exuded confidence and assurance.

'We're only here to do a job and by my reckoning we're not doing a very good one. I mean, to put on a lid on this town you need hundreds of thousands of troops and a long occupation. We're way too small. And the Iraqi police,' he looked over at the police cars and nodded his head, 'they are a mixed bunch. I mean, some of the guys are okay. But you never know who you're dealing with. One minute they seem okay. The next time you hear the guy has been arrested for embezzlement or whatever. We do our stuff, but, you know, we're not even scratching the surface. This place is beyond fucked up. I'm just looking forward to getting home. And I'm not coming back,' he said, turning and moving up the street.

Just then a shot rang out close to our position. All the soldiers crouched and made their guns ready. I moved into the shadows beside a doorway. Another shot was fired. Then another. Then a cacophony of rounds. Then return fire. Sergeant Mahon checked if anyone had fired from our side. No one had. Within seconds hundreds of shots were being exchanged and we were better able to get a fix on where they were coming from. The corporal manning the radio reckoned it was happening a few hundred metres down the road. Everyone waited and listened carefully.

Sergeant Mahon thought it was a battle between two Iraqi groups. 'You hear that? AK-47 fire. And that return fire is a heavy machine gun. You can also hear handguns. Yeah, I'm pretty sure it's a fight between Iraqis. Usually what happens is that someone is trying to get into a shop or something and the owner opens up. Then they have a big fight. That's what I think it is, anyway. They're not shooting at us, for sure,' he said.

The intensity of the battle lasted for four minutes and then ebbed away until one could hear only single rounds of AK-47 fire and then it ended. No one would investigate. It was just another mysterious battle between unknown people fighting over unknowable quarry.

I asked Sergeant Marshall what made him enlist in the services. He explained that he worked in aircraft maintenance in Iowa.

'After 9/11 I could see the recession coming. It was getting tough and I knew I had to do something. They were going to let a lot of people go, and I mean a lot. So I thought, if I joined the military, my employer had to keep my job open for me. So I went into the military to ride out the recession in the airline business. Simple as that. And I'm still fucking here,' he said with a rueful smile.

The search of the print works had yielded little. Sergeant Marshall re-emerged with a stack of paper.

'There's nothing in there, really. But we found the paper they're using to print the money,' he said.

He went to the radio and consulted his controller. Just then a tiny, wizened old woman emerged from an alleyway in a nightdress. The female translator attached to the military, Fatima, went over to her to hear what she had to say. They talked for a few minutes.

Fatima came over to brief Sergeant Marshall. 'She lives up that alleyway there and she says the man who works in the factory lives beside her. He escaped when he heard that we were here. She says they have been loading huge bundles of dinars onto trucks all day. They gave some of it out to the people around here to keep them quiet. They knew we were coming. She will show us the place where he lives,' she said.

We followed the little old woman up the lane. All the while she was talking and chattering. The middle of the lane was an open sewer and on either side one could hear the low whispers of fearful residents.

Fatima translated what she was saying. 'She says she is living in fear. Ali Babas are everywhere around here and she only feels safe when the Americans come,' she said. The soldiers all smiled.

Inside, the tenement building was a warren, with dozens of rooms and flats. The old lady led us to one door, which the soldiers immediately kicked in. Through a further maze of filthy rooms, they searched and searched until one soldier called out, 'We got it.'

What he had found was a folder with the plastic trans-parencies of the currency and a further folder with a transparency containing random serial numbers. The printer would use these to make a plate which would print the notes. It was as neat and simple as that, literally a license to print money. It struck me as odd that the man who looked after the factory would leave such useful evidence behind him as he fled, but then again, little surprised me in the new Iraq. Perhaps the gang had so many different ways of printing the currency that they had merely overlooked this set of templates.

The whole operation was neat. But perhaps just a little too neat. The thought occurred to me more than once that it had all been staged for the camera, to show that the Americans were winning the battle. Even though this felt a little far-fetched, bearing in mind the confusion over our rendezvous, it showed how my mind was working like an Iraqi's, seeing conspiracies in every action, wary of posi-tive developments.

I moved out of the tenement and made my way back to the vehicles and the film crew. As I walked back along the empty, eerie alleyway, whispered voices called out to me, 'Mister, mister.' I decided not to stop and called back, 'Everything okay.'

Back at the vehicles, the soldiers reported nothing unusual. They were still at a heightened state of alert. I wandered over to Private Wayne Wiley, who was again pirouetting with his gun, pointing at the shadows and getting ready for action.

In every large group there's always the character, the one who stands out as an eccentric or a comedian. Private Wiley was ours. All of his colleagues called him Papa because, in most cases, he was old enough to be their father. He was diminutive and with his helmet on and his scrunched-up facial features, he had the look of a cheerful elf. Tom, my cameraman, nodded as if to say 'now's the time for the interview with our character'. Every film has to have one, an individual who can lift the narrative. Tom switched on and we began the interview.

'After 9/11 I signed up. I said it was time to take a stand and help out the country. We can't have folks coming and attacking us at home. That's not right. So we're here. We don't want to occupy the country. Everyone knows that. We're just here so the folks can get back to normal. There are lots of bad guys here. We're here to show them that there are good guys as well. We're the good guys,' he said and smiled.

I asked him what a man of fifty-five was doing on the dangerous streets of Baghdad when he could be back in his hometown in Iowa, taking it easy and enjoying life. He looked at me through his bottle end glasses and shook his head.

'Can't rightly say,' he said.

I thought he might have misunderstood my question so I rephrased it and asked it again.

'Can't rightly say with the camera there,' he said.

I was puzzled, but decided to move on with the interview. He regained his fluency and we touched on many subjects: what he thought of Arabs (not much); what he thought of the war (not much); George W. Bush (nice guy), etc. He was likeable and amiable, but Papa wasn't a genius. He articulated a fundamental American truth: patriotic Americans heard the call of their government after the attacks in New York and would defend the homeland as best they could. This was all part of a grand American project to keep the country safe from evil people overseas who wanted to destroy the American way of life. Papa believed it all.

But there was still the small matter of the strange moment in our interview. Why had he refused to say what motivated him to come to Baghdad when he could be taking life easy back home? After the dust had settled on the interview, I approached him and asked him why he was so uncomfortable telling us about it.

'Well, you know there are some things you shouldn't say on television. And there was the lady there [referring to Janet, our flame-haired producer]. I didn't want to say it in front of her,' he said.

I was even more puzzled than ever.

'You see, when I take my gun and we head out on the Humvee on patrol, I get this big hard on. It lasts until I get back to base. I'm alive out there, man. It's better than Viagra,' he said and burst into a wickedly cackling laugh.

I was taken aback. What a strange, weird thing. Here was this fifty-something old timer, hanging around with teenagers and others in their early twenties. They were patrolling in the most dangerous city on earth and this tiny guy, the Papa of the troop, was getting a massive surge of sexual satisfaction from his work. I told the other members of the film crew and we all shared a rare moment of amusement. In fact, we laughed like Kilkenny cats.

We moved on to our final destination of the dawning day. This was a mansion near Sha'ab City on the outskirts of the metropolis. I recognised the area immediately. It was close to the open ground of foxholes and gun emplacements where I had been attacked by American cluster bombs at the end of the war in 2003. I told Sergeant Marshall about it and informed him that we were heading deep into Ba'athist territory.

The houses were large, gaudy affairs, clad in beige sandstone, overhung by large balconies and each with a massive satellite dish on their flat roof. The target property was identified and surrounded and the occupants didn't take long to surrender. A search revealed thousands of newly printed sheets of dinar notes. Again the haul was significant, but not enormous. The men who were arrested feigned ignorance of the loot. Adil again threw shapes around them, smiling in a sinister way, intimidating the men and mocking their denials.

It was early in the morning and it had been a very long night. Sergeant Marshall's cool, even temper, which had been so impressive all night, finally cracked.

'Shut the fuck up, Adil. And what are you doing with a rifle? Who said you could carry a weapon? You are not authorised to carry a weapon. Do you hear me? Do you hear me? You are not fucking authorised,' he shouted.

Adil cowered under the onslaught and showed his age by going into a deep sulk.

The Iraqi police took the men into custody. I asked where they would be taken. Sergeant Marshall told me that they would either go to the airport detention centre or to Abu Gharaib prison. I asked if he would be asked to give evidence in a hearing or court. He thought not.

'We leave all of that up to the Iraqi police. That's their job,' he said.

We headed back to the centre of the city for a debrief and some light refreshments. The troops were sent packages from home at regular intervals. They contained goodies and letters and treats. Each soldier had his or her own favourite treat and they shared them generously with the group. As we stood around Rusafi Square at about five o'clock, we snacked ferociously on Doritos tortilla chips, Hershey's chocolate and drank endless cans of Coke.

Corporal Rachel Looney showed me photographs of her family and explained that she was only in the military to earn credits so she could go to college. Her aim was to study social work. I remarked that it was an odd preparation, all this flying around the city pivoting on top of a Humvee with a massive machine gun. She laughed.

'I know it's kind of strange. But as long as I get out of here with my two legs intact, I'll be happy. We've got a good attitude about being here. We don't want to be here longer than we have to, but we're doing a job and, you know, somebody's got to do it. For me, I'll be happy to get home and be with my family. They don't like me being here and I won't stay longer than I have to,' she said.

'I thought I would be here for just a few weeks but, you know, the weeks have gone by and now it's months. I don't think the military will be here for another six months. At least I hope not,' she laughed, amused that the US Army could get bogged down in such a piddling conflict.

Sergeant Marshall was also in philosophical mode. 'Yeah, I'll be just as happy when this is all over. I'll give it a year or two and I think it'll have calmed down a bit. Then the military will pull out and leave it to the Iraqis. They need to get some money flowing and get the economy back up. That'll help a lot, cause I reckon a lot of the attacks are about money and, you know, guys with nothing to do. The devil makes work for idle hands. I'm quite optimistic, really, but I'll be happy to get home,' he said.

Sergeant Mahon was looking forward to a four-week break for leave. 'I'll get the fuck outta here. Fucking stinking hole of a shit hole. I'll pass through Shannon Airport and think of my relatives up in Mayo. Hell, it'd be good to go to Castlebar and drink some Guinness in a pub.' He stopped to relish the idea. 'Anyway, I'll get home and raise some hell for a couple of days. And see my girlfriend. If she's still my girlfriend, that is,' he laughed.

Private Wiley didn't seem so keen to leave Iraq, perhaps for obvious reasons. 'I've already signed up for another tour. So when we finish here in December, I'll have a couple of months back home and then I'll be back, probably in March or April next year. That's if we're still needed and if we're asked to come back. I'll do it. Hell, yeah. And if we're done here, I'll go somewhere else. Maybe Iran next time,' he said, suppressing an impish giggle.

We swapped numbers and e-mail addresses and went our separate ways. Our team went back to the Palestine Hotel and the friendly atmosphere of the journalist's hotel of choice in Baghdad, while our military friends went back to their base for six hours' sleep. They would be out again in twelve hours' time patrolling the streets and breaking down doors, trying to impose some semblance of law and order on the chaotic streets of Baghdad.

One doesn't necessarily expect ground troops to have a deep understanding of the war they are engaged in, and I didn't find it among the soldiers of the 18th Military Police. They approached their tasks with the wide-eyed acceptance of Americans who have been told to do something by their superiors. They were junior soldiers, all of them NCOs and enlisted men and women, mostly very young. It would be unfair to compare them to their more senior and more cosmopolitan British colleagues. There was little in the way of questioning among them about the motives of those who promulgated the war. This was true of virtually the whole American body politic and it wasn't until late 2005 that middle-Americans began debating the issues in any depth.

It certainly didn't happen on that warm October night in 2003.

Two days later I was again coming down in one of the rickety lifts of the Palestine Hotel when the doors opened and the Stetson man walked in. I greeted him like a long-lost friend and asked him how his trip down south had gone.

'Yeah, it was good. We did some good stuff down there. The whole prison system is a disaster, but, you know, we're doing our stuff and making changes,' he said.

I was puzzled and wanted to say that I thought he was working in the oil industry, but I held my counsel.

'What's it like?' I asked.

'They're all just thrown in together, you know. There's razor wire and some canvas cover. The Iraqis would finish them off, if they were let. But that's what we're here for,' he said.

He talked on until the lift reached the ground floor, describing the difficulties of keeping prisoners with some semblance of dignity in a desert camp.

'They'll tell you anything, except what you really want to know,' he continued, 'always making up stories and begging to be let out, pleading for their families. That's how you get what you want.'

As we strode across the lobby of the hotel, I stopped and looked at him and said, 'But you told me last week that you worked in the oil industry and that you were going to Nasiriya to sort out some projects,' I said.

He looked at me for a split second with wide, almost panicky eyes and then smiled quickly.

'Well, you wouldn't want to believe everything every-one says around here, now would you?' he said before tipping his hat in an old-fashioned way and striding purposefully out of the hotel and into the daylight.

EPILOGUE

The scale of the violence in Iraq is difficult to appreciate at a distance. On a single day in July 2006, I counted fifty separate 'incidents' in the troubled areas of central Iraq, including Baghdad and Anbar province, the most violent part of the country. Through trawls of the news agencies and the most reliable websites and blogs, a picture of carnage emerges. There were beheadings (three), car bombings (four), assassinations (two), IED attacks on convoys, mortars, rockets, small arms fire and abductions. Countless other incidents usually come to light weeks or even months after the event.

The morgue in central Baghdad cannot deal with the volume of bodies. Whereas before the war it had to deal with three or four violent deaths a month, now the numbers are more than fifty per day. In the old Iraq, the doctors painstakingly conducted elaborate post-mortem examinations to the same level as European hospitals. Today the death certificate is issued after only a cursory examination. Such is the volume of corpses that the temporary refrigerated trailers are full at all times. The identity of most of the victims is difficult to establish. Most are buried in anonymous mass graves without ceremony. Across the country it is reasonable to speculate that more than 100 people per day died violently during the summer of 2006.

A process of carving up the country into fiefdoms is at an advanced stage. The Sunni-dominated areas in the centre of the country are experiencing the greatest turbulence as insurgent groups fight to 'cleanse' their areas of non-Sunni elements. The reverse is happening in majority Shia areas.

Iraqis adjust their behaviour in response to the intense violence as best they can. On a daily basis the tactics change and it's wise to alter the pattern of living to try to avoid being caught up in the mayhem.

Abu Aseel tells me on the phone that the latest trend is for suicide squads to venture into the city very early in the day. They have a particular target in mind and when sufficient numbers of people have gathered at that place, the first bomber moves in. After he has done his work, the next suicide bomber waits for the arrival of the police and fire crews. They are legitimate targets because they are representatives of the Iraqi government, which the Sunni insurgent groups regard as illegitimate.

If an American patrol responds to the first attack, then the bombers regard this as a great blessing. But regardless of which agency responds, they will find themselves attacked by the second bomber.

A third bomber waits on the distant fringes of the scene and waits for the traffic to snarl up. Inevitably the incident causes a huge traffic jam and he heads to the densest part of this and delivers his deadly load.

The word has got out that these are the tactics used by the bombers. As a result, the emergency services try to cordon off an area and clear it of people and cars – a tall order in chaotic Baghdad. Ordinary people respond by fleeing the scene of the attack. Drivers will often abandon their cars in the middle of a traffic jam and disappear into side streets to hide from the subsequent bombs. The city grinds to a halt. No doubt refinements are being planned by the insurgents. Responses will be fine-tuned.

The forces behind the attacks are powerful and varied. Within the Sunni insurgency there are many divisions and rivalries. There is only one aim that the disparate groups could claim to have in common – an end to the US presence in Iraq. Most of the shadowy organisations that form the insurgency haven't articulated how they see the future after that, but a number of issues are clear.

Most believe they will be in a stronger position after they force the Americans out. Some groups believe they can use the power of violence to wrest a deal out of the new government – one that would be favourable to the Sunni constituency they claim to represent. They are using violence as a bargaining tool. This is the Sunni nationalist wing of the insurgency.

Others believe that in the event of an American withdrawal, they will be in a position to crush the Shia political parties and movements and reassert Sunni control over the whole country. There is a clearly Ba'athist character to this leg of the insurgency and it's strongest in the southern part of Baghdad and in the towns of the region the Americans call the 'triangle of death', Mahmoudiya, Babylon, al-Hilla.

Still others believe that the violence is part of a religious war in support of what they believe to be 'true Islam'. Once the Americans are out of the way, these fighters (along with their international brigades of suicide bombers) believe they will destroy the Shia government and take power. These Sunni extremists believe that the Shias are apostates. They despise them.

Once they have taken power, their aim is to re-establish an Islamic caliphate based in a 'cleansed' Baghdad. They see this as a fulfilment of destiny. Baghdad, they say, was the last location of a strong Islamic kingdom and the refounding of the caliphate there will herald a bright new age for the 'Umma'. There is an al-Qaeda flavour to their campaign.

All of the main groups are fungible. They change character over time and may even have common membership in some cases. What is true of the uprising today will not be true tomorrow. In a year's time, it seems certain the Sunni militant groups will have again mutated.

But it would be a mistake to see Iraq simply through the prism of the Sunni insurgents. In the south of the country, rival Shia groups are fighting a lower-level war for supremacy. Elements loyal to the different strands and personalities in the Shia pantheon are attacking each other. They are cleansing their areas of Sunnis and Christians.

Moqtada al-Sadr, the firebrand cleric, is continuing to flex his muscles. His Mehdi Army (Jaish al-Mehdi) has been dismissed by the coalition forces and the new government as an irrelevance. But it has shown itself to be capable of stirring up trouble. It has access to almost unlimited supplies of arms and is popular in the poorest and most deprived areas of Baghdad (notably al-Sadr City) and the south. As well as mining the age-old Shia psychology of defeat and martyrdom, the Mehdi Army exploits the sense of victimhood learned through years of discrimination and alienation at the hands of Saddam that is rife among poor Shias.

The Mehdi Army has been blamed for some of the most grotesque attacks on Sunnis. They denied they were responsible for the targeted killing of forty Sunni Muslims in the Jihad area of Baghdad in early July 2006. Militia members stopped a bus and checked the identity cards of those inside. Shias were spared. Sunnis were murdered on the spot. Al-Sadr City, on the edge of Baghdad – a vast slum which is home to more than two million people – has become a no-go area for Sunnis and even the police have to co-operate with the Mehdi Army in order to function there.

The tribes have also got in on the act. Under Saddam, the fortunes of the tribal elders waxed and waned, depending on the central government's needs. To appease them, on occasion Saddam would send money and food. If he detected disloyalty, he would send in his special forces and kill the leaders. In the new Iraq, the tribal leaders have exploited the vacuum of authority and reasserted their claims. Credible reports detail how they are attacking competing groups all over the centre and south. Their aim is primarily economic, but the blood rivalries of old have been given full vent.

Iraq is splintering into a thousand pieces. It has become a playground for the intelligence services of neighbouring countries. Everywhere they are said to be meddling, stirring up this group against that, encouraging one side with money and arms to fight against their perceived enemy.

Saudi Arabia is alarmed by the rise of Shia power. It has a significant Shia minority that has been traditionally kept down and it doesn't want to see a repeat of what happened in Iraq on its own soil. It has a hand in the mayhem.

Iran is delighted with the rise of Shia power, but is deeply uneasy at having so much US firepower on its doorstep. It sponsors some of the main political parties and is believed by Western intelligence agencies to have a hand in the violence in the south. The fractured nature of the regime in Tehran means that different forces are sponsoring different groups, muddying the picture considerably.

Syria has been the conduit for many of the most radical foreign Sunni elements that have joined the fight. Isolated for years because of its sponsorship of different terrorist groups, the Syrian government is trying to leverage some advantage for itself out of the Iraqi quagmire.

Much of the violence has come about as a result of the inevitable working out of big ideas on the unsuspecting Iraqi population. For nearly fifty years Iraq has been a great experiment. Big men with big ideas have worked out their strategies, regardless of the effects on ordinary people. They looked into Iraq and saw not a country but a laboratory, a place where they could conduct a grand experiment. Iraqi society could be manipulated and reshaped according to their uniquely brilliant vision.

In the case of Saddam Hussein, his idea of a grandiose Arab republic, a revolutionary force in the Arab world, was espoused as the highest ideal of the country during the decades of misrule: Iraq would oppose Shia fundamentalism from Iran; Iraq would be the most developed state in the region; Iraq would challenge the military might of Israel. Even as he mouthed the ideals of Arab unity and solidarity, he placed his own family in all the key institutions of state. When his family was exhausted, he moved his clan into positions of power and then his tribe, until all the people in senior positions in the country were related in one way or another to Saddam. His idea of Iraq as a beacon of revolutionary secularism was little more than rhetoric. He ended up creating a squalid country ruled by a bankrupt tribal elite.

Ironically, the Americans shared Saddam's idea of using Iraq as a force for change in the region. The war conspirators, Richard Perle, Paul Wolfowitz, Douglas Feith, Donald

Rumsfeld and Dick Cheney, saw Iraq as a way to change the dynamics in the region. They wanted success in Iraq to undermine the systems of rule in the region. They believed that a thriving, democratic Iraq would give them another friend in the Middle East. Its oil, properly managed under American tutelage, would help stabilise the price of the commodity on world markets. Iraq would be a more reliable ally than feudal Saudi Arabia, on which they are so dependent. Events on the ground have consigned that strategy to the dustbin of history.

Abu Musab al-Zarqawi was another outsider with grand designs on Iraq. Like his latter-day sponsor, Osama bin Laden, he saw Iraq as a way of changing Saudi Arabia and the other Muslim countries in the region. The establishment of a new Islamic caliphate in Baghdad would be the means. To achieve this, almost any method could be used. Suicide bombings and ritual killings were his favoured shock tactic and he made sure that he filmed as much of his work as possible so that it could be used for propaganda. The internet became his conduit. Unfortunately for the Iraqis, his ideas didn't die with him.

Iran has a big idea for Iraq, too. For the clerics that control Iran, the conquest of Iraq has removed the biggest threat to their state. Saddam has been replaced by a government composed of mostly Shias. Many of the new Iraqi ministers lived in exile in Tehran and Qom during Saddam's time and the Iranian Revolutionary Guard trained their militias. The Iranians have open and easy access to the Shia members of the government.

Ever wary of the United States and the potential for conflict in the future, Iran is believed to be the 'quiet hand' behind the more radical Shias, including Moqtada al-Sadr. By drawing US forces in Iraq into the chaos of the conflict, they have achieved their aim of tying down their long-term foe. They believe the American appetite for a war with Iran in the future has been blunted by what the Americans have experienced in Iraq. After all, what lunatic would dream of invading a country three times the size of Iraq after their punishing experience there?

The clerics can concentrate on their greater goal, their big idea. The dream of a Shia-dominated arc running from Tehran through Iraq to southern Lebanon is within their grasp. Already the south of Iraq has taken on many of the characteristics of Iranian rule. Sharia law is the legal code in many areas. The sale of alcohol is banned. Rules on the modesty of women are in place. In the case of alcohol and modesty, the strictures are being enforced by young zealots from the madrassas and mosques under the control of conservative Shia mullahs.

⌒

The 'big ideas' meant that the 'little people' didn't matter. If a few hundred or thousand were killed, it may have been regrettable, but it was understandable in the pursuit of a greater cause.

For the Americans, the deaths of ordinary Iraqis doesn't warrant much attention. During the invasion in 2003 the killings were reported as 'collateral damage', footnotes in a high-tech war. The deaths were regrettable but probably unavoidable. As the occupation unfolded, the US military didn't even keep a count of the number of Iraqis they killed at roadblocks or during combat operations. During their assault on the city of Fallujah in 2005, it was estimated that up to 5,000 were killed, but the Americans released no numbers, just a statement of regret for innocent lives lost. The estimates came from the Red Crescent and Red Cross.

To the radical insurgents, the deaths of ordinary Iraqis wasn't even a matter of regret. In their perverse world, the jihadis convinced themselves that those they killed were fortunate – they were doing them a favour in reuniting them with Allah. They would be in paradise sooner. True *Shaheen*, or martyrs, would be rewarded with seventy-two virgins to enjoy in the next life. If a woman was martyred, she would be miraculously transformed into a man, so as to enjoy the virgins. If those killed by the jihadis weren't Muslims or not 'proper' Muslims (for which, read Shia Muslims), then their life was of no account in the first place and their death meant nothing.

The little people of Iraq have been cowed – their silence is an affront. Apart from the briefest moments of optimism, they have had nothing to celebrate since their 'liberation' in 2003. We no longer view them as common inhabitants of a complicated world. Now we see them in the aftermath of a bomb attack, in tears, broken, running into hospitals with broken bodies, screaming with fear, their clothes stained in blood.

The Iraqis I hear on the radio or see on television or read about in newspapers today are not the Iraqis I have got to know over the last eight years.

As a rule, the Iraqis I have been lucky to know are neither brave nor cowardly, neither stupid nor exceptionally clever. Their ordinariness is their virtue – if that is what it is. None of the people I know in Iraq are 'big ideas' people. They don't want to remake the world, starting in Baghdad. They don't have the 'vision' thing.

In fact, for most Iraqis, the future is a blank – the possibilities too awful to contemplate. They have been at the receiving end of big ideas for nearly fifty years and it's accurate to say that they don't like what they have experienced.

For now, they muddle along. They make do. They hope the situation will somehow improve. The older ones can

RICHARD DOWNES

remember better times. There were periods of joy and
hope in the past. After the oil bonanza that began in 1973,
the country seemed blessed and lucky. The money
brought by oil led to a leap forward in development and
living standards. That was a good time. The brief weeks
after the liberation in 2003 when Iraqis realised that the
tyranny of Saddam was finally at an end counts as another
period of optimism. But these positive moments are only
sharp peaks on the otherwise declining line on the graph
of misery. They are against the trend, as an economist
might say.

Most of all, the Iraqis want to leave Iraq. Abu Aseel has
been tormenting me for more than a year to help get him
a visa to move to Europe. I have tried to explain that this
probably wouldn't be a good idea. Many people depend
on him, and if he left, they would be destitute. What would
his family do? I have patiently explained the life of a
refugee in Europe, the restrictions, the lack of support, the
loneliness. He was shocked by the realities, but it hasn't
put him off. He's determined to leave Iraq. He sees no
future in the only country he has ever known.

Like tens of thousands of Christians, David George
has left. I had no hand, act or part in his escape, but I
understand the reasons he got out. As one of the smallest
minorities in Iraq, the Christians have no one to defend
them. In an increasingly segmented and polarised
country, the Christians feel doomed. They have lost faith
in the future of Iraq.

David's brief sanctuary in Syria came to an abrupt end
in June 2006. While out walking one afternoon, he was
detained by the Mukhabarrat, the feared secret service of
Syria. He disappeared into a Damascus prison for weeks.
After his family found him, it took $3,000 in bribes to get
him released. Within days he was warming his toes in

Sydney Harbour in Australia. It's difficult to imagine David ever coming back to Iraq to find a bride, as he has always maintained he would do.

Art Newspaper reported in late 2006 that Dr Donny George, David's 'uncle', had fled Baghdad with his family. A combination of the intensity of the violence in Baghdad, poor funding from the Ministry of Culture and the growing influence of the radical Shia cleric, Moqtada al-Sadr, had made life impossible for Dr George and the Iraq Museum. The institution is surrounded by huge concrete barriers and there are serious concerns that a new round of looting could take place at any time. Speaking from a safe house in the Syrian capital, Damascus, he worried about the future of Iraq's unique antiquities, and in particular about the growing influence of Islamists within the government. 'I can no longer work with these people who have come in with the new Ministry. They have no knowledge of archaeology, no knowledge of antiquities. They are only interested in Islamic sites and not Iraq's earlier heritage,' he said.

Dr Mohammed Darweesh, like many Sunnis, is living through his worst nightmare. A Shia government is in power. The people he regards as lesser have been handed the government by the United States and he will never forgive them. He still works, but doesn't respond to messages or e-mails sent to him. Colleagues say he has withdrawn in on himself and is a shadow of the man I knew in the late 1990s.

The foreigners who have been in Iraq for the last three years are no less depressed. The soldiers talk endlessly of their next 'rotation', when they will get home. They dream of girlfriends and boyfriends, wives and husbands. They fantasise about raising hell in their hometowns. They think about leaving military service, of escaping the dangers of Iraq.

The Americans, John Marshall, Rachel Looney and 'Papa' Wiley, have left Baghdad. But they will be back. All talk of an American disengagement is bunk. Already they have spent as long in Iraq as the United States spent in Europe during World War II. They are in Iraq for the medium term. Until there is some substantial diminution in the threat to the new Iraqi state, they will stay, in some shape or form.

The British have withdrawn a substantial contingent of their Iraqi garrison, but this decision appears to have more to do with the needs of the British military than any improvement in the situation in southern Iraq. With large missions in Afghanistan and the Balkans, the British are already overstretched and the Iraqi operation is a substantial drain on their resources. They appear to be committed to staying the course in Iraq, although their enthusiasm is in serious doubt.

And for my own part, I have joined the ranks of the confused. I feel guilty that I'm not there, reporting on the mayhem, talking to Iraqis and reflecting their views. Yet I'm reluctant to go because of the dangers. When I'm there, embedded with the Americans or the British, I'm frustrated by the restrictions of having to report under military conditions. I hate being separated from the Iraqis in their own country. It seems absurd to have to use my mobile phone to call my Iraqi friends down the road to find out what's happening in the city. But most of all, I am afraid that I will be killed.

Nothing about Iraq is easy. There is no light at the end of the tunnel. In fact, the tunnel has collapsed and no one has a plan for rebuilding it. All of this makes me doubly angry because it is clear that no 'big idea' can rescue Iraq now.

INDEX

ACKNOWLEDGMENTS

This narrative is the truth and nothing but the truth, but it is not the whole truth. I have had to obscure certain locations and alter some names to protect the people in the book. While none of this impacts on the stories told or takes away from the veracity of the experiences, I regret having to do it. It would have been much easier to detail exactly where Abu Aseel lives or where Mohammed Darweesh spends his working day, but it would be dangerous for the people involved. They need protection.

My wife, Mairead O'Driscoll, provided stellar support during the writing of this book and read my drafts with a critic's eye. I would never have started or finished without her love and encouragement.

Writing a book while holding down a full-time job is difficult at the best of times and having a sympathetic boss is essential. Ed Mulhall, Director of News at RTÉ, allowed me extra time to complete the book and was supportive all the way through. Michael Good, Managing Editor, RTÉ News, embraced the idea of sharing my Iraqi friends with the world and proved to be a thorough critic of my early drafts. Hilary McGouran, Series Editor of *Morning Ireland* in RTÉ, was generous in her scheduling and immensely supportive of me during this project. Sincere thanks to all of them. Carolyn Fisher of the RTÉ press office helped with photographs.

My dear brother, Brian Downes, read the manuscript at a late stage and provided a detailed critique of its shortcomings at a crucial time. It is a better book because of his suggestions.

Likewise, Maureen Gilbert helped to mould the final shape of the book and our conversations clarified crucial passages in my mind.

My thanks are also due to the team at New Island, particularly Deirdre and Fidelma, who moved heaven and earth to get the book to market on time. Kristin Jensen edited the manuscript with a sharp and focused eye. I felt complete confidence in her suggestions and thank her warmly.

Finally, my heartfelt thanks to all the Iraqis who allowed me into their lives and who have found themselves incorporated, in one way or another, into the narrative. I hope I have shared a little of the joy and despair we experienced together.